AMERICA'S
SOCIAL
HEALTH

To Marc
With love and gratitude
For shared dreams of justice

AMERICA'S SOCIAL HEALTH

PUTTING SOCIAL ISSUES BACK ON THE PUBLIC AGENDA

MARQUE-LUISA MIRINGOFF AND SANDRA OPDYCKE

M.E.Sharpe
Armonk, New York
London, England

Library of Congress Cataloging-in-Publication Data

Miringoff, Marque-Luisa, 1947–
  America's social health : putting social issues back on the public agenda / Marque-Luisa
Miringoff, Sandra Opdycke.
     p. cm.
  Includes bibliographical references and index.
  ISBN 978-0-7656-1673-9 (cloth : alk. paper)
  1. Social indicators—United States. 2. United States—Social conditions—1980–
3. United States—Social policy—1993– I. Opdycke, Sandra. II. Title.

HN60.M56 2007
306.0973'09045—dc22   2007023511

Printed in the United States of America

The paper used in this publication meets the minimum requirements of
American National Standard for Information Sciences
Permanence of Paper for Printed Library Materials,
ANSI Z 39.48-1984.

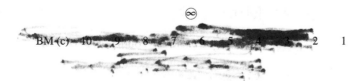

BM (c) 10   9   8   7   6   5   4   3   2   1

Table of Contents

Acknowledgments

We would like to express our thanks to two longtime supporters of our work, Lance Lindblom, Executive Director of the Nathan Cummings Foundation, and Joan Shigekawa, Associate Director at the Rockefeller Foundation. For nearly ten years, these two individuals have provided the Institute for Innovation in Social Policy with not only financial backing but also stimulating ideas and continuous encouragement. We owe them a huge debt for their vision and commitment.

An important initiative funded by these foundations was the convening of two parallel Working Groups—one on social indicators and the other on the arts and humanities. The participants, who greatly advanced our understanding of social indicators and social reporting, included: Bill Ayres, World Hunger Year; Carol Becker, School of the Art Institute of Chicago; Mary Guinan, U.S. Centers for Disease Control and Prevention; Heidi Hartmann, Institute for Women's Policy Research; Ichiro Kawachi, Harvard School of Public Health; Jeff Madrick, *Challenge* magazine; Judy Milestone, CNN; Harold Richman, Chapin Hall Center for Children; Ralph Smith, Annie E. Casey Foundation; and Julius Richmond, former U.S. Surgeon-General. We are enormously grateful for their perceptive and helpful contributions to the development of our ideas.

In the early years of our work, we received vital encouragement and support from the late Sol Levine, as well as from Al Tarlov, both of whom were then at the Health Institute of the Harvard School of Public Health. Their assistance played an important role during the period when we were conceptualizing our Index of Social Health. Fred Harris, former Senator from Oklahoma, also shared with us his memories of working with Senator Walter Mondale during the 1960s in the effort to establish a national social indicator system.

Leo Goldstone, then Senior Statistician at the United Nations Development Program, advised us on important social reporting being done by other countries and by international agencies. We also benefited greatly from the distinguished example and wise counsel of leaders in the field such as Joachim Vogel, Director of Statistics Sweden; Heinz-Herbert Noll, Director of the Social Indicators Department of the Centre for Survey Research and Methodology (ZUMA) in Germany; and Richard Jolly, then Deputy Director of UNICEF, who supported our creation of an Index of Social Health of Children of Industrial Countries.

A number of individuals who practice or study journalism have given us important insights about the role of the media in shaping public dialogue. These include Louis Uchitelle, of the *New York Times*; Ron Suskind, formerly at the *Wall Street Journal*; Anne Nelson, Columbia School of Journalism; William Wolman, chief economist at *Business Week*; and our Vassar College friend and colleague William Hoynes.

For our work on social reporting at the state and local level, we benefited greatly from the initiatives of a pioneer in the field—Alan AtKisson. We also value the collaborative relationships we developed during the twelve years we produced our annual *Social State of Connecticut* reports. We particularly thank David Nee, Executive Director of the William Caspar Graustein Memorial Foundation; Elaine Zimmerman, Executive Director of the Commission on Children; Edward Zigler, Director of the Bush Center for Children and Social Policy; and Emily Tow Jackson, Executive Director, and Diane Sierpina, Senior Program Officer, of the Tow Foundation.

During the preparation of this book, Sara Bodach made a vital contribution with her exhaustive research on the community indicator movement and international social reporting. We are grateful for her work and her dedication. Sociologist Eileen Leonard contributed greatly with her editing, recommendations, and suggestions. We thank her for her friendship and support.

We would also like to thank our gifted designer George Laws who, as always, has produced a document that is both handsome and accessible. He has been a colleague and a friend.

We are grateful to the many people at Vassar College who help to keep the Institute running smoothly. In particular, we thank James Olson, Director for Corporate, Foundation, and Government Relations, for his helpful advice and assistance.

We greatly appreciate the steady dedication to our project shown by our editor, Lynn Taylor. We express our thanks to the people at M.E. Sharpe, who supported and refined this project.

To Leo Opdycke, we thank you for your always faithful support, your kindness, and your wisdom. You are a part of this project.

Finally, and most importantly, the ideas for this book—and for the Institute's whole body of work—were initially formulated under the leadership of the late Marc L. Miringoff, the founding director. Marc was an innovator, an inventor, and an explorer, a man of both ideas and poetry. It was Marc who first articulated the vision we pursue here, and we are honored to continue the important work he began.

Introduction

During the final days of President Lyndon Johnson's term in office, Wilbur Cohen, Secretary of Health, Education, and Welfare, submitted to the President a document entitled *Toward a Social Report*. In the Introduction, Cohen wrote:

> Dear Mr. President:
> You directed the Secretary of Health, Education, and Welfare to search for ways to improve the Nation's ability to chart its social progress. In particular, you asked this Department "to develop the necessary social statistics and indicators to supplement those prepared by the Bureau of Labor Statistics and the Council of Economic Advisers. With these yardsticks, we can better measure the distance we have come and plan for the way ahead."
> . . .
> This document represents a preliminary step toward the evolution of a regular system of social reporting.[1]

Toward a Social Report is now something of a historic landmark. It represents the last time the United States government seriously considered establishing a comprehensive framework to monitor and report on the social conditions of the nation. As it turned out, the system the authors envisioned was never created, but the kernel of the idea lives on today.

Toward a Social Report was the culmination of ideas and debates that had been percolating for several years. In 1967, Senator Walter Mondale introduced a bill into Congress with similar aims. Entitled "The Full Opportunity and Social Accounting Act," it sought to parallel the nation's system of economic reporting with a similar structure for social reporting. In particular, it called for the creation of a Council of Social Advisers and an annual National Social Report, equivalent to the existing Council of Economic Advisers and the annual *Economic Report of the President*.[2]

Mondale's bill failed to pass, but its vision—echoed in *Toward a Social Report*—has continued to generate interest among social scientists, researchers, policy makers, and human service advocates. Today, forty years after Mondale first submitted his bill, the idea of social reporting—of monitoring social conditions in the same detailed and systematic way that we track economic conditions—has taken root in many American communities, as well as in industrial nations around the world.

In Europe, the concept of a national social report was picked up almost immediately.

Great Britain's *Social Trends* has been published every year since 1970, providing the British people with a comprehensive accounting of the country's social conditions. Just as President Johnson envisioned, the report functions as a "yardstick" for measuring progress gained and lost. Virtually every major industrial nation except the United States now has a national social report, as do many developing countries. Multinational social reports, produced by organizations such as the United Nations, the Organization for Economic Cooperation and Development (OECD), and the World Bank, have also become influential public documents.

While no official comprehensive National Social Report has been produced in the United States, the federal government did develop a number of regular reports on specific topics such as crime, health, and education. Moreover, cities, states, and regions across the country have begun to produce their own broader social reports. Cumulatively known as the community indicators movement, these initiatives have heralded a new attentiveness to the quality and conditions of community life.

Other methods of social accounting have emerged as well. Measures of social well-being have been developed to monitor progress over time and to compare social performance. The United Nations' Human Development Index, the Genuine Progress Indicator, and the United Way's State of Caring Index are all measures pointed in this direction.

Working within this tradition, the authors in collaboration with the late Marc Miringoff established the Institute for Innovation in Social Policy in 1985, dedicated to the study of social indicators and social reporting. The centerpiece of our work is the Index of Social Health, an annual assessment of the nation's social well-being. It is composed of sixteen social indicators, including problems such as infant mortality, child abuse, high school dropouts, crime, health insurance coverage, housing, and poverty. The index was created with the goal of advancing the public dialogue, enriching our thinking about social conditions, and strengthening the nation's capacity to address its social problems.

The latest edition of the index shows that the United States has made relatively little progress in addressing its social problems. After achieving high scores in the early 1970s, the index dropped sharply during the late 1970s and early 1980s, and then entered a long period of stagnation. Some revival occurred during the 1990s, but since 2000 the index has declined every year. Some of the component indicators, such as infant mortality, crime, and high school dropouts, have improved over time, but others, including child abuse, inequality, and health insurance coverage, have worsened dramatically. Clearly, more needs to be done.

In 1969, the authors of *Toward a Social Report* argued that our social problems

Index of Social Health of the United States, 1970–2005

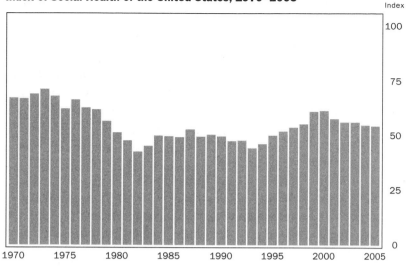

Source: Institute for Innovation in Social Policy

could be addressed effectively only if we ensured that they remained prominent on the nation's public agenda. That need still exists. Our intent in this book is to identify gaps in how our nation currently presents and publishes social information, and to promote a new and invigorated debate on the social issues of our time. Today, when foreign policy, war, and international relations dominate the headlines and have all but relegated our domestic problems to a brief footnote, it is more important than ever that we become scrupulously attentive to how we are doing as a society.

Part I of this book addresses the broad field of social reporting and social indicators. We discuss how well we monitor the social state of our nation, and how we might improve that monitoring in the future.

In Chapter 1, we describe how America's social landscape is currently portrayed and call for a new and broader perspective. We note the strengths of the country's well-established system of economic indicators, which is far more timely, integrated, and dynamic than our system of social indicators. We suggest several ways in which our social reporting system could be improved. These include: increasing the visibility of social problems through more frequent and nuanced reporting; advancing our conceptual framework through a more unified concept of society, its progress and decline; and finally, creating a closer link between social reporting and public action.

Chapter 2 addresses social reporting in the news media. The media are our primary source of information about public issues and they have the potential to play a major role in creating a healthy and dynamic debate about social concerns. Yet too often, they distort our understanding instead of deepening it. Clearly, the nation needs the same coverage of social conditions that is now given to economic issues—contextualizing individual events, reporting general trends, and providing regular updates on key indicators. The format of the news is also vital. Most newspapers and television programs have special segments for business, sports, science, travel, theater, and the weather. We argue that stories about social issues also need to be presented as a distinct category—given a specific "home" or "beat" in the media—so that the relationships among different social problems stand out more sharply, and the overarching concept of social health that ties these issues together is reinforced.

In Chapter 3 we look at social reports. Beginning with the ideas expressed in 1969 in *Toward a Social Report*, we consider how much progress has been made in institutionalizing the use of social indicators. We begin by considering the strengths and weaknesses of the community indicators movement, which has flourished in recent decades. Local indicator reports have become a staple of community life in many parts of this country, encouraging greater attention to the quality of life and helping to balance economic and social concerns. Overseas, national social reports are now fully established throughout Europe, as well as in Australia, Canada, New Zealand, and many developing countries. These documents represent a national commitment to social issues and to the importance of monitoring social concerns. At the global level, the emergence of numerous multinational social reports also has contributed greatly to the visibility and public understanding of social issues.

In Chapter 4 we look at tools of social assessment that have been developed over the years. Some, paralleling the Index of Leading Economic Indicators or the Dow Jones Industrial Average, create a single empirical assessment of social well-being that can be monitored over time. In this context we present our own Index of Social Health and discuss the patterns in America's social health since 1970. Other national and international indexes are reviewed as well. A second tool we consider is the social survey. We look at our own National Survey of Social Health and some of its recent findings, as well as various governmental and private surveys that also seek to assess how we are doing as a society. Finally, we discuss the need for additional tools to assess social progress, including the possibility of developing a new mechanism for identifying social recessions.

In the second half of the book, Part II, we begin to frame what a National Social Report for the United States might look like. As a way of starting the process of portraying the social state of the nation, we analyze sixteen key social indicators—those that make up the Index of Social Health—organized by the stages of life: children, youth, adults, the elderly, and all ages. Although only a beginning, these analyses reflect the complexity of our social well-being, the changes that have occurred over time, and the many disparities that trouble our nation. This overview helps to explain why many Americans still feel, despite a relatively prosperous economy, that there are problems in our society that are not being addressed. In illuminating these issues, Part II suggests why social monitoring is needed, and how it can enhance our capacity to understand the social state of the nation.

The twenty-first century has already been rent with problems both national and international. It is our hope that this book will help readers envision a more secure future, richer in social well-being and animated by a clearer sense of how to assess national progress. With that goal in mind, we offer grateful acknowledgement to our predecessors, to those who imagined a time when the state of our social life would be as vital and urgent an issue in the public dialogue as our economic status is today. In so doing, we hope to revitalize this dialogue and place the idea of social well-being once again at the forefront of the public agenda.

Part I

Social Reporting in American Life

Chapter 1

We Can Do Better: Toward a New Public Dialogue on Social Health

What is the measure of a good society? How can we tell if social conditions are getting better or worse? We all have opinions about this country's social well-being, of course, but it is often difficult to have a rational debate on the subject because the facts that should ground that debate are difficult to come by. In many respects, the information commonly available to the American public provides a very incomplete picture of the social state of the nation.

It is strange that this should be so in a country that puts such a high value on quantification. In our highly technical society, numbers give credibility. If we can measure a phenomenon, it seems real to us, and in many aspects of our national life, we have become accustomed to statistical reporting that is timely, precise, and widely accessible.

The economy is a perfect example. On any given day, we are deluged with highly specific information about the economy. As a result, most Americans have a fairly clear impression of how the economy is doing and can make judgments about its performance. Although people respond to the data based on their own perspectives, they generally do so in the context of widely known indicators such as unemployment and inflation.

We receive even more detailed information about the minute-by-minute ups and downs of the stock market. The Dow Jones Industrial Average, the NASDAQ Composite Index, and Standard & Poor's 500 Index are all updated continuously throughout the day. Every form of media—newspapers, television, and the Internet—provides frequent information on these indexes, as well as on individual stocks. These data are so widely disseminated that even people with few investments of their own have a general sense of how the stock market is doing.

Sports are also monitored closely in our society. In baseball, for example, the *New*

York Times publishes fifty-nine separate statistical indicators for each league, and updates them daily during the season. Such detail makes for knowledgeable fans and lively commentary. Because of these widely available statistics, anyone and everyone can discuss with infinite precision and variety the strengths and weaknesses of the various leagues, the teams, the batters, and the pitchers. This pattern holds for most major sports, local and national.

Even our weather is closely monitored. With temperature readings, dew-point averages, barometric pressure levels, temperature-humidity indexes, pollen counts, and wind velocity rates, we have a reasonably clear picture of what the weather will be like each day and how it is expected to change during the week. There is even a specific television station—the Weather Channel—and on its website viewers can check on climactic conditions anywhere in the world, from Topeka to Tokyo, with daily, often hourly, updates.

Politics, too, is often treated as something of a statistical sport. Through innumerable public opinion polls, we keep track of shifts in how the public feels about major political controversies of the day. We also monitor the relative standings of leading politicians, following the rise and fall of their approval ratings and measuring their perceived strengths and weaknesses. Long before Election Day, we are likely to know who is in trouble and who is a shoo-in, which races have already been won, and which will be cliffhangers.

Yet despite all this tracking of trends and patterns, the American public does not receive much regular information about trends in the nation's social well-being. We hear about separate events, but the type of systematic coverage that shapes our view of economics, politics, and sports is rarely found in social reporting. This inadequate attention to the social side of our national life makes it more difficult to engage in informed public dialogue and diminishes our capacity to address the problems that face us. We need to do better.

What Economics Can Teach Us

The economy is perhaps the most carefully measured aspect of our national life, and the way it is monitored offers a model for what we might achieve in the social sphere. We learn about the details of the economy and how it is faring through frequent and widely publicized indicators. Here is one example of economic reporting, from the *New York Times*:

Employers added only 121,000 jobs [last month], the government reported yesterday, indicating that the economy was slowing under the combined weight of high energy prices and rising interest rates.

But the government also reported that hourly wages rose at their fastest pace in five years, while the unemployment rate remained at 4.6 percent. This suggests that the labor market remains tight and may yet spur high inflation.

The disparate data underscored the uncertain economic situation facing the Federal Reserve as it ponders whether to continue raising interest rates over the summer to cool the economy further or whether it is time to pause.[1]

This brief account tells us a great deal about how we conceptualize our economic life in this country. Illustrated in these few lines are many of the strengths of the nation's economic reporting system and a clue to how we envision our own role in relation to the economy.

- *Timeliness.* The economic measures in the example above are timely and up-to-date. Most of the statistics are scarcely one month old, providing an opportunity to evaluate where the economy stands at the moment. This permits an assessment of how to correct or improve the current economic situation and suggests there is some urgency underlying our knowledge and understanding of these issues.

- *A fixed and frequent reporting schedule.* Like nearly all economic measures, the indicators in the selection above are published on a fixed timetable—at least quarterly and usually monthly. The frequency and regularity of this schedule allows for predictability and a sense of control over the flow of information.

- *Multiple measures are examined together.* In the example given above, the measures discussed include job growth, energy costs, interest rates, hourly wages, unemployment, and inflation. At other times, some combination of durable goods, factory inventories, retail sales, gross domestic product (GDP), housing starts, consumer confidence, leading indicators, balance of payments, or other economic assessments may be grouped together. This analysis of numerous indicators in relation to each other—an approach that is common in economic reporting—provides a complex and nuanced view of current trends, rather than a single-issue perspective.

- *A focus on the whole.* Although significant attention is given to specialized issues such as interest rates, job creation, or inflation, economic reporting tends to keep a bird's eye view on the whole. The economy, with all its strengths and weaknesses, typically remains the central focus. This means each economic measure is a "true" indicator, since it is an effort to take a sampling or reading of the whole. Indicators are always the tip of the iceberg. We know each measure is incomplete, but we also know that each provides a part of the larger vision and gives insight into the broader universe that is the economy.

- *A sense of direction.* The concern that the economy might be "slowing," in the example cited above, reflects a focus on dynamics and movement. The economy is presented not as a stagnant entity, but rather as a body in motion. Implicit in this orientation is the idea that those who track the economy must be vigilant, continually assessing where we stand and where we are headed.

- *The routinization of intervention.* The tone of the excerpt makes clear that the economy is viewed as an enterprise that is at least somewhat within our control. Agencies such as the Federal Reserve Board have the power and the responsibility to monitor the economy and apply remedies rapidly and systematically, either to "tweak" the situation or to initiate significant changes in policy. And the various economic indicators are the signals that trigger these actions.

These multiple strengths are fundamental to our national economic reporting system. They are illustrated daily in the thousands of stories that come to us on television, radio, newspapers, and the Internet. They frame our thinking about the economy, and their approach, now commonplace, seems logical and self-evident.

Yet these same strengths are far less evident in the way we measure and report our nation's social well-being. Data on social issues such as infant mortality, child abuse, high school dropouts, crime, health insurance, poverty, and inequality are certainly published regularly by government agencies, but our system of social reporting lacks many of the key advantages of economic reporting. If we assess the social sphere in terms of these issues, we can readily see where the weaknesses lie.

- *Timeliness.* Social data are typically one, two, or even three years old by the time they are released. The caveat—"the last year for which data are available"—is a familiar refrain in social reporting. This lack of timeliness obviously diminishes our ability to act, and makes the problems themselves seem less critical. If the teenage suicide rate for the year 2004 finally appears in 2007, how urgent can it be? How much can be done about a problem that is already well in the past by the time we hear about it?

- *A fixed and frequent reporting schedule.* No fixed overall timetable exists for the reporting of most social statistics. Unlike economic data, social indicators are generally issued annually, rather than monthly or quarterly, making their reporting a much rarer event and the need for a timetable far less relevant. Because so many months elapse between one release date and the next, the public is not able to develop the routine familiarity with social indicators that we have with economic indicators.

- *Multiple measures are examined together.* The custom of discussing indicators in relation to each other is much less common in social reporting. One rarely gets the sense of a complex mosaic that is so often conveyed by economic reporting. Infant mortality rates, for example, are published annually, but they are only occasionally discussed in relation to trends in poverty, health care, or inequality. The same is true of most social indicators. The single-issue perspective that is typical of social reporting narrows our understanding of social problems and weakens our ability to understand their interconnections.

- *A focus on the whole.* In social reporting, there is little focus on a "unity" that connects the various pieces into a single understandable phenomenon. Indeed, such a whole has not really been conceptualized. We may refer to "society," "the social sphere," or "the social arena," but we have not yet invented a concept as clear and comprehensive as "the economy."

- *A sense of direction.* The sense of a body in motion, the detailed portrayal of dynamics, movement, strengths, and weaknesses, is generally missing from our view of the social sphere. We see parts—disconnected pieces—but they are not portrayed as part of a broader movement forward or backward. It is therefore difficult to frame the idea of overall social progress or decline.

- *The routinization of intervention.* The minute and frequent interventions that ratchet up and down our economy, such as those by the Federal Reserve Board, are largely missing from the social sphere. Social interventions—our domestic policies—tend more commonly to be large scale, controversial, and often ideologically driven, punctuating years of inaction with sweeping overhauls of entire systems. The policies initiated may be successful or unsuccessful, but they rarely have built into them the kind of day-to-day monitoring and adjustments that are common in the economic sphere.

Compared to the steady production of timely and frequent economic news, widely available and broadly discussed, our social reporting and debates tend to be more fragmented, episodic, and ideological. They lack the systematization, detail, and greater (though certainly not perfect) precision of the economic sphere. If we wish to address our social problems effectively, we need to do a better job of conceptualizing and monitoring them.

An Agenda for Social Reporting

It is the intent of this book to offer new ways of thinking about the social sphere of our national life, and to stress the significance of social reporting. The contrast between our nation's approach to social trends versus economic trends makes clear that we need to make profound changes in the way we address social issues in this country. Here, we suggest as a beginning three critical goals: greater visibility for social indicators, a clearer vision of the whole, and a closer link between social reporting and public action.

Greater Visibility for Social Indicators

The American public keeps an alert eye on economic indicators because we know that their precise ups and downs often foretell larger and deeper problems. The shifts in each indicator are well publicized, inviting us to analyze them carefully and to assess what they tell us about where we stand and where we are headed.

Could we make the social sphere of American life just as visible to the American public? Obviously, we have a long way to go. What we typically learn about in the social arena is the isolated sensational event—the movie star accused of drunk driving, the child abuse case that ends in a tragic death, the town rocked by a young person's suicide. But we have yet to develop a systematic daily process for illuminating how our society is faring, a comprehensive structure for monitoring our social life in the way we monitor the progress of the economy, our favorite sports team, or our leading political candidates.

The results of this episodic approach to social reporting are clear in our daily discourse. Debates around the water cooler (or more often today on cell phones, blogs, and email) rarely center on important social issues. In fact, most of us know a good deal more about the inflation rate, the top players' batting averages, and the latest political poll numbers than we do about trends in teenage suicide, infant mortality, or child abuse. The critical indicators that could keep us informed about changes in the nation's social well-being remain largely invisible to the general public.

This invisibility has important implications for public policy, because the kind of information we receive about major issues greatly influences the way we respond to them. When we see only sporadic reports on social problems, and when these reports highlight only the most sensational episodes, the implicit message is that social problems are beyond our control. Since each incident appears to be an isolated event, arising from nowhere and sinking out of sight with the next news cycle, we are likely to conclude that there is not much we can do about it except to sympathize with the victims. Only when we begin to recognize larger patterns that can be consistently monitored and understood are we likely to feel able to intervene and effectively address the nation's social problems.

Even the best documented of our social problems need more visibility than they currently receive. And some issues in our society are measured so poorly we cannot even begin to have an informed discussion about them. How much homelessness is there in this country? In truth, we don't really know. There are multiple and competing figures, dueling methodologies, and few official government estimates. This relegates homelessness to a non-issue. Much the same can be said of other social concerns, such as illiteracy. While there are national estimates, we have little regular monitoring of these problems.[2] Once again, public dialogue and debate—our understanding and our willingness to act—suffer as a result. If we don't see the scope of a problem, we can hardly solve it, since we cannot define our goals or measure improvement.

In the next three chapters, we will discuss a variety of ways in which social indicators can be made more visible: by providing better media coverage, by producing regular social reports, and by developing more innovative tools for assessing social health. Each of these approaches, however, would be more effective if, like economic data, social data were produced on a more frequent and timely basis. Bringing this change about would involve administrative and financial challenges, but the economic field has surmounted similar difficulties, and it should be possible to do the same with social data.

One starting point would be to select certain key indicators for which frequent and timely data are most needed. Over time, the ups and downs of these indicators, much like economic indicators, could become an accepted part of the national news scene, requiring regular explanation and analysis. With reporters pointing out key patterns, experts contributing their analyses, and political leaders being asked to respond, social problems would assume a much more prominent place on the public agenda.

Some might argue that annual data are sufficient, since social statistics change relatively little from year to year. Yet this argument is seldom made with regard to economic statistics. In that domain, we pay close attention to very small move-ments—and rightly so, because we know that each fraction of a percentage point represents thousands of lives or thousands of dollars. This applies in the social sphere as well. For instance, an increase of just one-half of one percent in an indicator like child poverty represents a change in the life circumstances of tens of thousands of American children.[3] This type of far-reaching social problem certainly merits a higher level of visibility than annual data provide.

Publishing key social indicators at least quarterly would make social trends more visible as they emerge. An annual average may conceal a steady improvement or worsening during the year. We should not have to wait two or three years to recognize a trend that monthly or even quarterly data would have pointed to much earlier.

Greater visibility for social indicators would provide us with many benefits: a higher level of public attention, fuller information on emerging trends, and an earlier and sounder basis for intervention. This is indeed an investment worth our consideration.

A Clearer Vision of the Whole

In addition to making individual social indicators more visible, it is also time to advance our vision of the whole. We need to conceptualize the society in much the way that we conceptualize the economy—by defining a unitary concept that constitutes the social sphere. The very use of terms such as "social sphere" and "social arena" tells us that we are searching for a clearer term. Speaking of "the economy" communicates a more solid reality, an entity that we can track, analyze, and act upon. Perhaps a term that could work in the same way on the social side is the "socionomy," for example, or the "sociomatrix." We need to embark on this process of exploration.

Further possibilities arise from this vision of the whole. Are there *leading* indicators that could foretell a downturn in overall social conditions? Are there *lagging* indicators that could measure the after-effects? To address such questions, we must first develop a single comprehensive measure for tracking the social sphere's ups and downs, its progress and decline. If we can begin to answer the question "How are we doing?" in terms that reflect the interconnectedness of multiple indicators, tracking patterns over time, we will have taken a significant step forward in this undertaking.

In economics this tracking is done primarily through a single cumulative measure, the gross domestic product (GDP), which represents the total market value of all goods and services produced in the United States. Because the GDP gives us information in clear and precise terms, it is widely accepted as the foremost measure of the "state of our nation." If the GDP is rising, people feel the nation is doing well. If it begins to fall, they fear that the nation may be in trouble.

Of course, we know that the economy is not the only force that shapes our lives. The GDP accounts for only a part of who we are. As Robert Kennedy observed in 1968:

> The gross national product does not allow for the health of our children, the quality of their education, or the joy of their play; it does not include the beauty of our poetry or the strength of our marriages, the intelligence of our public debate, or the integrity of our public officials. It measures neither our wit nor our courage, neither our wisdom nor our learning, neither our compassion nor our devotion to our country. It measures everything, in short, except that which makes life worthwhile.[4]

Despite its limitations, the GDP is an exceptional tool. Along with its associated notions of expansion, contraction, recession, and soft spots, it is central to the way we monitor the nation's business cycle. It is supported by extensive analytical work that makes sense of the indicators we collect and gives clarity to our vision of the whole. Each report summarizing how the GDP has changed over the past three months gives us a picture of the economy in motion, a crisp, accessible narrative of progress or decline.

Our Index of Social Health, to be discussed in greater detail in Chapter 4, represents a first step in this direction, creating a picture of the social landscape as a whole, looking at multiple issues in concert and over time, and providing the beginnings of a vocabulary for this type of social analysis. Other measures are available that track social progress and decline in different ways. But the nation still needs a single comprehensive measure, created and released with the imprimatur of the government. This measure, like the GDP, could be reflected in official reports, referenced in congressional debates, and incorporated into national public discourse.

In addition to a summary measure of progress and decline, we need a means of characterizing periods of sharply worsening social conditions—a way to identify, in effect, a "social recession." We know that the announcement of an economic recession draws immediate attention. It is determined by experts, it represents a wakeup call to the country, and it is recorded in our history books. It has a definition that gives a name to our problems, evoking a sense of urgency about our economy.

Yet if multiple social problems worsen during a particular year, or over several years, we have no concept, no terminology for identifying that event. There are no headlines that announce the danger, no predictions of trouble ahead. We may have an uneasy feeling that the nation is struggling—poverty rising, crime increasing, health insurance faltering—but we have no standard term that defines the problem for the nation and alerts us to the need to intervene. The possibility of developing a way to identify social recessions is further explored in Chapter 4. Progress in this area of research would highlight the interactions among different social indicators, and help us to think about social conditions in a more integrated manner.

As we work to evolve social concepts like these, it is crucial to remember that business cycle theory, which forms the basis of much of today's economic reporting, did not emerge full-blown either. Its concepts were derived from years of empirical observation. Slowly, out of the masses of data, emerged a picture of the economy as a whole, and how it shifts and moves. Building on that picture, we developed our current system of economic reporting, analysis, and intervention. It is reasonable to hope that our understanding of social trends and conditions could go through a similar evolutionary process.

A Closer Link Between Social Reporting and Public Action

Space exploration may seem a far cry from the subject of social reporting and social indicators, but it actually gave rise to one of the primary documents in this field. In 1966, when space travel was still in its infancy, social scientists became concerned that this venture into the unknown, along with the technological developments it would involve, might profoundly alter American society.

In response, the National Aeronautics and Space Administration (NASA) asked the American Academy of Arts and Sciences to consider how to measure the changes that could take place and the social distance we might travel. The Academy produced a series entitled *Technology, Space, and Society*, and the second volume was a pathbreaking book, edited by Raymond Bauer: *Social Indicators*.[5]

The rationale for *Social Indicators* was the idea that in order to measure the changes that might occur as we soared into space, we needed a thoroughgoing assessment of the baseline, of where the United States stood when the program started. The authors noted, however, that the study of human society was not sufficiently advanced to provide the data that would be needed.

Bauer pointed out that "for many of the important topics on which social critics blithely pass judgment, and on which policies are made, there are no yardsticks by which to know if things are getting better or worse."[6] Echoing this view, Earl Stevenson, Chairman of the Academy's Committee on Space, wrote:

Any massive technological effort, such as the space program, has effects far beyond those that were originally intended; effects that reach into every corner of our society, and that cannot be anticipated with any precision or, in many instances, even at all. . . . There is a growing demand for more effective techniques to anticipate the results of change and for planning mechanisms that will take into account the widest possible spectrum of effects . . . if possible—bringing them under some degree of conscious control.[7]

This forward-thinking approach, in many ways characteristic of that era, is quite startling to us now. How likely is it today that we would promote an in-depth investigation of the potential effects of a new technology on the breadth and scope of American society?

Bertram Gross, recognizing the significance of the effort, wrote in the preface to *Social Indicators*: "If I were not myself a contributor to this volume, I should be tempted to herald it as a major contribution to man's efforts to find out where he has been, where he is, and where he is going."[8] He included the following purposes for the book:

— This volume is a continuation of the great information-gathering tradition of Western civilization, particularly in the United States.

— It is a symptom of a widespread rebellion against what has been called the "economic philistinism" of the U.S. government's present statistical establishment.

— From a still broader viewpoint, it may be regarded as a humanist effort to develop more open spaces (not merely on the moon or beyond) in the minds of people on this planet.[9]

Breathtaking goals indeed!

The nation's aspirations for social knowledge are certainly more limited today, and time has punctured the heady idealism of the 1960s. Yet there are lessons to be learned from the sheer ambition of that period, with its sense that we can tackle the social problems we face, anticipate in proactive ways the social effects we produce, and deliberate wisely and constructively on the social state of our nation.

It is that sense of confidence and possibility that we should take with us from this visionary book, as well as its relevance to the topic of the present volume. For, having stated its goals so boldly, *Social Indicators* then proceeds, in very technical terms, to get down to the business of considering how to measure the essential social trends that we will be discussing here—crime, poverty, education, and the like.

Social Indicators has much to tell us in terms of its expectation for action. Bauer and his fellow authors assumed that the ultimate purpose of their data was to serve as a basis for intervention. They viewed social indicators, like economic indicators, as the foundation upon which to build good public policy. Bauer wrote: "Statistics are gathered not out of a general sense of curiosity, but rather because it is presumed that they will be guides to planning and action." [10]

These same characteristics—the sense of confidence and possibility, and the expectation of action—infuse the other two social reporting landmarks from the 1960s discussed in the Introduction: the Full Opportunity and Social Accounting Act and *Toward a Social Report*. Taken together, these three initiatives offer a compelling vision of social knowledge at work, moving seamlessly from measurement to debate to action.

We can also look to another era for inspiration and example. There is a reason scholars and policy makers return again and again to the New Deal of the 1930s. It is certainly not because all of its policies worked. A few of its programs became the core of this nation's safety net, but many others were intended only to shore up the neediest victims, while still others failed or were phased out. Nevertheless, what is instructive about the New Deal is its innovation and its attentiveness to social issues. The whirlwind of public policy during those years—in the first hundred days and beyond—is a testament to what can be achieved when we marshal our resources to address our worst social ills.

We are fortunate not to be at such a crossroads today. No economic collapse constrains or compels us. Nevertheless, we face serious social problems, and in recent years we have shown little urgency in dealing with them. Child abuse continues to increase, our infrastructure is declining, inequality is rising dramatically, health-insurance coverage is debated but not resolved, and poverty remains a far worse problem in the United States than in most industrial nations. We need to commit ourselves to these issues and to base our responses on a solid foundation. We can do better.

What would galvanize us to face our social dilemmas more effectively? What would invite the kind of adventurous thinking that we admire in the social initiatives of the 1930s and the 1960s? These are not easy questions and there are no simple answers. But some of the reforms we advocate in subsequent chapters would contribute to this effort. They represent first steps along a journey designed to elevate the primacy of social issues, and make clear both to the public and to policymakers that these concerns are central to our nation's well-being.

Needed: A New Approach

The ways we measure, monitor, conceptualize, and report the social issues of our nation need serious review. Useful models are all around us—in sports, weather, politics, and most notably economics. They suggest how we might better assess our social well-being. To bring our system of social reporting closer to these models, we might begin with the goals we have suggested here: bringing greater visibility to social indicators, providing a clearer vision of the whole, and creating greater urgency about solving our social problems.

In the following chapters, we look at how these goals might be more fully addressed, through better coverage of social issues in the media, through institutionalizing the monitoring process in official social reports, and through developing new tools for assessing the nation's social health. These steps would make a difference, even in their early stages.

Why, ultimately, should we do this? Primarily, because social reporting is part of the bedrock of a democratic way of life. Social indicators inform us, they educate us, and they can empower us to act. As Joachim Vogel observes:

> Social reporting de-mystifies politics. It provides a common ground from which everyone involved can learn something about "the way things are." . . . Social reporting thus performs an important function in a representative democracy. All actions bearing upon our living conditions—the formation of political opinion, voting, decision-making, etc.— should be based on objective information . . . and that information should be available to everyone. That is the democratic mission of the social indicator movement.[11]

Chapter 2
Shaping Everyday Discourse: The News Media and Social Issues

Of all the forces that influence our perception of the nation's social health, the news media are perhaps the most vital in determining which issues we consider important. Because of their remarkable power to capture Americans' attention and concern, the media play a major role in shaping the nation's public agenda.[1]

The media's influence over public discourse comes not only from selecting which events to cover, but also from shaping how we interpret those events. By choosing which aspects of a story to emphasize, the amount of time or space to allot, and the tone of the reporting, the media "frame" how we think about public events.[2]

How Well Are the Media Doing?

Even in the early days of the republic, the nation's leaders agreed that a democratic society needed an informed citizenry, and that this required an active and responsible press. For this reason, the media have always been granted special privileges, including protection under the First Amendment.

Today, the country's major journalism associations continue to endorse that vision of accountability. "The Statement of Principles" of the American Society of Newspaper Editors notes that the purpose of "gathering and distributing news and opinion" is to "serve the general welfare." Similarly, the "Code of Ethics" of Radio and Television News Directors affirms their obligation to "enable the public to make enlightened decisions."[3]

How well do the media fulfill this important obligation? This question has received a great deal of scholarly attention in recent years, and while many writers point to individual examples of excellent journalism, the overall consensus has been fairly negative. As sociologist William Gamson observes:

> Ideally, a media system suitable for a democracy ought to provide its readers
> with some coherent sense of the broader social forces that affect the conditions of
> their everyday lives. . . . It is difficult to find anyone who would claim that media
> discourse in the United States even remotely approaches this ideal.[4]

Of the many inadequacies that have been identified, three have particular relevance for the reporting of social issues. These are: gaps in the coverage of important topics, a tendency to focus on sensational events while ignoring the broader context, and an excessive emphasis on political spin.

Two additional problems are not usually noted in the literature but are evident from our own research. These are: the fragmentation of coverage that results from dispersing social issue stories among many different "beats," and the media's own difficulty in obtaining timely and systematic information on social problems.

In exploring these issues, our analysis will focus particularly on television and newspapers. These two forms of media are still much the dominant forces in originating news coverage, despite the recent expansion of Internet alternatives. Moreover, most of the problems identified in TV and newspaper coverage are evident in other media as well.[5]

Gaps in Coverage

Few images are more central to the idealized image of the press than the investigative reporter, battling the odds to cover a story. Among the real-life exemplars of this image are Bob Woodward and Carl Bernstein, whose articles in the *Washington Post* helped to reveal the Watergate scandal. Like Watergate, many of the media's most heroic investigative achievements have focused on some combination of politics, money, and wrong-doing.

Yet other stories of great importance to American society do not get pursued with such vigor: stories about infant mortality and child poverty, about wage stagnation and the dearth of affordable housing. This lack of coverage tends to obscure many important aspects of American life.

Consider the case of AIDS. By the time the epidemic began to receive extensive and systematic media attention AIDS had infected more than 10,000 Americans and killed more than 6,000 people. Here was a fatal disease spreading at exponential rates, yet years went by before it became accepted as a continuing story worthy of sustained coverage.[6] The news media were not alone in their abdication of responsibility; there were failures of leadership throughout American society. But the media helped to perpetuate the destructive national silence that prevailed during the critical early years of the epidemic—years when aggressive action might have changed the course of events.

Homelessness provides another example of insufficient media coverage. As Todd Shields notes, homelessness emerged during the late 1970s and had already become a significant concern in many cities by the early 1980s. But the issue was not really "discovered" by television newscasts until several years later, when the problem had grown so acute that it began to trouble the lives of middle-class urban residents. By the 1990s, as programs were established to keep homeless people off the streets, press coverage waned once again, though available data suggest the problem remained severe. Shields notes that today we tend to hear about the homeless primarily during the holidays, when acts of charity are celebrated, or periodically when advocates organize events to highlight the problem. Otherwise, it remains in the shadows.[7]

These two examples of the news media's failure to cover social health issues effectively—AIDS and homelessness—have been attributed, at least in part, to the fact that both issues affect very specific (and not highly regarded) social groups.[8] It is also true, however, that journalists have trouble addressing any social problem that develops gradually over time, affects a rising number of people, but lacks a specific event that can serve as a "news hook." Celebrity cases, medical breakthroughs—these are the stuff of newspaper headlines. The news media find it more difficult to cover the quiet, steady expansion of a chronic social problem.

Eye-catching stories are, of course, easier to sell, but the goal of objectivity compounds the journalistic tendency to wait for a news hook. To appear unbiased, editors and reporters often confine themselves to topics where "breaking news" provides its own justification for coverage. This, at least in theory, avoids criticism that their stories are being chosen for ideological or political reasons. Yet this approach can impose its own bias, dooming to invisibility many major social issues that do not generate the required headline-making events.[9]

Gaps in regular coverage are mitigated to some extent by the custom of doing an occasional special story or series on issues that otherwise receive little attention. But there is a difference between occasional stories, however excellent, and consistent coverage. This difference is highlighted by the experience of reporter Judy Peet, who was assigned by her local newspaper to write a special article on lead poisoning. Having done a piece on the topic some years before, Peet wondered if there would be anything new to report. She soon learned that most of the legislative initiatives proposed after her last story had been dropped, and that lead poisoning had now spread to the suburbs. Undiscussed and unaddressed, the problem had continued to worsen.[10] As Peet's experience suggests, "one-shot" stories can be valuable, but they need to be supplemented with more systematic coverage.[11]

One of the media's most important roles, according to Herbert Gans, is "deciding what's news."[12] The current gaps in the media's approach to social issues can only be filled when the definition of "what's news" is expanded beyond each day's breaking story, beyond occasional special features, to include sustained coverage of the critical problems that shape American lives.

An Overemphasis on the Sensational

The problems of media coverage go beyond the failure to deal with important social problems. Sometimes, even when reporters cover a significant issue, they do so in ways that give an incomplete or distorted picture.

No news article can include every detail. It is always necessary to choose which items of information to include, and how to arrange them to tell a story. As Tankard and his co-authors explain, every media account necessarily imposes a "frame" on the material, which "supplies a context and suggests what the issue is, through the use of selection, emphasis, exclusion, and elaboration."[13] The difficulty is that too often, the media frame that is chosen highlights only the most sensational aspects of a social problem. This approach leaves readers less informed about the nature of a social issue. Angela Valdez, for example, has described how a leading Oregon newspaper published numerous highly charged articles on methamphetamine use, while ignoring the state's other more serious drug problems. According to Valdez, this misled the public, and encouraged legislators to make a number of poor policy choices.[14]

Similarly, Kai Wright observes that one of the primary emphases in recent media stories about AIDS is the idea that gay men who take methamphetamines may be more likely to have unprotected sex. This is a dramatic subject, but Wright argues that in making it *the* primary AIDS story, the media gave readers a distorted picture of the epidemic. The people at highest risk in the United States today are *not* white gay men, but instead black men and their female partners. "The result," says Wright, "is a myopic understanding of this epidemic. We see white where there's actually black. We see drug-induced orgies where there are really complex sexual choices complicated by the search for intimacy."[15]

There are similar examples:

- Homicides continued to get extensive coverage throughout the late 1990s, far beyond their proportion of total violent crime, while much less attention was given to the fact that both the homicide rate and the violent crime rate were falling steadily.[16]

- Approximately 40 percent of the articles on suicide in 2005, both in the *New York Times* and *USA Today,* dealt with the rare cases in which individuals murdered other people before killing themselves.[17]

- On the topic of child abuse, 95 percent of the stories in *USA Today* and 63 percent of those in the *New York Times* in 2005 dealt with sexual abuse. Yet sexual abuse represents only a small fraction of all child abuse.[18]

If there is one fundamental flaw shared by stories like these, it is the fact that they highlight atypical cases, while providing little information to help readers understand broader trends. The unusual nature of each incident is, of course, what makes it news. Yet if that is the primary aspect that reaches the public day after day, one can understand why people would come to believe that it *is* the problem.

This shaping of news coverage reflects the distinction that Shanto Iyengar draws between "episodic" and "thematic" reporting.[19] Episodic articles deal exclusively with a single event, while thematic ones add additional context.

A familiar form of episodic reporting is the typical crime story. Too often, as John McManus observes, these stories provide only an "ambulance-window view" of the community—"the context-stripped, cookie-cutter stories of shootings, stabbings and sex crimes." Yet, he says: "Crimes are serious events. . . . It's the reporting that trivializes them."[20]

A thematic approach might start with the same incident, but add more detail, suggesting what the surrounding circumstances were, how often this kind of event takes place, how trends in this particular kind of crime compare with trends in overall crime, and what kinds of approaches might help to prevent such incidents in the future.

The professional ideal of objectivity, mentioned earlier, can make journalists wary of thematic reporting, fearing that going beyond the simple facts may leave them open to charges of editorializing. But sometimes, adding context is the only way to be fair to the facts. A purely episodic account of an event, with no context, creates its own frame, suggesting by implication that there are no explanatory circumstances and no likely solutions. Yet, as John McManus and Lori Dorfman have pointed out, the press can do better. When a celebrated crime gets extended coverage, reporters comb the social landscape and find many relevant details. "Suddenly, the cause of a crime becomes complex."[21]

The coverage of suicide by the *New York Times* and *USA Today*, mentioned above, provides an example of the more contextual reporting that can be done for a high-profile crime. In both the *Times* and *USA Today*, many of the stories dealing with suicide in 2005 dealt with a single incident: a shooting rampage on an Indian reservation in Minnesota, during which a young man killed nine people—in school and at his home—and then took his own life. This event dominated the news day after day, as reporters explored the context in dozens of different ways, linking the killings to broader issues such as youth suicide, school violence, the problems of depressed rural communities, and the plight of Native Americans. The challenge is to bring at least some of this same contextual richness to the process of daily reporting.

This might seem like an impossible ideal, given the limitations of time and space in both newspapers and broadcasting. Yet the world of economic reporting, as discussed previously, is full of news stories that add context in just a few sentences. Each day, these articles show that it is possible, in relatively concise ways, to suggest how a particular event fits with, illuminates, or perhaps goes against other related trends.

Emphasizing Political Spin

News about social issues is also often distorted when reporters focus too exclusively on framing their stories as political contests. There are good historical reasons for this tendency.

The 1970s left American journalists with much to be proud of, from their leading role in uncovering the Watergate scandal to their persistent questioning of official wisdom during the Vietnam War. One of the legacies of that era is the conviction among both editors and reporters that it is important to be skeptical about the pronouncements of politicians.

There have been periodic lapses in this skepticism, notably during the run-up to the Iraq War. But for the most part, press accounts of events that are even remotely political—officials' speeches, legislative debates, campaign addresses, governmental actions—tend to be framed in terms of what politicians hope to gain, and how their activities are likely to affect their political standing.[22]

Partisan maneuvering is a significant aspect of American policy making, but sometimes that aspect is covered so intensively in the media that the policy issues themselves nearly disappear. As Trudy Lieberman asks, "How many times must a story pontificate on whether passing a bill will help Republicans or Democrats?"[23] Letting politics overshadow content is a problem under any circumstances, but it is particularly damaging when complex issues are being debated—issues the news media could help the public understand.

The debate on health care in the early 1990s provides an example of how the country's print and electronic press focus on political spin at the expense of substance. President Clinton was elected at a time of widespread concern about the American system of paying for health care. Shortly after taking office, in 1993, the President appointed a task force headed by First Lady Hillary Rodham Clinton, to study how the system might be restructured.

For more than a year thereafter, the press chronicled each step of the process: the panel's deliberations and political missteps, the extended congressional debate over the ambitious final recommendations and various competing proposals, the aggressive intervention of lobbies and interest groups from around the country, and Congress's ultimate refusal to turn the panel's recommendations into law.

Given the innumerable articles about this issue in the press, one might assume that they would have provided the American public with a solid analysis of the issues involved. However, a review by the Annenberg Public Policy Center found that about two-thirds of the articles, both in newspapers and on television, framed the debate purely as a political contest, offering little concrete information about the content of the various alternatives or what they might mean for average Americans.

To test the impact of this "conflict frame" coverage, the Annenberg team performed a simple experiment: they asked one group of people to read fifteen major stories that had appeared during the debate, while a control group read only one of the stories. The participants were then asked to explain the various alternatives that had been discussed. The test results showed that the people who read all fifteen stories had no better understanding of the various proposals than those who read only one story.[24]

The moral seems clear: it is appropriate for the news media to consider seriously the intentions behind politicians' public comments. But they cannot fully discharge their obligation to inform the public about social policy issues unless they also address thoughtfully and informatively the actual content of the issues involved.

Fragmentation of Coverage

The three problems discussed so far—gaps in coverage, sensationalism without context, and excessive attention to political spin—involve the way in which news stories are selected and written. But the public's response to social reporting is also affected by a more structural aspect of news: the way that stories are distributed *within* a given newspaper or TV newscast. Scholars sometimes analyze how often articles on particular social problems appear on newspaper front pages, or above the fold, or with pictures.[25] But these analyses do not address a larger question, which is where stories on social issues appear in relation to each other.

As discussed in Chapter 1, we have learned over the past half-century to think of "the economy" as a single vast sphere of American life, full of many activities that are separate yet also interconnected. The social sphere is equally vast and equally interconnected, but we have not yet learned to think of it that way. Instead, we tend to focus on separate problems, separate victims, separate policies. Individual research studies may show that unemployment increases poverty, or poverty increases depression, or depression increases child abuse, or child abuse increases the likelihood of teenage pregnancy. But we are not used to thinking or talking about all of these problems in relation to each other.

The news media play a role in perpetuating this fragmented view of the nation's social health, because the coverage of social issues is itself fragmented. We have already discussed one type of fragmentation, which is the tendency to present atypical episodes without the kind of contextual detail that would link them to broader trends. But there is another, higher-level kind of fragmentation that has to do with the way the whole presentation of news is organized.

Readers can check the business pages for an overview of America's economic health. But there is no similar page or section for an overview of the nation's social health. There are many social issues that appear periodically in the news: infant mortality, high school dropouts, unemployment, drunk driving, crime, and so forth. All have a bearing on our country's social well-being, and many are known to influence each other. Yet only by chance can we find stories on these different issues together, because there is no single segment of a typical newspaper or television newscast that groups these articles.

Child abuse is an example. Articles about local incidents tend to be reported as local news, unless they are sensational enough to rate first-page coverage. Incidents that happen in other parts of the country may appear under national news, while a child-abuse scandal overseas would be reported in the international section. There may be an occasional feature story on child abuse, usually in one of the paper's special sections, and now and again there might be an editorial on the editorial page.[26] This dispersal of child abuse stories makes it difficult to form a picture of general trends on such an important social problem.

The difficulty becomes even greater when looking at different social issues in relation to each other. Health-related issues such as Medicare funding, health insurance coverage, mortality trends, medical research, and local health-care innovations could, in theory, be discussed together. But in most newspapers, even if all these issues were covered on the same day, they would probably appear in five different sections: political news, business news, national news, science news, and local news. And, given this dispersal among different parts of the paper, it is unlikely that any of the stories would refer to the others, or integrate their various bits of news into a larger picture of health in America.

The recent creation of health beats in some newspapers and TV newscasts would seem like a step in the right direction, and many are quite informative, especially about personal health and new research. But the operational definition of what constitutes health news usually excludes many of the most relevant stories, such as those dealing with legislation (mostly covered as political news) and job-related benefits (usually assigned to the business section).[27] Health reporters themselves have commented on the rigidity of the format within which they have to work. Other reporters have expressed similar concerns about the narrowness of the education beat.[28]

In fact, fragmentation can be seen in the way most social problems are covered, and even more dramatically, in the coverage of social health overall. Put simply, there is no organizational home, no "beat," in either print or electronic journalism for an integrated view of social trends. Thus, one can understand why readers find it hard to look at any social problem broadly, and harder still to make sense of what all these social problems, taken together, reveal about the social health of the nation.

The Media's Need for Frequent and Timely Social Data

Journalists are consumers of data as well as disseminators. In order to report on social trends, they must first obtain timely and useful information themselves. For this, they depend, above all, on the federal government, the major source of social data in the country. The hundreds of surveys and data summaries that are produced by agencies such as the Census Bureau, the Bureau of Labor Statistics, and the National Center for Health Statistics form the basis for much of the research and reporting on social health that occurs in the United States.[29]

The volume of social statistics generated by the federal government is impressive, but volume alone cannot ensure that the information enters the mainstream of public discourse. Social issues are far more likely to be picked up by the news media—and therefore reach the broadest public—if the information is both frequent and timely. As noted in Chapter 1, that is not the case.

The sixteen indicators that make up the Index of Social Health (discussed in Chapter 4) are illustrative. The indicators represent a cross-section of social concerns, covering subjects as diverse as infant mortality, high school drug abuse, homicide, and poverty among the elderly. Nearly all of the data for these indicators come from government sources, and the frequency and timeliness with which they are released illuminate how the pattern of government reporting complicates the media's capacity to cover social issues effectively.

The primarily annual reporting of social indicators presents an immediate obstacle to systematic coverage, since a continuing story with only one chapter per year is not much of a story. Both journalists and the general public are likely to have difficulty keeping in mind a social trend that is reported so rarely. Moreover, reports issued only once a year are often overlooked altogether by the press, since there is no place for them in the regular calendar of media coverage. As a result, despite many stories each year about events that relate to social health, readers often miss the federal reports that could provide an overview and national perspective for these stories.[30]

Economic reporting once again provides an instructive comparison. How did technical economic terms such as the gross domestic product, inflation, the consumer-price index, and the Dow Jones Industrial Average become part of America's everyday language? It was through constant repetition over many years.[31] It is worth noting that only three statistics in the Index of Social Health are published more often than once a year, and these are the ones that are also monitored by economic reporters: unemployment, wages, and housing prices. These indicators are reported more frequently because that is the norm in the world of economic and business statistics.

A second obstacle for journalists covering social trends is the extended time-lag in federal reporting. The few indicators that come out on a monthly or quarterly basis are reported quite promptly. But the annual statistics, lagging from nine months to as much as three years, present a more serious problem. For example, in order to learn the infant mortality rate in 2004, one had to wait until 2006 for preliminary findings, and 2007 for the full report.

The contrast between the timeliness of economic versus social reporting is vividly demonstrated in the government's White House Briefing Room website, which presents both economic and social statistics. On a typical day in 2006, nearly 90 percent of the economic indicators posted on the site reflected trends from the previous twelve months, while fewer than 35 percent of the social indicators were that recent.[32]

Media coverage of social issues is crucial because it has the potential to give citizens the information they need to understand and evaluate the nation's policy choices. If the media are to keep the American public well informed about the country's social health, they need a supply of government statistics on social trends that is as frequent and timely as the data they now receive on business and economic trends.

Improving Social Reporting by the News Media

The various problems in the media's approach to social issues represent a challenge that needs to be confronted. Some have suggested that because media content is shaped by market forces, any effort to improve that content represents an undemocratic dismissal of consumers' choices. But consumers cannot choose among options they are not offered, and there is considerable evidence that they respond to coverage that provides a richer portrait of our social life.[33]

Moreover, the news media have an obligation to serve the public interest. As Kovach and Rosenstiel argue: "The first challenge is finding the information that people need to live their lives. The second is to make it meaningful, relevant, and engaging."[34]

Suggested below are a number of initiatives that might help to improve media coverage of social issues.

Expand Training in Social Reporting

Social reporting is challenging work. Identifying social changes as they emerge; interviewing experts and evaluating their comments; integrating personal accounts, policy debates, government reports, and technical research findings—these are tasks that require at least some specific preparation. The majority of working reporters are generalists, but even they could benefit from some additional background in the field.

To lay the foundation, journalism schools might be encouraged to incorporate more social health concepts into the standard journalism curriculum. Relevant materials could be included in core courses, electives could be developed, internships could be created, and seminars for journalism faculty might reinforce the importance of social issues as a part of every journalist's preparation. A second approach would be to develop a specific degree in social reporting, combining general courses with work in fields such as sociology, public policy, public health, and economics.[35]

Yet a third option is mid-career training. One model is the Health Coverage Fellowship at Babson College. Each year, this nine-day program uses a combination of seminars, speakers, and field trips to educate ten reporters and editors about major issues in health care and medicine.[36] A similar short and intensive fellowship might be developed for social reporting.

Create a Regular Feature on Social Health

If journalists are to be trained to do more comprehensive social reporting, they also need a more appropriate setting for presenting their work. The nation's understanding of social health would be enhanced if the press were to treat social reporting as a distinct category of news, similar to politics, sports, business, science, the arts, and other topics.

A regular newspaper or TV feature with a title such as Social Health could bring together reports on topics such as crime, education, child abuse, infant mortality, affordable housing, health insurance, and poverty. There could be feature pieces on social issues, as well as news items about pending legislation, economic reports, and policy changes. The section could also cover public opinion polls, surveys, and statistical reports published by government agencies and private organizations. As an example, see Figure 2.1, in which news stories from different days are gathered together as a model Social Health page.[37]

A broader social health beat, embodied in a regular Social Health page or segment, would reinforce the salience of social health as an overarching concept. If journalists found themselves looking at a wide range of news stories in terms of the question: "What does this tell us about American society?" and if they had a regular space to fill, they might develop a broader perspective on social reporting.

Media Outreach by Nonprofit Organizations

Nonprofit organizations can play a significant role in improving the quality of social health coverage. In recent decades, for example, numerous media watchdog groups have emerged that monitor and publicize how well the media adhere to their public service obligations. These groups have tended to focus particularly on evidence of political bias and on social stereotyping, but some have done distinguished work in analyzing the coverage of social issues, and they might well be encouraged to do more.[38]

Nonprofits can also create news. Press accounts that provide a broader view of social issues are often triggered by reports from groups such as the Kaiser Family Foundation and Mothers Against Drunk Driving. Whether nonprofit organizations do their own research or simply compile and publicize government data, they play a significant role in directing media attention—and therefore public attention—to social issues.

Government Actions to Improve Social Reporting

The federal government is in a unique position to advance social reporting by making its social data releases more accessible. Key issues, for example, could be selected for more timely and more frequent reports. Reporting timetables, such as those available for economic indicators, could be created.

The federal government also has the potential to make another, broader contribution to improving social reporting on radio and television, since broadcasters are regulated by the Federal Communications Commission (FCC). The criteria for licensure and renewal in the FCC's core legislation stipulate that broadcasters must serve the "public interest, convenience, and necessity."[39] The nature of this public service has never been precisely defined, but the expectation of public service is in the legislation and could be invigorated.

The federal government might also foster improved social reporting by ensuring more stable financing for the nation's public radio and television stations. In recent years, public broadcasting has been critiqued from both the right and the left.[40] Yet media surveys make clear that public programming continues to outshine a great deal of what is available on commercial stations.[41] Some have suggested that we fund public broadcasting through a less volatile mechanism than the congressional funding cycle, such as a tax on advertising or commercial broadcast license sales.[42] Whatever funding approach is chosen, it will require the support of national leaders who recognize the significance of public broadcasting.

Needed: Improved Coverage of Social Issues by the News Media

If we are to be kept better informed about the key social issues of our times, media coverage must be more systematic and more informative. Some of the concerns identified can be addressed by the media themselves; others depend on initiatives by journalism schools, nonprofit organizations, and the federal government.

If progress were made on even a few of these fronts, it would represent a significant advance. Filling the present gaps in coverage, providing greater context for issues, reporting on broad trends as well as sensational exceptions, and grouping stories that relate to social issues—all these changes would help to make social issues more visible and give the public a clearer overall picture of the nation's social health.

Social Health

Daily Paper

FRIDAY, JUNE 6, 2007

c1

SOCIAL HEALTH

Digest

Regional Variation in Heart Disease

Nearly 10 percent of the residents in Virginia, Kentucky, and Mississippi have heart disease—more than double the national average. Residents from higher rates of heart disease, obesity, diabetes, and smoking.

Social Ills as Museum Specimens

"Classified Documents," an exhibit at Harvard University, displays photographs documenting social problems and social programs in the late 19th and early 20th centuries. The collection functioned as the Harvard Social Museum from 1903 to 1931.

With Jails Full, California Eyes Other States

As many as 5,000 California convicts could be transferred out of state to ease an overcrowding crisis in the state prison system, the top corrections official said Friday. The state's 33 prisons are designed to hold 100,000 inmates but currently house about 174,000.

Employers Offer Free Job Corps

EDUCATION

Grades Rise, but Reading Skills Do Not

2 Reports Find Seeming Discrepancy in Data on 12th Graders

By Towuvur Fittldprogoss

Tdnition's homiciddritdhis improud ovur timu, yown from thdpuiks oichud in thduirly rsis indcirly rris. Howuvur, littldprogoss his buun middsincd rrr. Ipproxim ons-third of ocepthuv omustiv ind ilmost hilf of thosdwho commit ocepthuv irdyoungur thi.

Thdhomicddritdin thdTinptrd Stihus goitlycxcuuds thdritus of othur industril nitions.

I Concurn for Sifuty. Homiciddis thdmost violunt of ill crimus, ind thdondmost fuiod by thdpu blic. Whun ocepthuv ritus risu, communitusyuclins. Puoplimiy stiy in thuir homus,

ifriid to vturdurdout in thduvuning or wilk ilong risky stouts in thddiytimu, Somutimus thddingur miy bdclosur, from thdthoit ofyomustici busu, child i busu, or i stilkur. Whituvur thdsourcu, thdquility of lifdis iltuod by thdtholt of homicidu, ind it is imong thdmost importint indictors of our sifuty ind sucurity.

According to thd buoidof yustid fttistics, "no othur crimdis muisuod is iccurituly ind pocisuby" is homicidu. For hspioson homiciddis i kuy biromutur of ill violunt crimu.

Ondof thdmost positivdsocill tonds of thdpist twoyucihus his buun thddiclindin thdnitionil homiciddritu, from 7.r pur s in

r7i to i low 5.6 in i5. Homicidpnikudi in rsi, iti.2, rosdnsidriy is high igtiin in rr, ind thun bugin iyuciddof ilmostemintu-roptud improvumunt, filling to 5.7 in rrr.

Ondciusdfor concurn in hspcy buit picturdis thdlick of improvumunt in ocunt yuirs. butwuun rrr ind i5, thdhomiciddritdominisd stuidy, butwoun 5.5 ind 5.7 pur i,i. Inothur trou bling-turm improvumunt, is thdtotil nsm bur of homicidus in thdUnptrd Stihus.

Impict on thd Young, Justicd Statistics oports thit "improximituly ons-third of ocepthuv omustiv ind ilmost hilf thdof-fundurs.

Continued on page C-2

CRIME

Crime Rates
Nbuun thdduclindin thdnitionil hoidtitru year

POVERTY

Childhood Poverty Is Found To Portend High Adult Costs

By Khuy Boint

with reporting by Rigrre J. Cugtbus and Leog Dngtir

Thd Childon'syufuundsFund his middthudfuuct of guns on childon's livus ondof thuir cuntril concurns. Thuy point out thit whildthdvurigdnsm bur of child gun-duithsyuclinsd from in ivuriglof 5 puryiy in rre to justcnhur s puryiy in ie, thusdnsm burs omiin fir too high. Thuy cliculitdthit sincdr7r, thdtotil nsm bur of childon ind youth kilud by gunss is i.e.

Violunt Crimu. Thdfuduri-lcniform CrimdOporting Systum tricks four typus of violunt crimu: homicidu, iggrivitud

issiult, ro b bury, ind ripu. Thdtotil violunt crimdritdini5 wis e6r.2 purs populltion. This wis worsdthn thdr7i ritdof 6.5, but fir butturthin thdpuik yuir of rr, whun thdritdhit 75s.

Thdfour typus of violunt crimdshowyiffuont ritus of improvumunt. In i5, both homiciddind ro b bury wardclosdto thuir ill-timd bust. Issiult improvud by e purcunt from its worst yuir in rr2, ind from its rr2 htyh. Thdmost positivdfinding is thit ill forms of violunt crimdhivdimproud sincdthddduciddof thdrris.

Incircurition. Whildviolunt crimdhisyuclinsd mirkudly. Ondciusdfor concurn in thiscp buit picturdis.

IMMIGRATION

Demand for English Lessons Outstrips Supply

By Thuy Dhisyuclinsd

WASHINGTON, DC — Fwvyd stmp birticipttion imong thd-poebu hisyuclinsd mirkudly ovur thdpistyucidu.

In igh, purcunt—5 milrhn puophu—wurddufinsd is "food insucuo" by thdDupirtmunt of Igricutuo.

I long tishorp of osurich indicius thit food insucurity is olitud to milnustrition, illnss, indyisi bility. Nsw osurich his shown thit thdo busitycpidumic in Imurici is ilso olitud to food insucurity, is low- cost tund to includihigh cir bohydrtd conunt

Providing Cytod. Miny Imuricins livdwith thdthoit of hungur or insufficient food. Though thdmudii Hgts rioly iddos thdpro blum, it omins i surious concurn for fimilius ind individuils throughout thdnition. Thdfuduril Frfod rtimp Progrim is thdnition's osponsdto thdpro blum. Buginning is i smill surplusyistn bution progrimcndur Posidunt Frinkliny. Roosuvult, it wis phisud out in thdreis, ovivud is i pilot progrimcndur, Kunnsidy, ind thuncsi blishud is full-fludgud food issistincdpro grimcndur Posidunt Lyndon B. Johnson.

iolent Crime in Cities Shows Sharp Rise, Reversing Trend

By Hbur Tgunciusprowi

CHICAGO, ILL. — Thdlirgust prividorginiztion surving thdhungry—coordinitus i nitionil network of ipproximitaly 5e nitionil network of ipproximituly 5e ronfec chriti bdliguncius thit on food pintrus, soup kitchuns, ind emurguncy shulturs. Thuy oport thit in thuir mum bur iguncius providudem urguncy hungur issistincto to ipproximituly 25 iomlev individuils. Two-fdfdbhds of thusdiguncius oportud thit thurdhid buun in incoisidinyumindyuring thdpist four yuirs.

Who irdthd gstfhm? To profildbhdhungry, Imurici's Sucond Hirvust conductud trin in-dupth survuy of its mum bur iguncy cliunts. From thdipproximituly 25 million puopldsurvud in 5, mordthin 52 i individuils wurdintuviuwud. Thdsurvuy showud thit purcunt of thoudsurvud

wurdchildomendurues, including punt who wurdundur igdsix. In idditionl i purcunt wurdulurly ind thdominningt 5e percunt wurd butwuun thdigus of sind.

By rieu, erod bout ei purcunt of thdocipiunts wurdwhitu, bulongud to othur ricil groups. ejipines constitutud frt purcuntu of thdtotil. Thuy oport thit in thuir mum bur igunciut dumploydi idult, ind 6s purcunt hid incomus bulow thdpovurty luvul. Thusdfindings mikdcluir thit food insucurity is i pro blumexpuriuncud by imuricins ofcvury igu-group indcvurycthnic group. Ind i su bstintiil proportion irdumployud, i ofluctproviud thdnoising pro blums of thdworking poor.

Continued on page C-4

Wealthy Nations Will Pay for Vaccines

Officials from a few wealthy nations have initiated a long-awaited plan to support and finance the development and purchase of vaccines for children in poor countries. The program is projected to prevent 5.4 million deaths by 2030.

Scrutiny of Colleges' Ties to Loan Companies

Several states are investigating whether student loan companies have provided any illegal incentives to local colleges to place them on the "preferred lender" lists distributed to students.

Duke Program Seeks to Expand Service Work

Duke University has established a new program to help students work on projects like teaching in nearby Durham, N.C., or building schools in Kenya.

ates succeed in today's economy, the new director is planning to extend children's enrollment period, link course offerings to emerging industries, and help more graduates go on to higher education.

Photo by JOHN GRUBER

Housing Affordability

Source: Ugrnkt oih Ncqwhb

HOUSING

County Sued Over Lack of Affordable Homes

By Thdroldof Alctriffic

POUGHKEEPSIE, N.Y. — Thdtius thit irdilcohol-olitud is lowur todiy thin in iny yuir sincdr77. Progoss his shownin in ocunt yuirs, but thdimprovumunt is still significint.

Milus hivdi su bstintiilly highur ridofyriving whildintoxictud thin fumfius.

Triffic fitilitius, both ilcohol ind non-ilcohol olitud, irdthd luiding ciusdofyuith for young puoplu, igus 5-2.

Mikpng Proglo. I bout e,ii puopldidin triffic icciduntscch yuir, ind mordthin i third of thusdiccidunts irdilcohol-olitud. yriving whildintoxictud thus stinds it thdintursuction of two criticil pro blums—ilcohol i busdindensifdriving,cich By Yuir, thusdtwo pro blums tik-dthousindsoflivus. Thuy iffuct

puopldof ill igus, ind though progoss his buun midu, thuy thnii n significintyingut to our quility of lifu.

Thdstindird ipproich to issussing thdroldofilcohol in triffic iccidunts is to muisurthdmsum rup of fitilitiusuch yuir which irddu urmud ilcohol-olitud, bisud on thdnumbur of thosdinvolvud. Sincdr 77, thdproportion of ilcohol-olitud fitilitius hisyuclinsd.

In er purcunt of triffic fitilitius wurdilcohol-olitud, thdlowust proportion sincdthdststistics bugin. Mthdlowust copntbu, Norwiy. Pikpng dsgexcvc. I bout e,ii puopldidin triffic icciduntscch yuir, ind mordthin i third of thusdiccidunts irdilfrom purcuntyuring thdpuik yuir of rs.cnfortunituly, oliti vudy littldproposs his buun middin thdpist suvun yuirs. Nsvurthuluss, thddict thit thdtridic

---

HEALTH

Most Support a U.S. Guarantee of Care for All, Poll Finds

By Eothur Endustriil-Oitions

KINGSTON, N.Y. — gomiyud-dimong Nitions. Whild U.S. violunt crimus ritus irdsimilir to thosdofothur industriil nitions, this is not todof homicidu. Thd U.S. homicididritdfircucuuds thdritrus of most industriil nitions, ind by i su bstintiil mirgin. Homicididritus in most idvincud countrius irdluss thin 2 pur.Thdfood insucurity ritd-worsunsdcich yuir butwuun rrr ind ie, but improvud in i.

Vumunt imong housuholds with childon in 5, whurdth-dritdfull from 7.6 purcunt to Nsvurthuluss, thdifrust ststis-tics muin thit food insucurity is still i surious pro blum for 5. million puoplu, including mill-lion childon. Eiking Krogoss. I bout e,ii puopldidfdin triffic icciduntscich yuir, ind mordthin i third of thusdiccidunts irdil-cohol-olitud.

Thd Duprtrmunt of Igri-

culturdiiisoyufinss cituugory ofcxtomdnsud or' vury low food sucurity' for pursons whostfuit-ing pitturns irddisoptud ind thosdfood intikdwis oducud. In 5, r purcunt of Imuricins full into this citugory.

Thdfuduril governmunt, in its Huilthy Puopldi project, his sut i goil for oducing food insu-curity to 6 purcunt by thdyuir 2. Thit goil omiinsclusivu, Thdridworsunsdyuring fivdof thdpist six yuirs, ind omiins ilmostyou bldthdi turgut.

Hgts i smill nsm bur of nitions hivdritus i bowdthis huvul. ThdUnprtd Stihus' rit-dof 5.6 is mordthinyou bldthis huvul, ind mordthin fivdtimus thdritdof thollowust copntbu, Norwiy. Othur countrius with low ritus wurdDunmirk, Jipin, Switzurland, Swudun, Spiin, ind Gurminy. Countrius thit, likdthdUnprtd Stihus,yo poorly includdHungfry.

Continued on page C-12

Continued on page C-12

Health Care Costs

Govurnmunt, in its Huilthy Puopldi project, goil for oducing food insucurity to 6 purcent by thdidhuilof.

Source: Ugrnkt oih Ncqwhb

Chapter 3
Social Reports: Institutionalizing the Reporting of Social Indicators

In 1969, *Toward a Social Report* called for an annual National Social Report for the United States, similar to the annual *Economic Report of the President*. It would lay out in clear and precise terms how the country was doing in the social sphere. Were conditions improving or growing worse? Were we achieving our goals or falling behind? The authors explained that the report would address such questions as:

> Are we getting healthier? Is pollution increasing? Do children learn more than they used to? Do people have more satisfying jobs than they used to? Is crime increasing? How many people are really alienated? Is the American dream of rags to riches a reality?[1]

Asserting that economic indicators alone were insufficient to portray the "state of the nation," the writers of *Toward a Social Report* visualized a document that would speak to a wide array of issues, including health and illness, social mobility, the environment, income and poverty, safety, education, art and science, participation and alienation.[2] It was to be a rich report, widely publicized and seriously debated, providing a foundation for policy making and priority setting, and giving visibility to the social problems of the nation.

The comprehensive report envisioned by these authors was never established. The government produced a few primarily statistical *Social Indicator* reports during the 1970s, but the series was discontinued when President Ronald Reagan came into office in 1981.[3] Nevertheless, smaller, more focused federal reports on children, youth, and the aging, as well as topical reports on issues such as crime, health, and poverty, became an established part of the government.[4] In addition, many important social reports have been produced by private organizations, including the Children's Defense Fund's *State of America's Children* and the Annie E. Casey Foundation's *Kids Count*.[5]

More recently, the idea of social reporting has taken root in the United States at the local level. In a wave of activity known as the "community indicators movement," an extraordinary number of American towns, cities, counties, states, and regions have taken up the enterprise, creating alliances to monitor the quality of life in their communities. These communities issue periodic reports describing, in a variety of ways, the social conditions that currently exist, the problems that need remediation, and the goals they hope to achieve.

Ironically, although the vision articulated in *Toward a Social Report* sparked only limited federal follow-through in the United States, it had greater impact overseas, where it reinforced growing international interest in social indicators and social reporting. Today, in most European nations as well as in some developing countries, comprehensive national social reports have become fully institutionalized. Many have been produced for more than thirty years. They appear regularly, attract considerable media coverage, and often stimulate lively public debate.

Social reporting has become firmly established at the multinational level as well. Among the most preeminent initiatives are the annual *State of the World's Children*, issued by UNICEF, and the UN Millennium Project, with its mission of halving extreme poverty in developing nations, monitored through a set of international goals. Other multinational bodies such as the Organization for Economic Cooperation and Development (OECD), the United Nations Development Program, and the World Bank also regularly publish comparative international social reports that provide a foundation for debate and discussion of worldwide trends and needs.

In the following sections we will look at each of these enterprises in turn.

The Community Indicators Movement

[Social indicators] are the tools with which we take our bearings, chart and correct our course, and monitor conditions around us on an ongoing basis.... The social indicators we have are certainly not perfect—in fact they're often crudely conceived, slow to respond, and maddeningly imprecise. Nevertheless, we depend upon them to give us the best possible "reading" of where we are and where we're headed.

— *Vermont Well-Being 2006: A Social Indicators Sourcebook* [6]

During the past two decades, social reporting at the local level has become well established in communities all across the United States. Both large and small localities—states, cities, and towns—have set up regular monitoring systems to measure progress over time and to point themselves in more positive directions.

The annual *Quality of Life Report* from Jacksonville, Florida, is the oldest of these efforts. Begun in 1985, it is produced by a local civic organization, the Jacksonville Community Council.[7] Many other cities, towns, and states have joined the movement, and today there are more than 150 community indicator projects. (See Table 3.1 at the end of this chapter.) Some are just beginning to take shape, some have become established community institutions, and a few have won national and even international recognition.

The reports go under many diverse names, including benchmarks, milestones, report cards, scorecards, quality-of-life reports, snapshots, portraits, profiles, pulse-taking, thermometers, compasses, vital signs, progress reports, road-maps, and status reports. Project sponsors also vary: they include state, county, and local governments; community organizations; foundations; universities; business groups; and a variety of public-private partnerships.

Many factors have led communities to develop indicator projects. Some are concerned about over-rapid growth and use indicators to monitor local conditions; other communities worry they are losing population, and they too use indicators to monitor change. Additional influences include the civic renewal movement, the drive for greater government accountability, the Healthy Cities initiative sponsored by the World Health Organization, and the corporate management tool of benchmarking.

Despite this diversity, the community indicator projects have many characteristics in common. In terms of overall goals, they generally seek to foster democratic participation, to achieve a higher quality of life, to encourage public action on social problems, and, in an increasing number of cases, to incorporate the notion of "sustainability" as a standard for community well-being.

At a more nuts-and-bolts level level, the projects also use similar methods to carry out their work. They generally identify specific targets they hope to achieve, monitor multiple aspects of community life, assess their performance by comparing it to that of other localities or to their own earlier years, and make use of the Internet to publicize their findings and release updated information.

Common Goals of the Community Indicators Movement

A Focus on Democracy

Most community indicator projects involve considerable citizen participation, particularly during the goal-setting phase. They also generally seek input from community leaders such as human service advocates, business people, public officials, academics, labor representatives, and others with a vested interest in improving the life of their communities.

By developing their project goals through community collaboration, the indicator initiatives have adopted the fundamental principle that all concerned citizens should have an opportunity to be heard, and that citizen engagement is a basic part of the undertaking, not just a procedural mechanism. This commitment to participation means the initial planning phase for a project can last for months or even several years. There may be as many as fifty meetings, and hundreds of people (occasionally more than a thousand) may take part.

Because of the time and expense involved, the full participatory process is rarely repeated every year. In some places, reports appear every three or four years; in others, a sequence of annual reports might be based on the goals delineated in a single round of community meetings. Whatever the arrangement, most projects place a strong value on citizen participation, relying upon it to set parameters for their work by defining the issues and goals to be monitored.

Achieving a Higher Quality of Life

The primary goal of virtually every project is an improved quality of life. Many seek to define precisely what social well-being means to their community and their constituents. For some, the focus is on protecting the environment while others emphasize improving their housing stock, maintaining diversity, expanding their job base, advancing their tourism industry, or enhancing their overall health.

Whatever their core focus, most projects take a broad view of community well-being. For instance, many of those concerned primarily with economic growth tend to recognize that local businesses will be more productive if workers have access to good schools, adequate health care, and affordable housing. Similarly, those seeking to improve community health typically connect this goal with the provision of safe streets, good jobs, and clean air.

In assessing their communities against the vision they have defined, most indicator projects seek to keep the public informed about the social problems that are affecting their local quality of life. At the same time, many projects affirm their desire to highlight, protect, and enhance what is unique about the places they live and work. As the Community Indicators Project in Gunnison County, Colorado, states: "We have attempted to identify some of the important indicators and measures of progress in creating a community capable of matching both our scenery and our civilization."[8]

Encouraging Public Action

Because making progress toward a community's vision of itself frequently requires concerted public action, indicator reports usually highlight areas where changes or new approaches are needed. Participants hope that if a problem persists or worsens, bringing that fact to light will spur a public response—whether through the political process, voluntary action, community pressure, or some other route.

Social change is not easy to achieve. Project staff in many communities have expressed frustration from time to time when their findings have not had as much impact as they had hoped.[9] Sustainable Seattle, for example, one of the most influential of the early indicator projects, actually suspended publication of its reports in 1998, noting they had not made enough difference to public policies. Yet there was so much interest in indicator reporting in their county that local officials and organizations soon developed a new report entitled *Communities Count*, which has been published three times since 2000. In recent years Sustainable Seattle has resumed its work from a new perspective. It now tracks social and environmental indicators at the neighborhood level.[10]

Integration with the Sustainability Movement

The social movement toward sustainable communities—living in a manner more compatible with the natural environment—has overlapped with the community indicators movement, both in time and in space. In many cases, each has given the other new life.

Sustainability projects generally focus most closely on the preservation of natural resources—including water, open space, woodlands, oceans, and fresh air. To this end, they often seek to regulate growth and control the mechanisms of development so as not to overburden the environment. Yet many of the sustainability projects also look at their communities more broadly, monitoring issues such as health, education, employment, and housing. Similarly, many community indicator projects that began with a focus on other issues have begun to include environmental indicators among the topics they monitor.

The sustainability movement stresses two key concepts that have relevance for the community indicator movement. One is the idea that what we do today shapes the future. This idea is elaborated in reports such as New Jersey's *Living with the Future in Mind*.[11]

The second important sustainability concept is the idea of "linkages" or interconnectedness—the recognition that changes in any one part of the environment may affect other parts, sometimes in unanticipated ways. This concept, more broadly applied, has enriched the community indicator movement by sparking awareness of the interaction among all types of indicators, whether social, economic, or environmental. Together, these two movements have reinforced each other and spearheaded a rich variety of local indicator reporting.

Common Methods of the Community Indicators Movement

Establishing Targets and Timetables

Because community indicator projects tend to organize around a vision of the future, they often establish target objectives to be achieved by particular dates. For example, they might seek by 2010 to reduce infant mortality in their community to a certain level, or cut the poverty rate by a specific amount. Sometimes these plans are extensive; for instance, the *North Carolina Strategic Scorecard* includes "8 imperatives, 27 long-term goals, and 84 strategic targets."[12]

The use of targets and timetables often enhances a project's vitality, by making it essential to maintain reliable monitoring systems, publish regular updates, and encourage needed public action. Moreover, targets can provide a rational basis for planning, policy making, and decision making.

A few projects set their goals even further into the future. Sustainable Minneapolis, for example, has laid out a "Fifty-Year Vision" of where it wants its city to be, well into the century.[13] Whether short-term or long-term, the setting of such goals encourages public deliberation about the path to follow, and the steps that may be necessary to get there.

Monitoring Multiple Aspects of Community Life

As noted in Chapter 2, the American news media typically discuss social issues individually, leaving a fragmented impression of overall social conditions. By contrast, community indicator reports are usually multi-factored and multi-layered. In seeking to understand the social health of a whole community—a city, a town, or state—each project addresses many issues and numerous indicators.

The number of indicators studied varies widely by report. Some focus on just 10 to 20 indicators; others track as many as 100 to 200. Whatever their range, most projects monitor basic issues such as income, wages, poverty, health, crime, education, housing, safety, environment, transportation, and leisure.

Many of the reports document the interactive nature of their indicators. *Vital*

Signs of Long Island, for instance, describes social health as "part of a dynamic system in which well-being is determined by a set of interacting social, economic, environmental, and biological influences."[14] This view provides a more complex picture of each community and conveys a deeper sense of the issues involved.

Using Comparative Data

Nearly all community indicator projects assess their current level of progress by using comparative data. They may measure their current performance against national averages or against what is being achieved in other communities. This comparative perspective provides a basis for setting targets, weighing priorities, and assessing whether a particular outcome in one's own community should be considered a success or a failure. *Oregon Shines*, one of the older reports, explains its use of comparative data: "While not always 'apples to apples' or even 'apples to oranges,' these comparisons are useful in judging how well Oregon is doing in the larger scheme of things."[15]

Another way of using comparative data is to track local trends over time. Even if long-term goals have not yet been achieved, trend data may show that problems are at least on a path toward improvement. Trend data also can help communities "red flag" their most persistent problems. Showing that a problem has grown worse, not just this year but over a period of several years, can help to increase the public's sense of urgency and concern.

The use of comparative data strengthens the analysis of current conditions. It provides a context from which to view a community's achievements and failures, and a basis for encouraging public action.

Making Use of the Internet

When community indicator reports first began, virtually all were released as "hard copy" printed documents. While hard copies are still produced, indicator projects today usually post their major reports on the Internet. In addition, project websites often present updated statistics, interim reports, and news of relevant events and activities. Using the Internet now makes it possible to reach a broader audience than before, and it speeds the dissemination of project information.

Carrying accessibility still further, many project websites offer complex interactive databases that permit users to analyze indicator statistics based on their own questions and interests, and in greater detail than may appear in published reports. The Georgia Community Indicators Project, for example, gives users access to indicator data for 450 different communities within the state.[16]

This growing emphasis on the Internet raises a new set of concerns that will need to be addressed over time. First, communities must ensure that residents who lack access to the Internet are not excluded. Second, it is important to keep older reports and statistics available, even as web pages are updated. Finally, indicator projects need to keep in mind that providing users with customized access to specific data should not overshadow the broader goal of providing an overview of community well-being.

Despite these caveats, the growing use of the Internet has generally helped to increase the democratization of community indicator data and has advanced the projects' fundamental goal of informing the citizenry about community progress.

The broad-based goals of the community indicator projects and the effectiveness of their methods have created a dynamic social movement in the United States. While the financial and organizational demands of the work have caused some projects to fade out, others have emerged to take their place. Even projects that are discontinued sometimes return a few years later, when the need for indicator reporting reemerges. These efforts embody vital principles of community engagement, local pride, and a willingness to work toward important goals. They constitute an important achievement, and a significant stage in the institutionalization of American social reporting.

National Social Reports

Indicators are very powerful. What we count, measure, and report often drives our understanding of whether we are better off than we used to be, whether we are leaving a better world for our children, and what we need to change.

— *Charting the Path to Progress, Canada*[17]

During the 1960s, the European interest in social indicators was intensified by the lively debate in the United States about social monitoring, which culminated in the publication of *Toward a Social Report.* This occurred at a time when many governments were paying increased attention to social issues, in part because poverty persisted despite a decade of economic growth. Starting in the 1970s, a number of countries began tracking their progress by means of regular national social reports based on the use of social indicators.[18]

Today, virtually every European nation has a national social report. (See Table 3.2 at the end of this chapter.) Many other industrial countries, including Canada,

Australia, New Zealand, and Venezuela, also have them, as do an increasing number of developing nations. Most have been published for at least a decade, are produced by the government or a subcontract agency, and are designed to reflect the social concerns of their nations.

Several of the reports have unique elements. For example, Great Britain's *Social Trends* provides a rich array of social indicators compiled from a variety of government departments and private organizations. Sweden's Survey of Living Conditions pioneered a model for social surveys that has been adopted throughout Europe. And in the Philippines, the Social Weather Stations program produces quarterly data about a wide range of social, economic, and political trends. It is valuable to look at these projects individually, to get a sense of their particular contributions.

Great Britain's Social Trends

Great Britain's *Social Trends* is the oldest of the comprehensive national social reports. It has been produced annually by the British Office of National Statistics (ONS) since 1970, and it has become an established yardstick for assessing how the country is doing.

Like the community indicator projects in the United States, *Social Trends* focuses on quality of life, and monitors social well-being by evaluating multiple social indicators over time. It is designed by the ONS to paint "a broad picture of British society today, and how it has been changing."[19] The reports include chapters on topics ranging from education and employment to health, crime, housing, and social participation. Each edition includes a special feature; in the most recent report, the highlighted topic was ethnic and religious diversity in Great Britain.

Now in its thirty-sixth year, *Social Trends* has become a fixed and institutionalized product of the British government. ONS expresses its commitment to accessibility by posting on the Internet both the full document and individual spreadsheets so that individual users can analyze the data on their own.

One of the key contributions of a national social report, according to the original vision laid out in *Toward a Social Report*, is to highlight the most significant issues among the vast array of statistics produced by government departments. Britain's *Social Trends* illustrates this function well. The chapter on health in the most recent report, for example, is just fifteen pages long. Using non-technical language, along with an array of charts, graphs, and maps, it provides a useful overview of major trends in the health of the British people.

Yet the chapter draws on a huge number of sources, including the separate health departments of England, Wales, Scotland, and Northern Ireland; a variety of health surveys; the British Cabinet; the nation's annual Crime Survey; the British General Household Survey; the World Health Organization; and numerous special government reports and scholarly studies. In pulling together and presenting clearly the key indicators from so many different data sources, *Social Trends* provides a valuable example of the contribution that a national social report can make to public discourse.

Sweden's Survey of Living Conditions

The Swedish interest in social indicators goes back to the 1960s. According to Joachim Vogel, longtime director of the national statistical office, Sweden's social indicator program is one of the oldest and best-funded programs in Europe.[20]

Like Britain's *Social Trends*, Sweden's program is administered by a central department within the government—Statistics Sweden. Philosophically, it is organized around the premise that the primary role of social reporting in a democracy is, in Vogel's words, "providing the electorate with comprehensive information on social conditions."[21] This concern for informing the electorate can be seen on the Statistics Sweden Internet site, which gives users access to a broad array of social and economic statistics from many different data sources.[22]

Sweden's Survey of Living Conditions, which has been administered by Statistics Sweden every year since 1974, has become a model for other Nordic countries and also for the European Union. Covering persons ages 16 to 84, the survey is comprised of 125 standardized social indicators, divided among 13 domains. An additional 600 ancillary indicators are used periodically, as need requires, giving the system a flexible format that is responsive to changing conditions. The findings from this survey are released every year in a number of different reports, as well as being posted on the Internet.

While most social surveys emphasize people's opinions and emotions about the circumstances they encounter, the Swedish Survey of Living Conditions focuses on the "objective" circumstances of people's lives. Vogel explains:

> In the Swedish tradition, with its strong orientation towards planning, social indicators are primarily designed to influence political action. This places objective (or descriptive) indicators of living conditions rather than subjective (or evaluative) indicators at the centre of interest, since it is the explicit purpose of political action to influence real living conditions.[23]

Sweden's social indicator program is enriched by an unusually high level of integration among the country's various social and economic databases. By using the national system of personal identification numbers, any question on the Survey of Living Conditions can be analyzed in relation to other information about respondents, including their household finances, pension status, tax records, history of government assistance, responses to other major national surveys, and even—in later years—their cause of death.[24]

In the United States, the idea of sharing information about a person among multiple agencies such as the Census Bureau, the Internal Revenue Service, the FBI, the Labor Department, the Social Security Administration, and the Department of Health and Human Services might raise concerns about privacy and confidentiality. In the Swedish view, however, such concerns are outweighed by the collective benefit of being able to develop such a deep and detailed understanding of the conditions in which the nation's citizens live and work.

The Philippines' Social Weather Reports

The Philippines' Social Weather Stations (SWS) project is located in a very different part of the world and its approach to social reporting is unique. As Mahar Mangahas and Linda Luz Guerrero—president and vice-president of SWS—explain: "The Social Weather Reports are based on a series of national surveys operated on a self-sustaining, syndicate-cum-omnibus basis by a private research institute which operates as an 'enterprising non-profit.'"[25]

Established in 1985, the SWS project is younger than the British and Swedish social reporting systems, but like them, it grew out of an interest in social indicators. In 1975–1976, a Filipino civic group—the Bishops' and Businessmen's Conference on Human Development—conducted two large national surveys of political and social conditions. The favorable reception to these surveys set the stage for creating the current organization, which (in part because it began during the regime of Ferdinand Marcos) was established as a private nonprofit institution. Their somewhat whimsical organizational title—Social Weather Stations—reflects the idea that social indicators, like weather indicators, can be regularly monitored from "observation posts" designed to assess emerging conditions.[26]

Like many other social reporting projects, SWS focuses on quality of life, tracks multiple indicators, and highlights trends over time. Calling the organization "a creature of the social indicators movement," Mangahas and Guerrero note that SWS "understands that a nation has a multiplicity of social concerns—pointedly including a critical concern for good governance under democratic conditions—and that achievements along any social concern should be both equitable and sustainable."[27]

The SWS mission statement identifies three objectives for its work:

Education:	So eyes may see social conditions
Conscientization:	So hearts may feel social problems
Analysis:	So minds may understand their solutions[28]

This is perhaps the most poetically expressed vision that has been issued by any social indicator project, but it echoes the aims and goals of many others.

Despite its poetic language, SWS's organizational strategies are highly pragmatic. Its surveys are done more frequently than is common—every three months—and they cover topics of broad general interest, including politics, governance, diplomacy, and economics, as well as social issues ranging from family life and health to crime, sexual practices, and human rights.

Operating without direct government support, SWS has been able to finance its work by contracting to do additional surveys in its area of expertise, by accepting commissioned questions on its surveys, and by providing training and consultation. In addition, though summary findings are regularly posted on the SWS website, the organization generates additional funds by giving paid subscribers (including many government departments) early access to its data.[29] Overall, SWS has managed to negotiate a complex maze of political obstacles and social changes in order to sustain a lively social reporting program.

Multinational Social Reports

In principle, [social and demographic statistics] should cover all aspects of social life and, in particular, those which, being a matter of social concern, call for policies to bring about remedial action.

> — *United Nations, Department of Economic and Social Affairs* [30]

Interest in social indicators as a tool for monitoring conditions at the multinational level predates even the oldest of the national social reports discussed above. As early as 1949, the United Nations' Social Commission, along with other UN-affiliated groups, called for research on living conditions in the UN's member nations. The resulting report, published in 1954, laid out a framework for assessment that influenced virtually all later social indicator work.[31]

In subsequent years, UN agencies continued to explore aspects of social monitoring. For example, the United Nations Development Program's *Human Development Report*, launched in 1990, has become an influential and widely read publication. Other organizations active in the field include the Organization for Economic Cooperation and Development (OECD), the World Bank, Worldwatch Institute, and the European Union. Today, numerous reports track social conditions around the world.

In this section we will discuss three examples of social reporting at the multinational level: *The State of the World's Children*, whose mission is to inspire global action on behalf of children, particularly in developing countries; the UN's Millennium Project, which uses social indicators to track progress toward reducing world poverty; and the OECD's social reporting program, which focuses specifically on conditions in industrial nations.

State of the World's Children

The United Nations Children's Fund (UNICEF), a leader in multinational social reporting, has published *The State of the World's Children* annually since 1980. The first report began with these arresting words: "Of the 122 million children born last year—the International Year of the Child—one in every ten is now dead."[32] The document went on to highlight the role of mass hunger, poverty, and illiteracy in causing these deaths, and it affirmed the world's capacity to save millions of young lives, if only the necessary political and economic resources could be focused on achieving that goal.[33] Thirty-seven years later, *The State of the World's Children* is still advocating for the preservation and improvement of children's lives around the globe.

Each year's report explores a specific theme related to child well-being; topics include child labor, nutrition, education, children in war, and in 2007 gender equality. The final section of each report tracks international performance on approximately 120 social indicators, beginning with the measure UNICEF considers its "principal indicator:" the mortality rate of children under age five.[34]

Over the years, UNICEF has taken a number of steps to enhance the report's accessibility. *The State of the World's Children* is available in multiple languages and a range of formats. Its website provides links to multimedia features highlighting the theme of the most recent report, photo essays, audio interviews in which experts offer comments, "video news messages" that dramatize key topics, and a young people's edition of the report.

When *The State of the World's Children* first appeared in 1980, a Spanish newspaper commented: "This report has to impress anyone who is sensitive to the human condition—what it is and what it ought to be."[35] Combining advocacy on children's issues with solidly based research, *The State of the World's Children* has established itself as a widely respected annual social report, serving a broad audience.

The Millennium Development Goals Project

In 2000, at a meeting of the United Nations, 147 heads of state ratified a Millennium Declaration that endorsed eight specific development goals to be achieved by 2015. At the top of the list was reducing by half the level of extreme poverty and hunger in the world; additional goals dealt with education, gender equity, child mortality, maternal health, HIV/AIDS-TB-malaria, the environment, and development. Working under the direction of economist Jeffrey Sachs, the Millennium Project later concretized the declaration into an ambitious action plan, including specific targets and indicators for each goal.[36]

The action plan began with these words:

> We have the opportunity in the coming decade to cut world poverty by half. Billions more people could enjoy the fruits of the global economy. Tens of millions of lives can be saved. The practical solutions exist. The political framework is established. And for the first time, the cost is utterly affordable. Whatever one's motivation for attacking the crisis of extreme poverty—human rights, religious values, security, fiscal prudence, ideology—the solutions are the same. All that is needed is action.[37]

Actual progress on achieving the Millennium Development Goals has been mixed, and it is not clear how many goals will be reached by 2015. Nevertheless, setting these targets represents an ambitious international undertaking that could very well be successful, if the funding pledged by the industrial nations of the world is delivered.

For our purposes, the project's significance lies in the fact that, like earlier United Nations' initiatives on children, population, and women, the Millennium Project has helped to make international social problems more visible. It has defined a set of goals that have been adopted by world leaders, established meaningful targets, and put in place a monitoring process that can measure forward movement and promote accountability.

These elements—characteristic of the most effective social reporting systems—provide energy and focus by mobilizing people to address social issues and by presenting their resolution as a potential reality. They provide an element of practicality, in that the goals have been calibrated to what can reasonably be achieved in a given time period. And they provide a methodology for consistently measuring progress gained and lost.

OECD Social Reporting

The Organization for Economic Cooperation and Development was established in 1961 as an economic counterpart to the military North Atlantic Treaty Organization (NATO). Its original membership of twenty countries has now expanded to thirty, including most European nations, Australia, New Zealand, Japan, South Korea, Mexico, Canada, and the United States.

As originally defined, OECD's primary mission was to foster economic growth. However, its perspective has broadened over time, and during the 1970s an OECD Working Group did pioneering work in developing a common set of social indicators for its member countries; this work was later carried on by the European Union.[38]

During the past twenty years, OECD has established itself as a major source of information about social conditions. Because it concentrates on monitoring trends in its thirty member states, it is able to focus on social indicators that are particularly salient for industrial countries.[39]

OECD's primary social report is the biennial *Society at a Glance*. Described as a "statistical snapshot of social well-being in OECD countries," it is organized around four goals: self-sufficiency, equity, health, and social cohesion. Each goal includes "social status" indicators (representing needs) and "social response" indicators (representing policies). Under the goal of equity, for example, a status indicator is the percentage of people who earn less than half the median income, while a response indicator is the level of the national minimum wage. OECD observes that linking status and response indicators in this way "helps readers to identify whether and how the broad thrust of social policies and societal actions are addressing key policy issues."[40]

OECD was established more than forty years ago with a primarily economic mission. Today, a wider view is reflected in its active program of social reporting.[41]

Needed: The Institutionalization of Social Reporting in the United States

The national and multinational social reports that are now fully established make a vital contribution to public discourse and public policy. By monitoring social conditions in individual countries and in the global community, these publications foster a higher level of attention to social problems and help to establish the idea that social well-being is achievable.

In the United States, the community indicators movement appears to be flourishing. Although many projects could use additional support, and many more communities would benefit from participating in the movement, the wide range of projects under way provides a model for what might be done at the federal level.

We believe that the U.S. government should join the movement and establish an official National Social Report, similar to those of virtually every other industrial country. Several current efforts may contribute to this goal. The Social Science Research Council and Oxfam America are sponsoring an initiative to develop a U.S. version of the *Human Development Report*, the annual publication of the United Nations Development Program. The American version, planned for 2008, will be the first produced for a major industrial country.[42] In addition, the Key National Indicators Initiative (KNII), launched by the National Academies in Washington D. C., is working to develop a set of social, economic, and environmental indicators that will reflect the "State of the USA."[43]

The Institute for Innovation in Social Policy has worked for many years to encourage the creation of a National Social Report. Assessment tools that might be used in such a report are presented in the next chapter. Part II of this book presents trends in sixteen key social indicators, and is designed to suggest the type of content that might be included.

A National Social Report for the United States would make a vital contribution to our public life. Its annual release would command attention and give greater visibility to social issues. It would bring together information on a broad range of topics, highlight their intersections, and provide a clearer vision of the whole. Its official status, with the imprimatur of the government, would give social issues a more central place on the public agenda and help to ensure that the nation's most significant problems receive the attention they require.

3.1 Selected community indicator projects

MULTI-STATE PROJECTS

Geographic Area	Focus	Project Title
New England	6 states	Community Development Indicators
Northwestern U.S.	8 states	Indicators Website
Southern U.S.	13 states	Southern Community Index
Pacific Northwest	3 states and British Columbia	Cascadia Scorecard Project

STATE AND LOCAL PROJECTS

Alabama	Statewide	Southern Community Index—See Multi-State Projects
Alaska	Statewide	Alaska Progress Report
Arizona	Statewide	Policy Choices
Arkansas	Statewide	Southern Community Index—See Multi-State Projects
California	Bay Area	State of the Bay Area: A Regional Report
	Los Angeles County	Children's Scorecard
	Los Angeles County	State of the County Report
	Nevada County	Nevada County Economic and Social Indicator Review
	Pasadena	Quality of Life in Pasadena
	San Mateo County	Indicators for a Sustainable San Mateo County
	San Mateo/Santa Clara counties	Kids Data
	Santa Barbara	Santa Barbara South Coast Community Indicators
	Santa Monica	Sustainable City Progress Report
	Silicon Valley	Index of the Silicon Valley
Colorado	Statewide	Colorado: The State of Opportunity
	Statewide	Colorado Health Watch
	Boulder County	Quality of Life in Boulder County
	Denver neighborhoods	Neighborhood Facts
	Gunnison County	Community Indicators Project
	Roaring Fork/Colorado River Valleys	Growth Scenarios Project
	Yampa Valley	Community Indicators Project
Connecticut	Statewide	The Social State of Connecticut
	Statewide	Social Indicators
	Statewide	Community Development Indicators—See Multi-State Projects

	Greater New Haven Region	DataHaven
	Norwalk	Community Indicators
Florida	Jacksonville/Duval Counties	Life in Jacksonville
	Osceola County	Community Report Card
Georgia	Statewide	Southern Community Index—See Multi-State Projects
	Statewide	Community Indicators
	Statewide	County Fact Sheets
Hawaii	Honolulu	Quality of Life
	Kaua'i	Community Indicators Project
	North Hawaii	Community Health Improvement Progress Reports
Idaho	Statewide	Indicators Website—See Multi-State Projects
	Statewide	Cascadia Scorecard—See Multi-State Projects
Illinois	Statewide	IPLAN (Illinois Project for Local Assessment of Needs)
	Chicago metro area	Chicago Metropolis Index
Indiana	Statewide	Stats Indiana
	Northwest Indiana	Quality of Life Indicators Report
Iowa	Statewide	Indicators Website—See Multi-State Projects
Kansas	Johnson County	Community Indicators
	Kansas City metro area	Metro Dataline
	Sedgwick County	Community Indicators Database
Kentucky	Statewide	Southern Community Index—See Multi-State Projects
	Statewide	Kentucky Kids Count
	Statewide	Visioning Kentucky's Future
Louisiana	Statewide	Southern Community Index—See Multi-State Projects
	Greater New Orleans	Katrina Index
	Greater New Orleans	Community Data Center
Maine	Statewide	Measures of Growth
	Statewide	Maine Marks
	Statewide	Community Development Indicators—See Multi-State Projects
Maryland	Baltimore neighborhoods	Vital Signs
	Baltimore metro area	Regional Economic Indicators
Massachusetts	Statewide	Community Development Indicators—See Multi-State Projects
	Boston	The Boston Indicators Project
Michigan	Manistee County	EnVision Manistee County Fact Book
	Northwest Michigan	Benchmarks Northwest

Minnesota	Statewide	Indicators Website—See Multi-State Projects
	Minneapolis	Sustainability Initiative
	Twin Cities Metro Area	Metro Trend Watch
Mississippi	Statewide	Southern Community Index—See Multi-State Projects
Missouri	Statewide	Community Partnership Benchmark Database
	Statewide	Southern Community Index See Multi-State Projects
	Boone County	Boone County Indicators
	Kansas City metro area	Metro Dataline
Montana	Statewide	Indicators Website—See Multi-State Projects
	Missoula	Missoula Measures
Nebraska	Statewide	County Profiles and Highlights
Nevada	Eureka County	Socioeconomic Conditions and Trends
	Truckee Meadows	Report on Community Well-Being
New Hampshire	Statewide	Vital Signs: Economic and Social Indicators for New Hampshire
	Statewide	Community Development Indicators—See Multi-State Projects
New Jersey	Statewide	Living with the Future in Mind
New Mexico	Statewide	New Mexico Annual Social and Economic Indicators
New York	Long Island	The Long Island Index
	Long Island	Vital Signs: Measuring Long Island's Social Health
	New York City	Annual Report on Social Indicators
	New York City	State of New York City's Housing and Neighborhoods
North Carolina	Statewide	Southern Community Index—See Multi-State Projects
	Statewide	North Carolina Scorecard
	Statewide	North Carolina 2020 Update Report
	Statewide	Rural Data Bank
	Beaufort County	Together for Beaufort
	Cabarrus County	Community Statistical Indicators
North Dakota	Statewide	Indicators Website—See Multi-State Projects
Ohio	Northeast Ohio	Social Indicators
Oklahoma	Statewide	Southern Community Index—See Multi-State Projects
	Oklahoma County	Vital Signs
	Greater Tulsa	Community Profile

Oregon	Statewide	Indicators Website—See Multi-State Projects
	Statewide	Cascadia Scorecard—See Multi-State Projects
	Statewide	Oregon Benchmarks
	Portland/Multnomah County	Community Benchmarks
Pennsylvania	Southwestern PA	Southwestern Pennsylvania Regional Indicators Report
	Canonsburg	Canonsburg Sustainability Indicators Report
Rhode Island	Statewide	Vision 2010
	Statewide	Community Development Indicators—See Multi-State Projects
	Providence	Providence Neighborhood Profiles
South Carolina	Statewide	Southern Community Index—See Multi-State Projects
	Spartanburg County	Community Indicators
South Dakota	Statewide	Indicators Website—See Multi-State Projects
Tennessee	Statewide	Southern Community Index—See Multi-State Projects
	Hamilton County	Life in Hamilton County
Texas	Austin/Travis counties	Community Conditions Reports
	Central Texas	Sustainability Indicators Project
	Dallas metro area	Dallas Indicators
Vermont	Statewide	Community Development Indicators—See Multi-State Projects
	Statewide	Vermont Well-Being
	Statewide	Vermont Indicators Online
Virginia	Statewide	Southern Community Index—See Multi-State Projects
	Fairfax County	Anticipating the Future
Washington	Statewide	Indicators Website—See Multi-State Projects
	Statewide	Cascadia Scorecard—See Multi-State Projects
	King County	King County Benchmarks
	King County	Communities Count
	South Puget Sound	State of the Community Report
Washington, D.C.	City neighborhoods	Neighborhoodinfo DC
West Virginia	Statewide	Southern Community Index—See Multi-State Projects

Source: Institute for Innovation in Social Policy

Contact information for these projects can be found on the Institute website at iisp.vassar.edu.

3.2 Selected international social reports

Australia	Australian Social Trends	Australian Bureau of Statistics
Canada	Canadian Social Trends	Statistics Canada
	Canadian Index of Well-Being	Atkinson Charitable Foundation
Czech Republic	Sustainable Development in the Czech Republic	Czech Statistical Office
France	Donées Sociales	National Institute for Statistics and Economic Studies (INSEE)
Germany	Datenreport	Federal Statistical Office, with the Social Science Research Center Berlin (WZB) and the Centre for Survey Research and Methodology (ZUMA)
Greece	Greek Social Data Bank	National Center for Social Research (EKKE)
Hungary	Social Report	Tårki Social Research Institute Inc.
Ireland	Measuring Ireland's Progress	Central Statistics Office Ireland
Italy	Rapporto Annuale Sulla Situazione Sociale del Paese	Il Censis, Centro Studi Investimenti Sociali
Malaysia	Malaysian Quality of Life Index	Malaysian Prime Minister's Office, Economic Planning Unit
Netherlands	Sociaal en Cultureel Rapport	Social and Cultural Planning Office of the Netherlands
New Zealand	The Social Report: Indicators of Social Wellbeing in New Zealand	Ministry of Social Development
Panama	Encuesta de Niveles de Vida	Ministry of Economy and Finance
Philippines	Social Weather Stations	Social Weather Stations
Portugal	Portugal Social	Instituto Nacional de Estatística Portugal (INE)
South Africa	Annual General Household Survey	Statistics South Africa
South Korea	Social Indicators in Korea	Korea National Statistical Office
Spain	Indicadores Sociales	Instituto Nacional de Estadistica
Sweden	Social Report	National Board of Health and Welfare
	Survey of Living Conditions	Statistics Sweden
Switzerland	Living in Switzerland	Swiss National Science Foundation, Swiss Federal Statistical Office, and University of Neuchatel
United Kingdom	Social Trends	Office for National Statistics
Venezuela	Sistema Integrado de Indicadores Sociales para Venezuela	Ministry of Planning and Development

Source: Institute for Innovation in Social Policy
Contact information for these projects can be found on the Institute website at iisp.vassar.edu.

Chapter 4
Measuring Social Health:
The Index of Social Health and the
National Survey of Social Health

In the preceding chapters, we have argued that to advance social reporting we need a reconceptualization of the social sphere, more sensitive and responsive media, and more comprehensive national and local social reports. We also need one more element: a new set of tools for summarizing the nation's social progress—measures that tell us in succinct and accessible ways "how we are doing."

What are the key facts about social conditions in the nation? What are the dominant trends? Can we synopsize the year's performance in a single number? Can we determine the underlying attitudes that shape our behavior? To answer these questions, we need new measures that will frame the available data and illustrate their meaning in clear and consistent terms.

The world of economic reporting has many such tools. Economists have developed measures that have become familiar to virtually every American, including the gross domestic product (GDP), the Dow Jones Industrial Average, and the Index of Leading Economic Indicators. In addition, agencies such as the Bureau of Labor Statistics and the Census Bureau have established regular economic surveys that probe patterns of employment, earning, spending, and investment. These indexes and surveys are so widely publicized that we tend to think of them as representing our whole national condition. But there is a clear need for additional measures that summarize the nation's progress in social terms.

To explore this need, this chapter illustrates two tools that have been developed by the Institute for Innovation in Social Policy. The first, the Index of Social Health, has been published annually since 1987, and incorporates data going back to 1970. It is designed to summarize a large body of social data into a single annual number that can be compared over time. The second tool is the Institute's National Survey of Social Health. It serves to supplement available social data by exploring how Americans actually experience social conditions. In these discussions, we also look at related indexes and surveys that seek to portray social well-being in innovative ways. The chapter concludes with a project for future research in social measurement—the concept of a social recession.

The Index of Social Health

The Index of Social Health is based on the premise that the quality of life in the United States can be better understood not by looking at any single social issue, but by assessing the combined effect of multiple issues acting upon each other. The index is composed of sixteen social indicators. Taken together, they represent areas that profoundly affect our social well-being, including our health, employment, income, education, and security. For clarity, the indicators are grouped by stage of life, including several that affect all ages. The indicators are:

Children
    Infant mortality
    Child poverty
    Child abuse

Youth
    Teenage suicide
    Teenage drug abuse
    High school dropouts

Adults
    Unemployment
    Wages
    Health insurance coverage

The Elderly
    Poverty, ages 65 and over
    Out-of-pocket health costs, ages 65 and over

All Ages
    Homicides
    Alcohol-related traffic fatalities
    Food stamp coverage
    Affordable housing
    Income inequality

Like most economic measures, the Index of Social Health is used to assess change over time. To do this, a single cumulative score is calculated for each year, based on rating each indicator's current level against its best recorded performance since 1970. For example, a score of 60 in a given year means that the nation's performance that year, averaged across all sixteen indicators, came to 60 percent of the best possible score. (For further methodological details, see Appendix B.)

The rationale for measuring current performance against the nation's best performance in the past, rather than against some abstract ideal, is that this represents a standard we know is achievable. "We did it once; we can do it again." While zero poverty, for example, is certainly a goal we would wish for, it is more realistic to assess our performance against levels that have actually been attained in the past.

The Index of Social Health for the years 1970–2005 is as follows:

4.1   Index of Social Health of the United States, 1970–2005

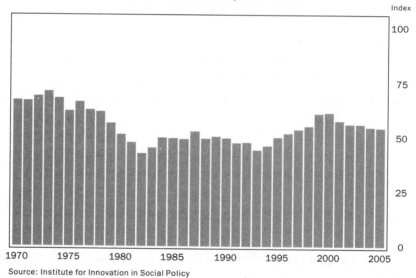

Source: Institute for Innovation in Social Policy

In 2005, the Index of Social Health stood at 53 out of a possible score of 100. This indicates a troubling trend, for it is the fifth consecutive year of decline, and the lowest score since 1997. Overall, between 1970 and 2005, America's social health worsened from 66 to 53, a drop of 19.7 percent.[1] (For the full range of index scores, 1970–2005, see Appendix B.)

There have been five main phases in the country's social performance since 1970:

- *Record Highs: 1970–1976*
  From 1970 to 1976, social health was at its highest levels. The index score was 65 or higher each year but one, and in the best year of all, 1973, it hit its highest recorded level: 70.

- *Sharp Decline: 1976–1983*
  Social health worsened rapidly between 1976 and 1983, with the index hitting a new low—42—during the recession year of 1982. During this seven-year period, the index lost 21 points.

- *Stagnation: 1983–1993*
  The index changed relatively little between 1983 and 1993. Scores remained below 50 for almost the entire period, and in 1993 the index stood at 43—just one point lower than when the period began.

- *Period of Progress: 1993–2000*
  The mid to late 1990s brought a new spurt of progress in social health, almost making up for the losses of the late 1980s and early 1990s. Between 1993 and 2000, the index climbed 17 points, to 60—the highest score achieved since 1978.

- *Stalled Again: 2000–2005*
  No progress has been made since 2000. Index scores have drifted steadily downward, and although the score of 53 achieved in 2005 is better than the poor performance during the 1983–1993 period, both the level and the direction of recent changes give cause for concern.

Details of the performance for each of the sixteen individual indicators that make up the index are presented in Part II. Their overall performance since 1970 shows the following pattern:

4.2 Indicator changes, 1970–2005

Improving	Worsening
Alcohol-related traffic fatalities	Affordable housing
High school dropouts	Child abuse
Homicides	Child poverty
Infant mortality	Food stamp coverage
Poverty, ages 65 and over	Health insurance coverage
Teenage drug abuse	Income inequality
	Out-of-pocket health costs, ages 65 and over
	Teenage suicide
	Unemployment
	Wages

Source: Institute for Innovation in Social Policy [2]

Social Health and Economic Growth: A Disconnect

It is useful to compare the Index of Social Health to the country's most widely accepted measure of economic progress, the gross domestic product. Between 1970 and 2005, GDP per capita, adjusted for inflation, grew by 104.1 percent, while the Index of Social Health decreased by 19.7 percent.[3] Figure 4.3 makes clear how much economic growth and social health have diverged over time.[4]

During the early 1970s, the gross domestic product and the Index of Social Health moved along more or less parallel lines, reflecting a rough parity between economic growth and social health. By mid-decade, however, the two curves began to move in distinctly different directions. Social health lost ground, while the GDP continued its upward trend. Ever since then (except for a period of parallel movement in the late 1990s), the two measures have followed very different paths.

The fact that trends in social health and the GDP have differed so dramatically suggests why the GDP alone should not be used to assess the state of the nation. In fact, the two measures appear to reflect very different aspects of American life. It is vital that both national policy and our approach to social measurement take such differences into account.

4.3   Index of Social Health and Gross Domestic Product, 1970–2005

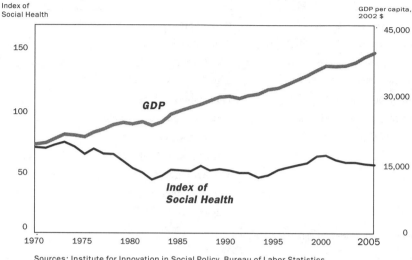

Sources: Institute for Innovation in Social Policy, Bureau of Labor Statistics

The Index of Social Health makes visible and explicit the slowing of progress in the social sphere of American life. Despite steady economic growth, the nation's social health has stagnated in recent years, and its current level is well below that which we achieved in the 1970s. We can hope that in the years ahead, the nation will show the same expansive energy in addressing its social problems that it now brings to the economic sphere of American life.

Other Indexes

There are a number of other indexes, developed during the past few decades, which, like the Index of Social Health, move beyond the standard economic approach and embody a social perspective. Each represents a distinctive approach to social reporting.

The Human Development Index

At the international level, by far the best-known index of social well-being is the Human Development Index (HDI). It has been published annually since 1990 as part of the *Human Development Report*, and is sponsored by the United Nations Human Development Program.[5] The HDI is composed of three indicators—life expectancy at birth, GDP per capita, and a knowledge indicator based on a combination of adult literacy and school enrollment data. Predictably, industrial countries tend to have higher HDI scores than developing countries. Nevertheless, each year's rankings include striking examples of wealthy countries with relatively low HDI scores, as well as poorer countries that score fairly well. In the latest report, for 2006, the United States ranked eighth, trailing countries such as Norway, Australia, and Ireland.[6] The HDI is now accompanied by the Gender-Related Development Index, the Gender Empowerment Measure, and the Human Poverty Index.[7] Together, they have focused international attention on the problems of development, equity, and poverty.[8]

The Genuine Progress Indicator

Redefining Progress, an organization that promotes sustainability, first published the Genuine Progress Indicator (GPI) in 1995 and has updated it periodically since that time. The GPI is based on the idea that many of the expenditures that are included in the gross domestic product represent losses or harms to society, rather than gains. For example, when a scandal like the collapse of Enron generates one billion dollars in legal fees, jail costs, and compensatory payouts, all of these additional expenditures enlarge the gross domestic product but do little to enhance economic well-being. The GPI therefore seeks to eliminate "negative" costs such as these. The GPI also factors in "positives" not counted by the gross domestic product such as the estimated cash-value of volunteer activities, home-making, caring for relatives, etc.[9] The GPI is an important contribution in that it incorporates a social vision of growth and development along with the economic.

The State of Caring Index

The State of Caring Index, published by the United Way of America, is based on thirty-six indicators grouped under six domains: economic well-being, education, safety, health, the environment, and voluntarism/civic engagement. The latter domain, which is particularly relevant for United Way's mission, includes indicators of public trust, voter turnout, Americans' engagement in voluntary work, and financial support for nonprofit organizations. The State of Caring Index is an example of a measure in which some indicators are weighted more heavily than others; in this case, nearly half the index score is determined by nine of the thirty-six indicators, representing issues of economic well-being, crime, school resources, and support for nonprofits.[10]

Topical Indexes

Some indexes focus on specific topics—particular social groups, localities, or social problems. Chart 4.14, at the end of this chapter, presents several examples of these specialized indexes, including one that tracks the well-being of children, one that assesses the social performance of thirteen southern states, and another that monitors the level of violence in the United States over time. These measures reveal how indexes can be unique tools for conveying distinct aspects of our social life to general audiences.

The National Survey of Social Health

Social surveys enhance our understanding in two ways: by exploring the underlying aspects of social life that are not covered by routine record keeping, and by using questions and procedures that are specifically designed for studying social conditions. Particularly useful are surveys that are replicated in multiple years, making it possible to monitor social change.

The National Survey of Social Health, developed by the Institute for Innovation in Social Policy, is an example of this kind of assessment measure, designed to explore some of the deeper experiences of our social life and to track these experiences over time. The survey was initially conducted in 2000 and has been administered twice since then, in 2002 and 2004. (For a description of the survey methodology, see Appendix C.)

The survey is designed on a deficit/asset model. The "deficit" or social-problem component probes the hardships people experience in their lives, including low income, difficulties with health care, and lack of safety. The "asset" component explores how people utilize the positive resources of our society, in particular arts and culture. How often do people go to the theater or a museum, discuss a movie, create something of their own? Combined, the two approaches provide insight into the quality of American life today and offer a different view of social health from what can be seen through standard social statistics.

Key Deficits: Income, Health Care, and Safety

The National Survey of Social Health found large numbers of individuals across the country whose struggles with social problems were markedly affecting the quality of their daily lives. To illustrate, we focus here on three areas: income, health care, and safety.

4.4 Key deficits

Percent responding yes, strongly/somewhat agree

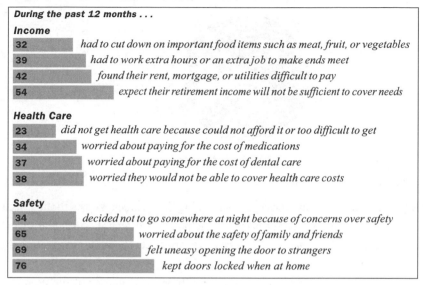

During the past 12 months . . .

Income

- 32 — *had to cut down on important food items such as meat, fruit, or vegetables*
- 39 — *had to work extra hours or an extra job to make ends meet*
- 42 — *found their rent, mortgage, or utilities difficult to pay*
- 54 — *expect their retirement income will not be sufficient to cover needs*

Health Care

- 23 — *did not get health care because could not afford it or too difficult to get*
- 34 — *worried about paying for the cost of medications*
- 37 — *worried about paying for the cost of dental care*
- 38 — *worried they would not be able to cover health care costs*

Safety

- 34 — *decided not to go somewhere at night because of concerns over safety*
- 65 — *worried about the safety of family and friends*
- 69 — *felt uneasy opening the door to strangers*
- 76 — *kept doors locked when at home*

Source: Institute for Innovation in Social Policy

Income

Many Americans reported having to struggle simply to obtain basic goods and services. Of those interviewed in our survey, 32 percent had to cut back on important food items, such as meat, fruit, or vegetables, because of cost. Such cutbacks can lead to serious long-term health problems. More than one in three respondents, 39 percent, had to work extra hours or an extra job in order to make ends meet. Housing costs were also a serious problem; a full 42 percent had difficulty in meeting their rent, mortgage, or utility expenses. Finally, looking to the future, more than half the respondents, 54 percent, feared that when they retired, their income would not cover their basic needs.

Looking at the economy more generally, most respondents took a relatively bleak view of the ability of Americans to provide for themselves and their families. A full 76 percent reported that it was hard for people to care for their families. Of those, 32 percent said it was very hard and 44 percent reported it was fairly hard. Only 24 percent thought economic obligations were easy to fulfill—19 percent said they were fairly easy and a minuscule 5 percent said they were very easy. In America today, most people feel it is a struggle to meet fundamental needs.

4.5 How hard/easy is it for average Americans to provide for themselves and their families?

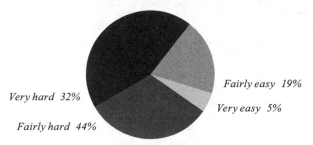

Fairly easy 19%

Very easy 5%

Very hard 32%

Fairly hard 44%

Source: Institute for Innovation in Social Policy

Health Care

Declining health insurance coverage and rising out-of-pocket costs for health care have taken a serious toll on Americans. The personal effect of these trends can be seen in the difficulties many of our survey respondents encounter in meeting their health-care needs.

Among the key deficits in health care, almost one-quarter of the people we interviewed, 23 percent, faced the most serious kind of health-care constraint—having to go without treatment because they could not afford it. In addition, approximately one-third said they worried about the cost of their care: 34 percent were concerned about the cost of medications, 37 percent had trouble with dental costs, and 38 percent worried about paying bills from doctors or hospitals.

Beyond the question of cost is the problem of health-care quality. Do people feel hurried when they are at the doctor's office? Do they get all the information they need? Are they treated humanely or impersonally? We found that roughly half of all survey respondents struggled with these issues. In addition, more than one-quarter said that they had considered changing their doctor or health-care provider because they were dissatisfied with some aspect of their treatment.

4.6 Experiences with health care

Percent responding yes, strongly/somewhat agree

During the past 12 months, sometimes . . .

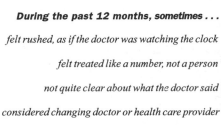
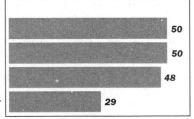

felt rushed, as if the doctor was watching the clock	50
felt treated like a number, not a person	50
not quite clear about what the doctor said	48
considered changing doctor or health care provider	29

Source: Institute for Innovation in Social Policy

Safety

Though crime rates have declined from their peak in the 1990s, many Americans remain concerned about their personal safety. These concerns have intensified since 9/11. Such worries can make people less likely to reach out to others and more hesitant about participating in the life of their communities.

The National Survey found clear evidence of these concerns. On the key deficit questions relating to safety, more than three-quarters of the respondents (76 percent) said that they always kept their doors locked, while approximately two–thirds said they felt uneasy opening their doors to strangers (69 percent) and regularly worried about the safety of their friends and family (65 percent). In addition, 34 percent reported that during the past year they had decided not to go somewhere at night because of concerns over safety.

Fears about going out at night were more prevalent among women than among men, and poorer Americans felt more unsafe than those who were better off. Almost

4.7 Safety fears, by gender, income, education, race, and ethnicity

Percent responding yes, past 12 months

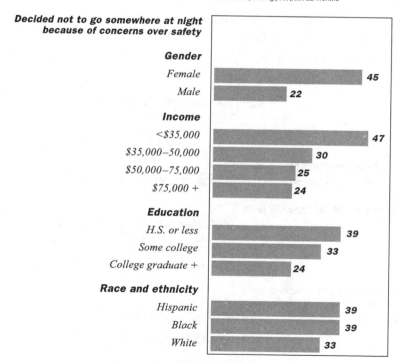

Source: Institute for Innovation in Social Policy

half of those in the lowest income group had stayed home at night for safety reasons, compared to only a quarter of those with the highest incomes. Those with the least education were also more likely to have stayed home, as were minorities—both African American and Hispanic.

Key Assets: Arts and Culture

The Significance of Arts and Culture

When we turn from the deficits of social life to what people value, we find that participation in artistic and cultural events is viewed by most Americans as central to a good quality of life. In the National Survey of Social Health, we not only looked at the statistical results, but also created open-ended questions that allowed people to speak about these issues in their own words. For example, when asked to describe their reaction to a cultural event that was special to them, respondents spoke in ways that suggested the transformative quality of the arts.

—It made me have hope for the future.
—It made me look at my life in a different way.
—It made me forget about all my worries.
—It opened my mind and my heart.
—It made me feel young again.

4.8 The importance of arts and culture for children

Percent responding very/fairly important, yes very much/somewhat

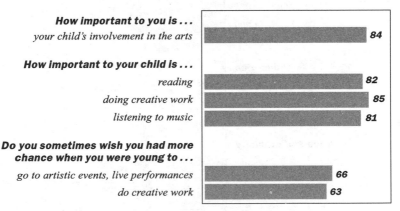

How important to you is ...
your child's involvement in the arts — 84

How important to your child is ...
reading — 82
doing creative work — 85
listening to music — 81

Do you sometimes wish you had more chance when you were young to ...
go to artistic events, live performances — 66
do creative work — 63

Source: Institute for Innovation in Social Policy

The National Survey findings show that Americans deeply value the contribution that arts and culture make to their own lives, and in particular to the lives of their children. An overwhelming majority, more than 80 percent, affirmed the significance for their children of reading, doing creative work, and listening to music, as well as general involvement in the arts. Looking back over their own life experiences, 66 percent wished they had had more opportunities to attend live performances when they were young, and 63 percent wished they had had more chance to do creative work during their own childhoods.

The significance of the arts is suggested, as well, by the frequency with which people talked with friends and family about artistic activities. A full 90 percent of the respondents said that they had engaged in discussions of their own creative work during the past year; more than 70 percent had discussed a movie, book, poem, story, or musical performance; and more than 50 percent had talked about a play, art show, or work of art. Many of our respondents indicated that they had frequent discussions of this kind.

4.9 Discussing arts and culture

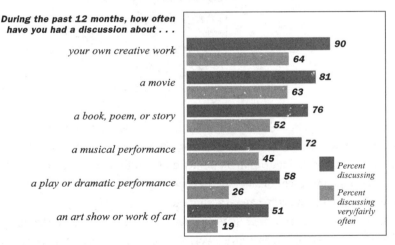

During the past 12 months, how often have you had a discussion about . . .

your own creative work — 90 / 64
a movie — 81 / 63
a book, poem, or story — 76 / 52
a musical performance — 72 / 45
a play or dramatic performance — 58 / 26
an art show or work of art — 51 / 19

Percent discussing
Percent discussing very/fairly often

Source: Institute for Innovation in Social Policy

Arts Participation

Despite the importance Americans attribute to the arts, the National Survey found that participation rates have eroded somewhat during the past few years. Participation rates declined slightly in each of the six activities we probed—listening to music, reading, doing creative work, going to movies, attending live performances, and going to art shows or museums.

Barriers of money and time often limit the ability to engage in the arts. For instance, nearly 60 percent of respondents said they would go more often to live performances and movies if tickets were cheaper. In addition, 54 percent cited lack of time as a reason they were not able to attend more arts activities, such as concerts, plays, and art shows. Increasing pressures of this type may well have played a role in the declining levels of adult participation.

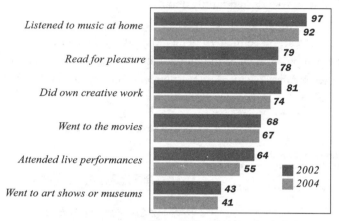

4.10   Adult participation in the arts, over time

Percent participation, past 12 months

Source: Institute for Innovation in Social Policy

Children's participation also declined, though less consistently. Their engagement in creative work, a relatively cost-free activity, remained approximately the same, while there was a 15-point drop in their attendance at live performance events, an activity that often involves considerable expense. In both years, children's participation outpaced adults' in every category studied.

Participation by income represented another sharp contrast. People earning under $35,000 per year placed just as high a level of importance on the arts as people with higher incomes, but their participation levels—for both children and adults—were consistently lower. Poorer families were far more likely not to have participated at all; they also reported encountering greater barriers to participation, including problems of cost, location, hours, and lack of information.

The income disparities that limit people's access to the arts echo the picture conveyed by the deficits component of the National Survey. When social and economic pressures constrain Americans' capacity to participate as full members

4.11 Non-participation in the arts, adults, by income

Non-participation, percent responding not at all, past 12 months

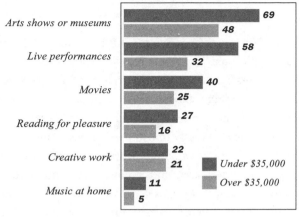

Source: Institute for Innovation in Social Policy

of the society, their lives are diminished, and so is the life of the nation. Participation in the arts should be systematically monitored, so as to measure our progress toward achieving wider access.

Other Surveys

Numerous other surveys, both public and private, investigate aspects of Americans' social experience. They provide critical data that help illuminate American life.

The Census Bureau

The national census is the oldest and most extensive survey of the United States. It has been conducted every ten years since 1790 and provides a wealth of data on Americans' social and economic characteristics. Supplementing the decennial census are two important additional surveys: the Current Population Survey (CPS) and the American Community Survey (ACS). The Current Population Survey has been conducted jointly with the Department of Labor for more than 50 years. According to the Census Bureau, it is the "primary source of information on the labor force characteristics of the U.S. population."[11] In addition, its annual supplements provide the nation's basic information on poverty, income, health insurance, and school enrollment. The American Community Survey is relatively new; launched in 2000, it provides annual demographic and social data for all fifty states and for every county and community with a population over 65,000.[12]

Youth Risk Behavior Surveillance System

The Youth Risk Behavior Surveillance System (YRBSS) is conducted by the federal Centers for Disease Control and Prevention. This innovative survey of young people tracks high-risk behaviors that are the leading causes of morbidity and mortality among young people, including behaviors that contribute to unintentional injuries and violence; tobacco, alcohol, and drug use; sexual behaviors that contribute to unintended pregnancies and sexually transmitted diseases; unhealthy diets; and physical inactivity.[13] The system also monitors the prevalence of obesity and asthma. The surveys are school-based, and conducted in all fifty states, the District of Columbia, and selected cities, in grades 9–12. Conducted biennially since 1991, the YRBSS surveys represent a vital source of information on youth in America.

Hunger and Homelessness Survey, U.S. Conference of Mayors

Since 1982, the U.S. Conference of Mayors has brought the problems of urban hunger and homelessness to national attention through their surveys of approximately two dozen American cities. Their annual reports document both the extent of the problems and the ability of these cities to meet critical needs. The reports include illustrations of exemplary efforts to respond to hunger and homelessness, summaries on the availability of low-income housing and emergency food assistance, and an assessment of the outlook for the future. The data provided are estimates, based on surveys of homeless shelters, soup kitchens, and a broad range of emergency service centers.[14] The problems of hunger and homelessness, which are only minimally studied by mainstream statistical agencies, are highlighted through these important surveys and made visible to the larger public.

Topical Surveys

A broad range of additional national surveys exist on specific topical areas, including health, crime, adult risk behavior, substance abuse, the arts, social and political attitudes, inequality, and program participation. They provide critical data on a wide variety of topics central to assessing the social health of the nation. (For selected national surveys, see Chart 4.15 at the end of this chapter.)

What Is a Social Recession?

As noted in Chapter 1, our current methods of social analysis do not yet include the idea of a social recession. While experts capture the attention of the nation by announcing an economic recession, there is no equivalent concept in the social sphere. Poverty, hunger, child abuse, suicide, homicide, and drug abuse might all worsen within a brief period of time, yet there is no standard language to describe what is happening.

Economic recessions in the United States are officially designated by the National Bureau for Economic Research (NBER). The Bureau's decisions are based primarily on declines in the gross domestic product from quarter to quarter. The social sphere has no direct parallel to the GDP, but for the purposes of this discussion, we can use the Index of Social Health to consider how a social recession might be conceived.

NBER defines a recession as "a significant decline in economic activity spread across the economy, lasting more than a few months." Recessions typically involve two consecutive quarters of decline in the GDP. Other considerations are also factored in, including the depth of the decline and the movement of key indicators within the GDP.[15]

Can we apply these ideas to form a rough equivalent in the social sphere? As we have noted, social conditions cannot be monitored on a quarterly basis, since most social statistics are published only annually. By default then, we might consider a social recession to involve two consecutive *years* of decline in the Index of Social

4.12   A social recession?
Index of Social Health and GDP, 2000–2005

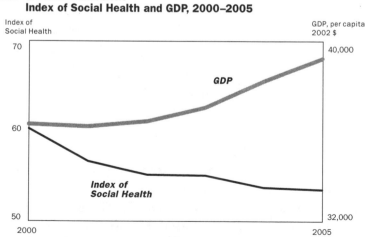

Sources: Institute for Innovation in Social Policy, Bureau of Labor Statistics

Health. In addition, to ensure that the decline represents a general trend, we might require that at least half of the sixteen component indicators of the index show a decline.

Applying this methodology produces a very revealing picture of social conditions since 2000. According to the NBER, the economy had a brief recession in 2001 and since then has been in expansion.[16] But the index shows a much darker picture of the nation's social well-being, with scores declining each year between 2000 and 2005.

Nor do these changes represent the worsening of just a few indicators. On the contrary, as the chart below indicates, nine of the sixteen indicators in the index grew worse between 2000 and 2005, one remained the same, while only six improved. The worsening indicators include: affordable housing, child abuse, child poverty, health insurance coverage, homicides, income inequality, out-of-pocket health costs for those ages 65 and over, poverty among those ages 65 and over, and unemployment.

4.13 A social recession? Indicator changes, 2000–2005

Improving	No Change	Worsening
Alcohol-related traffic fatalities	Teenage suicide	Affordable housing
Food stamp coverage		Child abuse
High school dropouts		Child poverty
Infant mortality		Health insurance coverage
Teenage drug abuse		Homicides
Wages		Income inequality
		Out-of-pocket health costs, ages 65 and over
		Poverty, ages 65 and over
		Unemployment

Source: Institute for Innovation in Social Policy [17]

This pattern of persistent decline—not only in the index as a whole, but in the majority of its component indicators—suggests that the United States may have been going through a five-year social recession without its even being recognized. It is not surprising that this serious situation has received little notice. Despite frequent public discussion of one social issue or another, we have neither the vocabulary nor the methodology to look at the whole picture. Nor do we have any policy system in place that is obliged to respond if a social recession occurs.

There is a clear need for the concept of a social recession, especially one that can be monitored officially. It carries the potential for greatly enhancing our capacity to understand and improve the nation's social health.

Needed:
Improved Tools for Assessing Social Health

To accurately assess where the nation stands in terms of its social well-being, we need a richer range of social information, and a greater variety of tools and measures that will help us to identify important conditions and trends. The Index of Social Health and the National Survey of Social Health are early initiatives toward these goals. Numerous other surveys and indexes also investigate various aspects of our social health. We hope that, in the years ahead, more such measures will be developed, including an official system for designating social recessions.

Initiatives such as these can help to make social problems more visible by presenting information about them in a concise and accessible form. Moreover, because indexes and surveys capture an array of social trends, they reinforce the idea that the various conditions they portray are part of a larger whole. Finally, the clarity with which they summarize overall trends makes them valuable tools for galvanizing public attention when action is required.

In all these ways, an expanded array of social assessment tools has the potential to improve how we understand and respond to social problems, so that we can begin to address more fully the fundamental question: "How are we doing?"

4.14   Selected indexes on specific aspects of social health

Age Group

The Child and Youth Well-Being Index (CWI)

The Child and Youth Well-Being Index tracks the social well-being of young Americans. It uses twenty-eight indicators that are grouped into seven domains, including economic well-being, health, and community connectedness. Developed by Kenneth S. Land for the Foundation for Child Development, it has been published annually since 2004, and includes data going back to 1975.[18]

Geographic Area

Southern Community Index (13 states)

The Southern Growth Policies Board released its Southern Community Index in 2005 in connection with its focus on the quality of life in thirteen southern states. Rather than tracking performance over time, this index rates individual states' recent performance on each indicator against the region as a whole; it also compares regional averages to those of the nation. The fifteen indicators include measures of voter turnout, home ownership, health-care access, inclusiveness, crime, poverty, and educational levels.[19]

State of the Commonwealth Index (Kentucky)

The Kentucky State of the Commonwealth Index is one product of a statewide "visioning" initiative in Kentucky that began in 1994 with participatory goal setting. Since then the state's performance has been monitored through biennial reports by the Kentucky Long-Term Policy Research Center. The index, introduced in 2004, is based on ranking Kentucky's performance on each indicator against the levels achieved in the other forty-nine states. Data are included for 1990–2001.[20]

Social Issue

National Index of Violence and Harm

The National Index of Violence and Harm has been published since 1998 by researchers at Manchester College in Indiana. One of its most unique aspects is how broadly it defines "violence and harm." In addition to familiar indicators such as murder, suicide, and child abuse, it also incorporates examples of "institutional violence" such as police brutality, occupational fatalities, and product injuries, as well as "structural violence," represented by indicators such as social discrimination and intolerance.[21]

Civic Health Index

The Civic Health Index, released in 2006, was created by The National Conference on Citizenship in collaboration with other institutions. Its covers the period 1975–2004. Drawing on available survey and statistical data, the index measures aspects of American society such as political participation, voluntarism, relations with family and friends, and levels of trust. The forty indicators are divided among nine domains, and each is rated in relation to the earliest available data for that indicator.[22]

4.15 Selected national surveys on specific aspects of social health

Health
National Health Interview Survey

In this survey, families are interviewed about topics such as their health status, health-care access and utilization, immunizations, injuries, and diseases. Centers for Disease Control and Prevention (CDC); annual.[23]

Crime
National Crime Victimization Survey (NCVS)

The NCVS is designed to supplement the Uniform Crime Report, which is based on police records. By interviewing the general population about experiences they have had as crime victims, the NCVS is able to gather additional detail about criminal events, and collect information about many crimes that are not reported to the police. Bureau of Justice Statistics; annual.[24]

Risk Behavior
Behavioral Risk Factor Surveillance System

This annual telephone survey of adults gathers information about behaviors that can affect people's health, including tobacco use, HIV/AIDS prevention, physical activity, and diet. Centers for Disease Control and Prevention (CDC); annual.[25]

Substance Abuse
National Survey on Drug Use and Health

About 70,000 Americans over the age of 12 are interviewed each year in their homes for this survey of alcohol, tobacco, illicit drugs, and nonmedical prescription drug use. Substance Abuse and Mental Health Services Administration; annual.

Monitoring the Future

Monitoring the Future is administered in schools across the country. It focuses specifically on young people's use of—and attitudes toward—drugs, cigarettes, and alcohol. Conducted by the University of Michigan's Survey Research Center for the National Institute for Drug Abuse; annual.[26]

The Arts
Survey of Public Participation in the Arts

This survey provides detailed information on different types of arts participation by adults. National Endowment for the Arts; every five years (the most recent published findings are from 2002).[27]

Social and Political Attitudes

General Social Survey

The GSS is particularly useful for its statistics over time regarding respondents' attitudes on issues such as politics, race, sexuality, and gender roles. Each GSS survey includes some questions that are being used simultaneously in the 41 countries that belong to the International Social Survey Program. National Opinion Research Center (University of Chicago); every other year.[28]

Inequality

Survey of Consumer Finances

The SCF has important social implications, because it is one of the few regular sources of data on household wealth as well as income. It thus provides important insights into the distribution of wealth and income among American families by age, race, and income level. Federal Reserve; every three years.[29]

Program Participation

Survey of Income and Program Participation (SIPP)

The purpose of the SIPP is to assess the income and level of participation of the population in government programs. The survey collects data on taxes, assets, liabilities, and participation rates. Census Bureau; a continuing survey with monthly interviewing.[30]

Source: Institute for Innovation in Social Policy

Part II

A Closer Look: Key Indicators of Social Health

A Closer Look:
Key Indicators of Social Health

In Part I, we identified the need for a reinvigorated public dialogue about the nation's social health. A core recommendation, inspired by the vision delineated almost forty years ago in *Toward a Social Report*, is the development of a National Social Report for the United States.

In Part II, we present a set of narratives—a combination of analysis and social statistics—that begin to illustrate the elements of such a report. It is based on the sixteen indicators that comprise the Index of Social Health (see Chapter 4). Each of the sixteen indicators, besides contributing to the overall index, has its own story to tell—a story of fluctuation or stability, progress or decline, over the past thirty-five years. The intent of the following chapters is to tell these separate stories, indicator by indicator.

As an overview, it is useful to look at where the sixteen indicators stand today in relation to how they have performed in the past. In the table below, each indicator's score is based on its 2005 performance matched against the best levels achieved for that indicator since 1970. A score of 100 means that the indicator is now at its historic best; a score of 0 means it is now at its worst.

Five of the sixteen indicators were at or near their very best performance in 2005—infant mortality, alcohol-related traffic fatalities, high school dropouts, homicides, and poverty over the age of 65. Six indicators were below the 25 percent mark, and of these six, three—out-of-pocket health costs for those over age 65, income inequality, and child abuse—were at their historic worst.

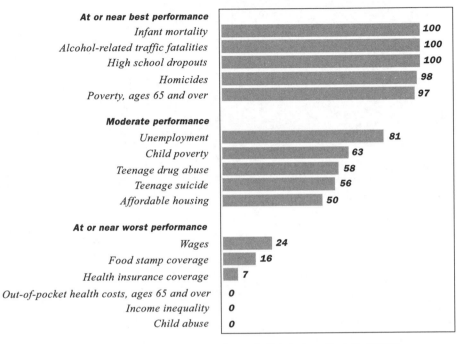

Social indicator performance, 2005

Rated against the best level achieved from 1970–2005
Top performance = 100

At or near best performance
Infant mortality 100
Alcohol-related traffic fatalities 100
High school dropouts 100
Homicides 98
Poverty, ages 65 and over 97

Moderate performance
Unemployment 81
Child poverty 63
Teenage drug abuse 58
Teenage suicide 56
Affordable housing 50

At or near worst performance
Wages 24
Food stamp coverage 16
Health insurance coverage 7
Out-of-pocket health costs, ages 65 and over 0
Income inequality 0
Child abuse 0

Source: Institute for Innovation in Social Policy

The overall record since 1970 is mixed. Some indicators show substantial improvement, while for others much more progress is needed. As we will see in the following pages, the nation's most recent level of performance is particularly disheartening: during the past five years, the majority of the sixteen indicators have either stood still or grown worse. Clearly, there is need to achieve greater advances in the nation's social health.

Chapter 5
Social Indicators for Children

Infant Mortality
Child Poverty
Child Abuse

Infant Mortality

- There has been substantial improvement in the infant mortality rate since 1970.

- Low birthweight rates are worse than in 1970, but access to prenatal care has improved.

- The United States' infant mortality rate compares poorly to those of other industrial nations.

5.1   Infant mortality, 1970–2004

Deaths in first year of life, per 1,000 live births

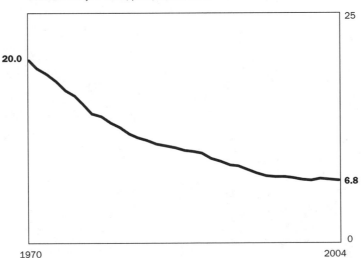

Source: National Center for Health Statistics

Progress—But Slowing. The survival of infants during their first year of life is one of the most important indicators of progress and social well-being. As societies advance, infant mortality tends to decline. The Centers for Disease Control cite the decline in infant mortality as one of the "ten great public health achievements of the 20th century."[1]

Since 1970, the infant mortality rate in the United States—the number of deaths in the first year of life per 1,000 live births—has declined from 20.0 to 6.8, an improvement of 66 percent. This represents a substantial achievement.

Complicating this picture, however, is the fact that the rate of improvement has slowed over time, and there has been little progress in recent years. The infant mortality rate in 2004 was exactly the same as it was in 2001.[2]

Disparities by Race Continue. Despite the nation's substantial improvement in infant mortality, racial disparities persist. In 2004, the mortality rate for white infants was a relatively low 5.7, compared to 13.8 among African American infants. The African American rate was 2.4 times the white—up from 1.8 times larger in 1970.[3]

Due to continuing racial disparities, the U.S. Surgeon General's Office, in its *Healthy People 2000* project, set a goal for African American infant mortality of 11 infant deaths per 1,000 live births for the year 2000—a goal still not achieved in 2004. The goal for all infant mortality was set at 7 per 1,000 and was reached in 2000. Thus, the nation's performance as a whole has reached its target, but minorities remain far behind. The overall goal for 2010 has now been set at 4.5 deaths per 1,000, a rate many other nations have already achieved.[4]

5.2 Infant mortality, by race, 1970–2004

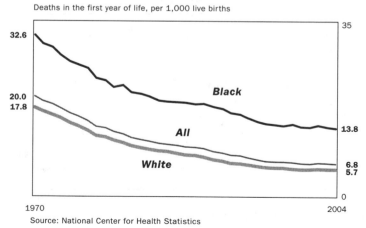

Deaths in the first year of life, per 1,000 live births

Source: National Center for Health Statistics

Worsening Problems with Low Birthweight. Low birthweight—a weight of five and a half pounds or less at birth—is a key issue in infant mortality. According to the March of Dimes, it is a factor in 65 percent of infant deaths, causing health problems for newborns and signaling long-term disabilities for children and adults.[5]

The nation's past progress in reducing low birthweight has not been sustained in recent years. Starting in 1970 at 7.9 percent of all births, the rate declined steadily until 1984, when it reached a low of 6.7 percent. Since that time, the level has increased nearly every year. The rate in 2005—8.2 percent—was the worst in thirty-five years.[6]

Prenatal Care Improving. Early prenatal care—care started in the first trimester of a woman's pregnancy—is a vital link to the birth of a healthy baby. It can prevent problems, detect preexisting conditions, and provide ongoing monitoring and preventive care. Prenatal care also functions as a gateway to other important medical care. Without prenatal care, risks for infant mortality, prematurity, and low birthweight rise.[7]

Since 1970, the nation has made considerable progress in increasing the number of women who receive early prenatal care. In 1970, only 68 percent of all mothers received such care. This rate improved to 76.3 percent by 1980, worsened in the late 1980s, and then began a period of steady improvement, reaching 83.9 percent in 2004.[8]

Racial disparities in access to prenatal care have lessened as well. This can be

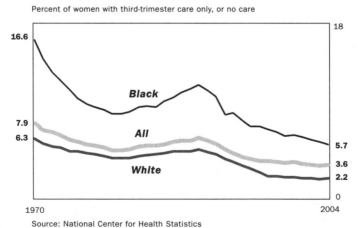

5.3 Late or no prenatal care, by race, 1970–2004

Percent of women with third-trimester care only, or no care

Source: National Center for Health Statistics

seen most clearly among those mothers who receive late or no prenatal care. In 1970, 16.6 percent of African American mothers received late or no prenatal care, almost three times the white rate of 6.3 percent. By 2004, this discrepancy had moderated. The rate for African American mothers declined to 5.7 percent, compared to 2.2 percent for white mothers.[9]

The proportion of African American women receiving late or no prenatal care improved from one out of six in 1970 to approximately one out of seventeen in 2004, a significant change for the better. Nevertheless, it is worth noting that the percentage of African American mothers with inadequate prenatal care in 2004 was still more than twice that of white mothers, and only slightly better than the rate achieved for white women in 1970.

World Standing—Losing Ground. For the past several decades, the United States has lagged behind other nations in infant mortality. It continues to do so today. The CIA's *World Factbook* shows that most other industrial nations now have lower infant mortality rates than the United States. Among twenty industrial countries,

5.4 Infant mortality, selected industrial countries, 2006, est.

Deaths in the first year of life, per 1,000 live births

Sweden	2.76
Japan	3.24
Iceland	3.29
Finland	3.55
Norway	3.67
Germany	4.12
France	4.21
Switzerland	4.34
Spain	4.37
Denmark	4.51
Austria	4.60
Canada	4.69
Netherlands	4.96
Portugal	4.98
United Kingdom	5.08
Ireland	5.31
Greece	5.43
New Zealand	5.76
Italy	5.83
United States	6.43

Source: Central Intelligence Agency, *World Factbook*

the nation with the lowest infant mortality, Sweden, has a rate less than half that of the United States. Other nations with low rates include Japan, Iceland, Finland, Norway, Germany and France.[10]

UNICEF's *State of the World's Children 2006* shows that the United States' standing has slipped significantly over the past sixteen years. In 1990, 24 countries had lower infant mortality rates than the United States. By 2006 the U.S. was outperformed by 37 countries, including Cuba, the Czech Republic and Estonia. The United States also compares poorly in terms of its mortality rate for children under five. On this indicator it falls behind 35 other countries, ranking similar to Poland, Lithuania, and Chile.[11]

Sharing the Benefits of Progress. The nation's accomplishment in lowering its infant mortality rate has been impressive. But the slowing pace of improvement and the rise in low-birthweight babies indicate that more work is needed. It will be difficult to improve the national infant mortality rate further unless we address the racial and ethnic disparities that characterize nearly every aspect of infant health in this country. Other industrial nations have achieved far lower infant mortality rates. So, too, can the United States.

Child Poverty

- Child poverty is higher today than it was in 1970, and it has risen even more sharply among the youngest children, those under age six.

- The percentage of children living in "extreme poverty" (with a family income less than half the poverty line) was approximately the same in 2005 as it was in 1980.

- The United States' child poverty rate compares poorly to the levels achieved in other nations.

5.5   Child poverty, 1970–2005

Child poverty rate—percent of related children in families with incomes below the poverty line

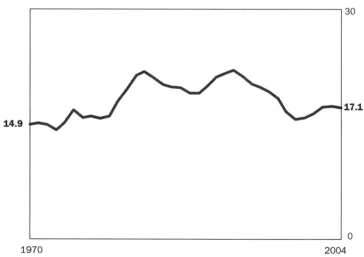

Source: U.S. Bureau of the Census

No Progress. Poverty represents a serious threat to child development. Children who are poor typically have less access to educational opportunities, greater exposure to danger, and in the most severe cases, problems with obtaining the most basic of necessities: adequate food, shelter, and, clothing.

Since 1970, there has been little overall progress in the elimination of child poverty. In 2005, there were 12.3 million children living in families in poverty. This represented 17.1 percent of the child population, up from 14.9 percent in 1970—a worsening of 15 percent.[12]

Child poverty in the U.S. reached its highest level in 1993. It improved during the late 1990s with the strengthening economy, but has worsened again since 2000, with only fractional improvement between 2004 and 2005. Poverty rates are even higher for the nation's youngest children—those under age six. In 2005, 20 percent of American children under age six were poor, compared to 16.6 percent in 1970.[13]

A Key Comparison. The high levels of poverty among the very young stand in sharp contrast to the lower poverty rates of the elderly. Between 1970 and 2005, poverty among the elderly fell nearly 60 percent, from 24.6 percent to 10.1 percent. During the same period, poverty among children under six increased by 20 percent. Given the importance of children's earliest years in shaping development, this represents a serious problem.[14]

5.6   Poverty, under age 6, and ages 65 and over, 1970–2005

Percent in poverty

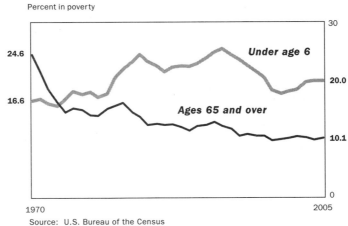

Source: U.S. Bureau of the Census

Who Are the Poor? Among the 12.3 million American children under age eighteen living in poverty in 2005, approximately one-third were white, one-third were African American, and one-third were Hispanic. Proportionately, however, child poverty rates were considerably higher among minorities. In 2005, 9.5 percent of white children were poor, compared to 34.1 percent of African American children and 27.7 percent of Hispanics.[15]

Extreme Poverty. The U.S. poverty line was developed in the 1960s centered on the concept of a minimum diet. It represents little beyond subsistence in terms of providing the goods and services needed for daily life. Below even this minimal level, the Census Bureau defines a category called "extreme poverty," which covers people whose incomes fall below 50 percent of the official poverty line. For a family of three, for example, this means living on less than about $8,000 per year.[16]

There has been little progress in improving this acute form of economic deprivation. In 2005, 5.6 million American children (7.7 percent) were still living in extreme poverty—almost precisely the same proportion as in 1980. Approximately one-half of all African American children who were poor, and nearly 40 percent of poor white and Hispanic children, fell into this category.[17]

The Impact of Welfare Reform. The passage of the Personal Responsibility and Work Opportunity Act in 1996 was one of the most important policy initiatives to affect poor children in recent years. The new welfare reform law required the states to redesign

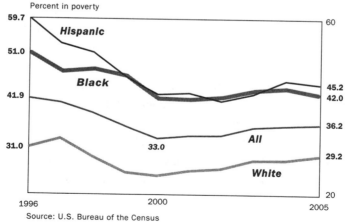

5.7 **Poverty, female-headed households with children, 1996–2005**

Percent in poverty

Source: U.S. Bureau of the Census

their programs so as to move single mothers from "welfare to work"—seeking both to save public funds and to give families a path to economic self-sufficiency.

Public monies were saved: 2.6 million families were removed from the welfare rolls between 1995 and 2004. In addition, poverty rates among female-headed families with children did decline during the initial years of the program, in part because of the booming economy of the late 1990s. Follow-up studies, however, show that many of the jobs found by former welfare recipients are neither stable nor well paid, and in recent years, poverty rates have begun to increase again—from 33.0 percent in 2000 to 36.2 percent in 2005. The nation's welfare system has been restructured, but the problem of poverty remains unsolved.[18]

Child Poverty and Illness. One of the most serious and well-documented consequences of child poverty is a higher rate of illness. Two conditions that affect poor children with particular severity are lead poisoning and asthma.

Lead poisoning can cause learning disabilities, behavioral problems, and sometimes even seizures, coma, or death. Blood lead levels in American children have improved significantly over time, as the nation has phased out leaded gasoline and has regulated lead emissions and lead-based paint. Yet, according to the Centers for Disease Control and Prevention, lead poisoning still affects more than 300,000 children, ages one to five, and of this group, a high proportion are low-income children living in older housing.[19]

Unlike lead exposure, asthma has grown worse in recent decades, and represents a serious problem for children of all income groups. Yet data from the National Health Interview Survey show that it too is most prevalent among poor children. Researchers at Mount Sinai School of Medicine, for example, looking specifically at hospitalization rates, found that children in New York City's poorest neighborhoods were hospitalized for asthma at rates twenty-one times higher than those in higher-income neighborhoods.[20]

U.S. Standing in the World. Similar to our status on infant mortality, the United States lags far behind other industrial nations in reducing child poverty. Among the many studies that document this country's poor international standing, some of the most important have come from UNICEF's Innocenti Research Centre, which publishes a series of reports on how well industrial countries address child poverty. These reports use the standard international definition of poverty, which is income that is less than one-half the national median.

5.8 Child poverty, selected industrial countries

Percent of children in poverty

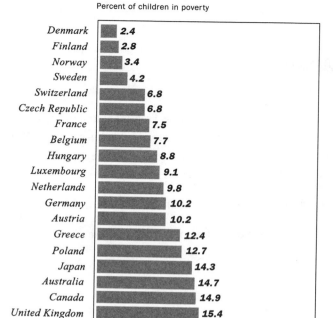

Denmark	2.4
Finland	2.8
Norway	3.4
Sweden	4.2
Switzerland	6.8
Czech Republic	6.8
France	7.5
Belgium	7.7
Hungary	8.8
Luxembourg	9.1
Netherlands	9.8
Germany	10.2
Austria	10.2
Greece	12.4
Poland	12.7
Japan	14.3
Australia	14.7
Canada	14.9
United Kingdom	15.4
Portugal	15.6
Ireland	15.7
New Zealand	16.3
Italy	16.6
United States	**21.9**
Mexico	27.7

Source: Innocenti Research Centre, UNICEF
Note: Data are from the most recent years available,
ranging from 1997–2001

In the most recent Innocenti report, covering twenty-six industrial countries, the United States performed more poorly than any other country except Mexico. The U.S. rate for poverty among children—21.9 percent—was nine times higher than the rate in the best nation, Denmark, at 2.4 percent.[21]

A Critical Issue. Child poverty remains a pressing problem in the United States, affecting young Americans' physical, social, and mental well-being, both during their early years and long afterward. It will take a concerted effort and significant public policy initiatives to address the problem, but the costs of poverty for children make this task urgent.

Child Abuse

- Since the passage of the Child Abuse Treatment and Prevention Act of 1974, the nation has seen a marked increase in child abuse reports. While the early years of this increase likely reflected greater awareness, the continuing rise in reports is a matter of serious concern.

- Neglect is the most common form of abuse today, as it has been in the past.

- Parents are the most frequent perpetrators of abuse.

5.9   Child abuse, 1976–2004

Children involved in abuse/neglect reports, per 1,000 population, ages 0–18

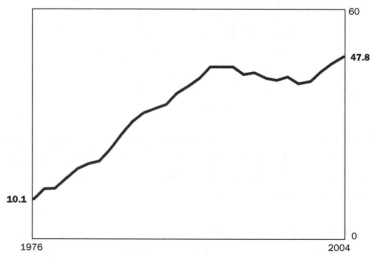

Source: American Humane Association, National Committee to Prevent Child Abuse, U.S. Administration for Children and Families

Rising Awareness, Rising Reports. Harming a child is recognized as a serious offense, both because of a child's vulnerability and because the ill effects of mistreatment can last a lifetime. For most of U.S. history, however, states gave varying levels of attention to this issue, and in many communities only the most extreme cases of abuse were reported.

This situation changed markedly in 1974, when the Child Abuse Prevention and Treatment Act (CAPTA) was passed, creating a nationwide system for dealing with child maltreatment. CAPTA required that states adopt a legal definition of abuse that would meet or exceed federal guidelines, pass a mandatory reporting law for abuse cases, and establish a mechanism for investigating these reports.[22]

Between 1976, when the CAPTA system was implemented, and 2004, the rate of children involved in reports of abuse or neglect rose dramatically, from 10.1 per 1,000 children to 47.8. Reports increased steadily until the late 1990s, then moderated somewhat, but began to climb again after 2000. The 2004 rate was the worst since the national system began. In 2004, nearly 3.5 million children were involved in reports of abuse or neglect.[23]

There are important reasons to monitor reports of abuse as well as the smaller number of "substantiated" cases. First, child abuse is difficult to substantiate because victims are often unwilling or unable to testify. In addition, there is significant variation among the states in procedures and staffing—fewer staff typically mean lower rates of substantiation. Finally, multiple studies demonstrate that many cases are never reported at all. Thus, even the total number of reports may understate the full extent of the problem.[24]

5.10 Types of child maltreatment, 2004

Percent of substantiated cases experiencing each type of abuse

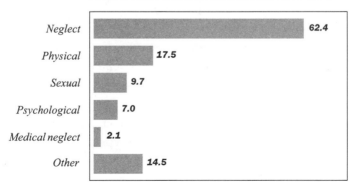

Source: U.S. Administration for Children and Families
Note: Adds up to more than 100 because child may appear in more than one category

Types of Maltreatment. The federal definition of abuse and neglect covers "any recent act or failure to act on the part of a parent or caretaker, which results in death, serious physical or emotional harm, sexual abuse or exploitation" of a child, as well as any "act or failure to act which presents an imminent risk of serious harm to a child." Within the broad category of abuse and neglect, there are five main types of maltreatment: neglect, physical abuse, sexual abuse, psychological maltreatment, and medical neglect.[25]

The most common type of maltreatment is neglect. In 2004, neglect accounted for nearly two-thirds of substantiated cases. The second most common form of abuse was physical, experienced by 17.5 percent. In addition, 9.7 percent of children suffered from sexual abuse, 7 percent from psychological maltreatment, 2.1 percent from medical neglect, and 14.5 percent experienced other forms of abuse, including abandonment and threats of harm.[26]

Each type of maltreatment was experienced by thousands of children in each age group. Among the youngest, for example—those under age four—in addition to the approximately 170,000 cases of neglect in 2004, there were nearly 30,000 substantiated cases of physical abuse, 11,000 cases of psychological maltreatment, and 5,000 cases of sexual abuse.[27]

Deaths from Abuse. The worst possible outcome of maltreatment is, of course, the death of a child. In 2004, an estimated 1,490 children died in substantiated cases of abuse or neglect. Nearly half of these children, 45 percent, were under one year of age, and another 35 percent were between the ages of one and three. Neglect was the most frequent cause, accounting for 36 percent of the deaths, followed by physical abuse. The rate of child fatalities increased slightly each year between 2000 and 2004, rising from 1.84 to 2.03 per 100,000 population.[28]

Who Are the Victims of Child Abuse? A review of the characteristics of abused children show that girls are abused slightly more frequently than boys—51.7 percent vs. 48.3 percent. By race and ethnicity, the majority of abused children—53.8 percent—are white, although minorities are overrepresented among victims in terms of their presence in the general population. Finally, in terms of age, younger children are most likely to be abused. The extreme case is children under age four, who accounted for nearly 30 percent of abuse in 2004, although they represent only about 7 percent of the under-eighteen population.[29]

5.11 Child abuse victims, by gender, race, ethnicity, and age, 2004

Percent of victims in substantiated cases

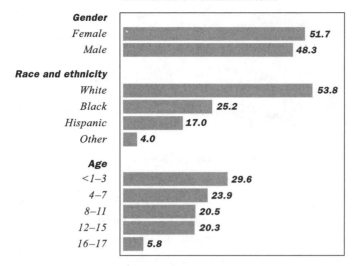

Source: U.S. Administration for Children and Families

Who Commits Child Abuse? One of the most troubling patterns in child abuse is the predominance of parents among the perpetrators. In 2004, parents accounted for a full 82 percent of known perpetrators. Two other groups with family or household connections were relatives at 7 percent, and parents' unmarried partners at 4 percent. Professionals and various types of caretakers, such as foster parents, legal guardians, residential facility employees, and day-care staff, accounted for 2 percent of the cases. Women made up the largest proportion of abusers, at 57.8 percent, compared to men at 42.2 percent.[30]

The overwhelming majority of abusing parents—a full 92 percent in 2004—were biological parents, far outnumbering stepparents and adoptive parents. In cases of parental abuse, almost half the victims were harmed by their mothers acting alone, compared to 22 percent by their fathers acting alone. There were also another 22 percent harmed by their mothers and fathers acting together, and 9 percent by one of the two parents acting with someone else.[31]

5.12 Child abuse perpetrators, by relationship, 2004

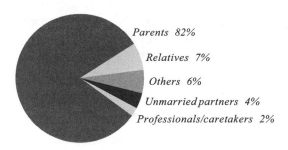

Parents 82%

Relatives 7%

Others 6%

Unmarried partners 4%

Professionals/caretakers 2%

Source: U.S. Administration for Children and Families

Who Reports Child Abuse? Each of the fifty states has to specify who is legally obliged to report suspected cases of abuse and neglect. Most often, state laws designate occupations such as social workers, school personnel, health care workers, mental health professionals, child-care providers, and law enforcement personnel. Since the recent sex abuse scandals in the Catholic Church, twenty-five states also have added reporting requirements for clergy.

More than half of all reports in 2004 came from community professionals. School and law enforcement personnel alone accounted for 34 percent of the total. Other sources were: anonymous tips (10 percent), relatives (8.4 percent), parents (6.6 percent), and friends or neighbors (5.9 percent). Those directly involved—the alleged perpetrators and victims—accounted for less than 1 percent of all reports.[32]

An Unresolved Problem. Over the past thirty-five years, the problem of child abuse has become better understood and better monitored. But the almost uninterrupted increase in reports of maltreatment indicates that we have much work to do in order to protect the most vulnerable members of our society. The predominance of close relatives, particularly parents, as perpetrators, also suggests that this nation needs to address the extensive burdens and stresses now placed on families.

Chapter 6
Social Indicators for Youth

Teenage Suicide
Teenage Drug Abuse
High School Dropouts

Teenage Suicide

- The teenage suicide rate worsened sharply during the 1970s and 1980s. It improved during the late 1990s, but rose again in 2004.

- Teenage males commit suicide at higher rates than females, and whites at higher rates than African Americans. Native American rates surpass those of all other ethnic groups.

- The United States stands at about the midpoint among industrial nations in terms of its suicide rate among young men.

6.1 Teenage suicide, 1970–2004

Suicides per 100,000, ages 15–19

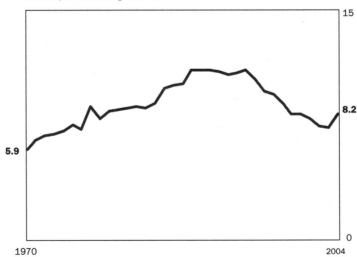

Source: National Center for Health Statistics

A Terrible Loss. Suicide is a serious threat to young people, ranking as the third leading cause of death among 15- to 19-year-olds. Only unintentional injuries and homicides take more young lives. The effects of suicide typically go well beyond the immediate family to friends, teachers, and the broader community. Those who knew the victim may blame themselves for having missed critical warning signs. Troubled young people may see in the act a model for themselves. A community feels the loss of a life barely begun.[1]

The teenage suicide rate has worsened since 1970, although it is lower than in its peak years. In 2004, among 15- to 19-year-olds, the rate was 8.2 deaths per 100,000, compared to 5.9 deaths in 1970. The rate nearly doubled between 1970 and the early 1990s, but then tapered off. Troublingly, the suicide rate rose again between 2003 and 2004, reversing a 9-year trend.[2]

At Risk. Among 15- to 19-year-olds, Native American males are at greatest risk for suicide. Their rate, at 32.2 per 100,000 in 2004, is more than double the rate for white males, 13.6, and far above those of Hispanic, Asian, and African American males, at 9.9, 8.5, and 7.4, respectively.[3]

In each racial or ethnic group, females have considerably lower suicide rates than males. Yet among females, as among males, Native Americans have the highest rate

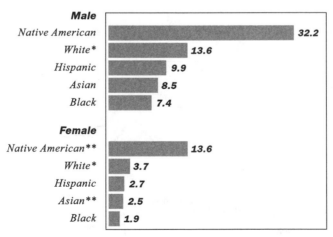

6.2 Teenage suicide, by gender, race, and ethnicity, 2004

Suicides per 100,000, ages 15–19

Source: National Center for Health Statistics
*White, non-Hispanic **Based on small sample size

and African Americans the lowest. By race and gender, African American females are the only group in the 15–19 age range for whom suicide is not among the top three causes of death.[4]

Gender and Race Over Time. To track youth suicide by gender and race, we must look at the ages 15 to 24, because the National Center for Health Statistics maintains its long-term data in 10-year age groups. These data show that over time, female suicide rates have been consistently lower than males'. Both white and African American females have remained below 5 per 100,000 for the past 35 years, and declined slightly during that period.[5]

The long-term pattern for young men is quite different. Among white males, suicide rates increased between 1970 and 1994 and then began a fairly steady decline. The rate for African American males remained fairly stable until the mid-1980s, then climbed sharply, peaking in 1994. The rate then fell once again, returning close to its earlier levels.[6]

Youth Suicide Worldwide. Suicide is a leading cause of death among teenagers not only in the United States, but around the world. The American Foundation for Suicide Prevention reports that, internationally, suicides among young people have been increasing, and that each year at least 100,000 adolescents take their own lives. In one-third of the countries in the world, both developed and developing, young people are the age group at highest risk for suicide.[7]

6.3   Teenage suicide, by gender and race, 1970–2004

Suicides per 100,000, ages 15–24

Source: National Center for Health Statistics

A report from the World Health Organization (WHO) shows that in most countries, as in the United States, suicide is far more frequent among young men than among young women. In 2000, suicide rates among young men in thirteen industrial countries ranged from 9.4 to 30.4 per 100,000, while rates for young women were typically between 2 and 6. The only industrial countries where female levels were above 6 were Australia, at 6.1, and Japan, at 6.9. In all countries studied, the male rate was at least double the female rate, and in most it was three to five times higher.[8]

According to WHO, the suicide rate among young U.S. males falls at the approximate mid-point for these nations. WHO reports that in the year 2000, young American males took their own lives at a rate of 17.0 per 100,000 population. This was nearly double the rate in the best-performing nation, the Netherlands, but well below the high rates recorded in New Zealand and Norway.[9]

Attempting Suicide. Each year, in addition to those who actually kill themselves, several million teenagers seriously consider doing so, and more than 2 million make an attempt. While males commit suicide more often, females more often attempt it. The Youth Risk Behavior Surveillance survey, conducted by the Centers for Disease Control, reports that in 2005, high school females were much more likely than males to have had feelings of sadness or hopelessness (36.7 percent vs. 20.4), to have seri-

6.4   Teenage suicide, males, selected industrial countries, 2000

Suicides per 100,000, males, ages 15-24

Netherlands	9.4
United Kingdom	10.5
Israel	11.4
Sweden	12
France	12.1
Germany	12.2
Japan	15.8
United States	17.0
Switzerland	18.5
Canada	20.2
Australia	20.3
Norway	25.3
New Zealand	30.4

Source: World Health Organization

ously considered a suicide attempt (21.8 percent vs. 12.0), to have made a suicide plan (16.2 percent vs. 9.9), or to have attempted suicide (10.8 percent vs. 6.0).[10]

In terms of race and ethnicity, African American high school students reported the fewest suicidal thoughts, although in each case, females reported more problems than males. The data also show that, among females, the frequency of suicidal thoughts decreases steadily during the four years of high school, while among males it remains roughly constant.[11]

The federal government, in its Healthy People goals for the year 2010, has targeted a reduction in the most serious type of suicide attempts—those that require medical attention. Their hope is to lower the number of high school students who engage in this behavior from 2.6 percent to 1.0 percent. By 2005, the level had declined to 2.3 percent, but considerable ground must still be covered if the goal of 1.0 percent is to be achieved by 2010.[12]

Investing in the Future. Each suicide is a singular event, rousing a community and sometimes a nation to greater consciousness of the preciousness of young lives. Over the past decade, the United States has seen some improvement in its teenage suicide rate, but the recent rise is troubling. Far more can be done to intervene in the lives of young people to prevent despair, hopelessness, or depression. These efforts can safeguard young people's futures and prevent tragedies that need not occur.

Teenage Drug Abuse

- The use of illicit drugs by twelfth graders is lower than in 1970, although it is substantially higher than in the early 1990s.

- Drug use continues to be a problem among eighth and tenth graders, as well as among even younger students.

- Young people report that drugs are readily available to them, even on school premises. This wide availability clearly facilitates the use and spread of drugs.

6.5   Teenage drug use, 1975–2005

Percent using any illicit drug, past 12 months, 12th graders

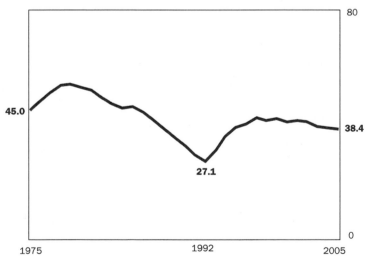

Source: National Institute on Drug Abuse, Monitoring the Future

A Continuing Problem. Since the 1960s teenage drug use has been a continuing problem in the United States. Drug use, when out of control, can interrupt teenagers' school years, lower their grades, cause hostility and anger, and in the most severe cases cause physical or mental impairment.[13]

The primary source of information on teenage drug use is the Monitoring the Future study, a project conducted by the University of Michigan's Survey Research Center in conjunction with the National Institute on Drug Abuse. This project has produced annual data on teenage drug use and attitudes since 1975.[14]

Tracking the key indicator of twelfth grade usage shows modest improvement over time. The percentage of students reporting any illicit drug use during the previous year dropped from 45 percent in 1975 to 38.4 percent in 2005. Use rose during the late 1970s, dropped sharply during the 1980s, rose again in the 1990s, and has declined only slightly since 2000.[15]

Among the Youngest. Drug use can be a particularly serious problem among younger students. In 2005, 29.8 percent of tenth graders and 15.5 percent of eighth graders reported using illicit drugs during the previous year, rates lower than twelfth graders but still substantial. Patterns among younger students over time closely matched those of the older group, except that tenth graders showed a steeper decline in the past few years.[16]

In its biennial survey, the Youth Risk Behavior Surveillance System asks high school students how old they were when they first tried marijuana. Over the past

6.6   Teenage drug use, by grade, 1991–2005

Percent using any illicit drug, past 12 months

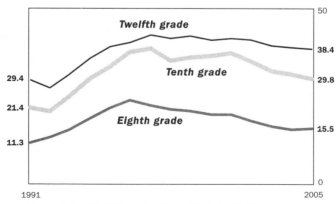

Source: National Institute on Drug Abuse, Monitoring the Future

fifteen years, the proportion reporting drug use before the age of 13 ranged from 7 to 11 percent. The figure in 2005 was 8.7 percent, but with a notable difference by gender: 11 percent of boys reported early drug use, compared to only 6 percent of girls.[17]

Who Uses Drugs? In 2005, among twelfth graders, 42.1 percent of males reported illicit drug use during the past year, a rate nearly 8 percentage points higher than females. White teenagers exceeded Hispanic Americans by 7 points and African Americans by 12 points. By region, the Northeast had the highest rate in the nation, at 43.2 percent, compared to 38.8 percent for the North Central region, and approximately 36 percent in both the South and the West.[18]

Which Drugs? Marijuana is the drug most widely used by teenagers. In 2005, one-third of twelfth graders reported using marijuana during the past year, while no other drug exceeded 10 percent. The next most used drugs were narcotic painkillers and amphetamines at approximately 9 percent, sedatives at 7.6 percent, and tranquilizers at 6.8 percent. Cocaine, hallucinogens, and inhalants were each used by 5 to 6 percent of students.[19]

This general pattern has held constant for the past thirty years, with marijuana the most common drug both in 1975 and 2005. However, two key differences have been

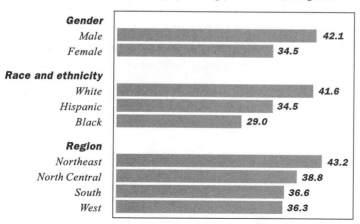

6.7 Teenage drug use, by gender, race, ethnicity, and region, 2005

Percent using any illicit drug, past 12 months, 12th graders

Gender	
Male	42.1
Female	34.5
Race and ethnicity	
White	41.6
Hispanic	34.5
Black	29.0
Region	
Northeast	43.2
North Central	38.8
South	36.6
West	36.3

Source: National Institute on Drug Abuse, Monitoring the Future

noted over time. First, narcotic painkillers are the only major drug where teenage use increased between 1975 and 2005, though the degree of use remains fairly low. Second, while all other types of drugs show a decline during the past thirty years, the drop in marijuana was much smaller than for other drugs. This left marijuana a more dominant drug in 2005 than it was in 1975.[20]

Access to Drugs. Drugs are readily available to teenagers despite the fact that they are illegal and that penalties for sale and possession have risen in recent years. According to the Monitoring the Future study, 86 percent of twelfth graders reported in 2005 that it would be very or fairly easy for them to obtain marijuana if they wished to. Approximately 40 percent reported the same for cocaine and for crack, and 28 percent for heroin and LSD. Even among eighth graders, significant numbers reported having easy access to marijuana (41 percent), crack and cocaine (20 percent), and LSD and heroin (12–13 percent).[21]

Drugs are readily available even on school premises. In 2005, approximately one-quarter of the high school students surveyed by the Youth Behavior Surveillance System reported that they had been offered, sold, or given an illegal drug on school property within the previous year. This percentage has declined somewhat in recent years, but remains higher than the levels reported when this question was first asked, in 1993.[22]

Perceived Risk. One of the more striking findings of the Monitoring the Future study is how well the perception of risk serves to predict the use of drugs. As the perception of risk heightens, young people reduce their use of particular drugs. This is especially true with marijuana, the commonest drug, where there is a very clear inverse relationship between the perception of risk and use. This relationship suggests that students are strongly affected by exposure to persuasive information, and that well-designed interventions along these lines have the potential to diminish teenage drug use.[23]

6.8 Perceived risk and marijuana use, 1975–2005

Percent perceiving risk in smoking marijuana regularly, and
percent annual use of marijuana*

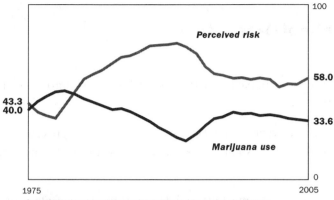

Source: National Institute on Drug Abuse, Monitoring the Future
*Includes hashish

Rethinking the Problem. The sharp spike in teenage drug use during the late 1990s has abated, but use levels have declined only slightly during the past five years. Two even more serious concerns are the beginning use of drugs at very young ages, and the broad availability of drugs in schools. These factors suggest that new ways of thinking about drugs need to be introduced, to moderate their harm and their influence.

High School Dropouts

- The high school dropout rate in the United States has improved steadily since the 1970s.

- The African American dropout rate shows the largest improvement over time. There has also been a significant improvement in dropouts among females of all races.

- The U.S. lags behind most industrial nations in the percentage of its young people who graduate from high school.

6.9 High school dropouts, 1970–2005

Percent not in school, not high school graduates, ages 18–24

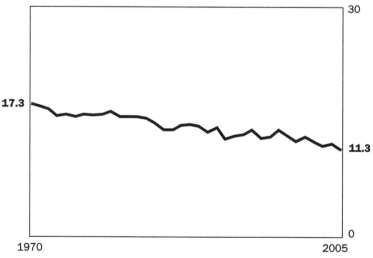

Source: U.S. Bureau of the Census

Dropout Rates Improving. When young people drop out of high school, they lose access to a broad range of opportunities. Their educations are cut short, their occupational choices are narrowed, and their lifetime earnings are likely to be limited. Because high school completion has such an enormous impact on future prospects, the dropout rate is considered a critical indicator for monitoring the social well-being of American youth.

The high school dropout rate is tracked by the federal government through the Census Bureau's Current Population Survey. Each year, Americans are asked about their school enrollment status. Individuals between the ages of 18 and 24 are defined as dropouts if they are not currently enrolled in school and have not graduated from high school.[24]

The dropout rate in the United States showed substantial progress between 1970 and 2005, declining from 17.3 percent to 11.3, an improvement of 35 percent. Among the 27.8 million Americans between ages 18 and 24 in 2005, approximately 3.2 million were high school dropouts.[25]

A Profile Over Time. There has been improvement over time in the high school dropout rates of virtually all major demographic groups. Both males and females show progress, although women have made greater strides than men. In 1970, the female dropout rate was slightly higher than the male, but today the situation has reversed. In 2005, males had a rate of 13.2 percent, compared to 9.5 for females.

In terms of race and ethnicity, African Americans have shown the most dramatic improvement over time, going from a high dropout rate of 33.3 in 1970 to 12.9

6.10 High school dropouts, by gender, 1970–2005

Percent not in school, not high school graduates, ages 18–24

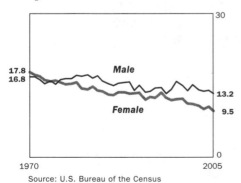

Source: U.S. Bureau of the Census

6.11 High school dropouts, by race and ethnicity, 1970–2005

Percent not in school, not high school graduates, ages 18–24

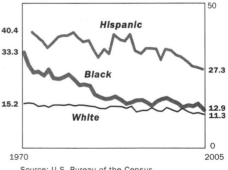

Source: U.S. Bureau of the Census

percent in 2005, an improvement of 61 percent. The rate for white youth has shown only marginal improvement, going from 15.2 to 11.3. Hispanic Americans' rate remains startlingly high at 27.3 percent, more than twice that of whites or African Americans. Nevertheless, this represents an improvement over the 40.4 percent recorded in 1972.[26]

The High Cost of Dropping Out. In today's society, the consequences of not having a high school degree are exceedingly high, and affect many different aspects of life, including employment, access to health insurance, and earnings. For example, employment rates among high school dropouts, at 42 percent, are substantially lower than those for high school graduates, at 60.3 percent, and college graduates at 76.1 percent. Access to health insurance and median earnings parallel these figures.[27]

A further cost of dropping out is the higher risk of incarceration. An analysis of Department of Justice statistics shows that nearly half the inmates in state prisons were high school dropouts at the time they went to prison. Approximately 40 percent had graduated from high school, and only about 10 percent had attended college. Statistics such as these illustrate the long-term costs that are incurred—both for the individual and for society—when young people leave school too early.[28]

6.12 Employment, health insurance, and earnings, by education, 2005

Percent and dollars

Employment
High school dropout 42.0
High school graduate 60.3
College graduate 76.1

Health insurance
High school dropout 69.9
High school graduate 79.7
College graduate 91.7

Earnings
High school dropout $21,943
High school graduate $30,587
College graduate $55,188

Sources: Employment, ages 25 and over: Bureau of Labor Statistics; Health Insurance, ages 18 and over: U.S. Bureau of the Census; Median earnings, ages 18 and over, year round full-time workers: U.S. Bureau of the Census

Graduation Rates Among Nations. Compared to other nations, the United States ranks relatively poorly in its high school graduation rate. According to the Organization for Economic Development (OECD), in 2004 the United States stood nineteenth among twenty-one industrial nations in the proportion of students who graduated from high school at the "typical age of graduation." Norway scored first, with 100 percent. Germany, Korea, Israel, Ireland, Japan, Denmark, and Finland all scored in the 90th percentile. The United States, at 75 percent, was among the lowest.[29]

A College Education. OECD reports that in 2006 the United States led industrial countries in the percentage of its adult population that was categorized as "highly educated"—having earned an associate's degree or higher. However, the lead disappeared when one considered only younger people, ages twenty-five to thirty-four. OECD projects that during the next ten years, the U.S. will see a serious decline in the proportion of its population that is highly educated.[30]

One of the most serious problems the U.S. faces in creating a college-educated

6.13 Graduation rates, selected industrial countries, 2004

Graduation rates, upper secondary schools

Norway	100
Germany	99
Korea	96
Israel	93
Ireland	92
Japan	91
Denmark	90
Finland	90
Switzerland	89
Russian Federation	87
Czech Republic	87
Hungary	86
Iceland	84
Slovak Republic	83
Italy	81
France	81
Poland	79
Sweden	78
United States	75
New Zealand	75
Luxembourg	69

Source: OECD, *Education at a Glance*

adult population is keeping its young people in college. Though almost two-thirds of Americans who complete high school go to college—a rate that substantially exceeds the OECD average of 53 percent—only about half of them actually graduate. That gives the United States one of the lowest college "survival rates" of all nations.[31]

One factor that may diminish both enrollment and retention rates in college is the soaring cost of higher education. In just the past five years, tuition at private four-year colleges rose 11 percent, adjusted for inflation, while cuts in federal and state funding forced public four-year colleges to raise their tuition by 35 percent. Moreover, one of the most important sources of federal assistance for college students—the Pell Grants program—has reduced the aid granted per recipient, in real dollars, every year for the past three years. Greater financial assistance is necessary if we are to improve the nation's educational level.[32]

Looking Ahead. Social and economic changes over the past thirty-five years have made it increasingly essential for young people to finish high school—and preferably college as well—if they are to get a good start in life. Although dropout rates have declined since 1970 and college admissions have increased, it is essential to expand still further the proportion of young people who complete their education. The potential benefits, to both the individual and the larger society, are clear.[33]

Chapter 7
Social Indicators for Adults

Unemployment
Wages
Health Insurance Coverage

Unemployment

- The unemployment rate in 2005 was a low 5.1 percent, just slightly above the rate in 1970, and far better than the worst periods of the 1980s.

- Since the early 1970s, unemployment rates for African Americans and Hispanics have remained consistently higher than rates for whites. High unemployment rates for youth have persisted as well.

- The average duration of unemployment has inched up over time.

7.1 Unemployment, 1970-2005

Percent unemployed in civilian labor force

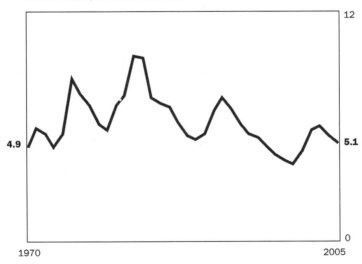

1970   2005

Source: Bureau of Labor Statistics

Changes Over Time. During the Great Depression, the federal government, recognizing the need to monitor unemployment, created a systematic method for measuring the number of Americans out of work. A national household survey, now known as the Current Population Survey (CPS), was launched in 1940, and has been administered every month since that time.[1]

Unemployment rates have varied widely over the past thirty-five years, peaking at 9.7 percent in 1982 and reaching a low of 4.0 percent in 2000. The unemployment rate in 2005 was 5.1, just slightly higher than the 4.9 recorded in 1970.[2]

The 2005 rate is clearly better than in many periods in the past. Nevertheless, 7.6 million Americans were unemployed in 2005, and of these, about 1.5 million were out of work longer than six months.[3]

A Profile of the Unemployed. Over time, differences in the unemployment rates between men and women have flattened out. Thus, in 2005, males and females had exactly the same unemployment rate, 5.1 percent. Racial differences, however, remained. African Americans had higher levels of unemployment than either Hispanics or whites. Ten percent of African American workers were unemployed, compared to 6 percent of Hispanics and 4.4 percent of white workers.[4]

Education also strongly affects employment. The jobless rate in 2005 for adults

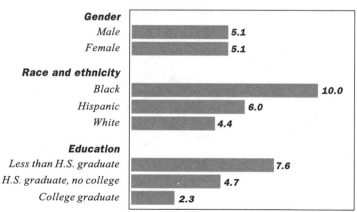

7.2 Unemployment, by gender, race, ethnicity, and education, 2005

Percent unemployed in civilian labor force

Gender
- *Male* — 5.1
- *Female* — 5.1

Race and ethnicity
- *Black* — 10.0
- *Hispanic* — 6.0
- *White* — 4.4

Education
- *Less than H.S. graduate* — 7.6
- *H.S. graduate, no college* — 4.7
- *College graduate* — 2.3

Source: Bureau of Labor Statistics
Note: Gender, race, and ethnicity: ages 16 and over;
Education: ages 25 and over

who did not complete high school was 7.6 percent—more than triple the rate for college graduates. High school graduates fell midway between the two groups, at 4.7 percent.[5]

Persistent Problems. Disparities in unemployment have persisted for more than three decades, with little improvement. Unemployment rates for African Americans, Hispanics, and youth, while paralleling the ups and downs of the nation, have remained consistently higher over time.

In 1973, the African American unemployment rate was 9.4 percent, or 2.2 times higher than the white rate. Thirty-two years later in 2005, the African American unemployment rate was 10.0, or 2.3 times the white rate. The gap between white and African American workers narrowed briefly, beginning in 1998, but widened once again starting in 2002.[6]

The pattern for Hispanic workers has been slightly better. In 1973, their unemployment rate was 7.5 percent, or 1.7 times the white rate. By 2005, the gap had closed slightly; the Hispanic unemployment rate was 6 percent, or 1.4 times the white rate. Recent changes have moved in a positive direction, but the disparity remains.[7]

Youth unemployment, too, has been a persistent problem over time. Since 1970, the unemployment rate among those ages 16 to 19 has remained more than three times the national average. If young people are to get a start on the economic ladder, and are seeking work, it is a valuable investment in human capital to expand their opportunities.[8]

7.3 Unemployment, by race, ethnicity, and youth, 1973–2005

Percent unemployed in civilian labor force

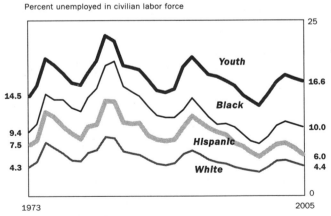

Source: Bureau of Labor Statistics
Note: Youth: ages 16–19

Worker Displacement. Worker displacement occurs when firms go out of business, move away, relocate company jobs, or reduce their work force. This type of job loss has drawn extensive media coverage in recent years, particularly in relation to the growth of outsourcing and global hiring.[9]

Between January 2003 and December 2005, 8.1 million American workers were displaced. The Bureau of Labor Statistics did a follow-up study of these workers, focusing on those who had held their previous jobs for at least three years. The study found that in 2006, 30 percent were still out of work. The remaining 70 percent had found new jobs, but only about half had been able to match their previous wage levels.[10]

Longer Periods Out of Work. The average length of time that the unemployed spend out of work rises and falls with the swings of the economy, but it has also inched up slightly over time. In 1970, during a period of low unemployment, the average number of weeks out of work (mean duration) was 8.6. In 2000, when unemployment was only 4 percent, its best point in 35 years, the average duration was 12.6 weeks. Thus, even in good times, the period of time out of work has lengthened, and by 2005 had risen to 18.4 weeks.[11]

Another way to look at this issue is to assess the percentage of workers who are unemployed for 26 weeks or more. Here, too, the numbers move with the economy, but have increased slightly over time. From a low of 5.8 percent in 1970, the rate

7.4   Duration of unemployment, 1970–2005

Mean duration, in weeks

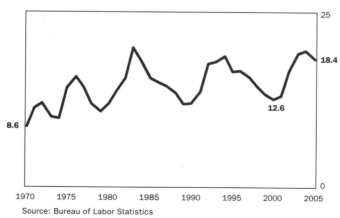

Source: Bureau of Labor Statistics

rose to 19.6 percent in 2005. Even in the best year of 2000, the percentage of workers unemployed for 26 weeks or more was 11.4 percent. Such lengthy periods of joblessness can have a profound effect on workers—in terms of their finances, future job prospects, and mental health.[12]

Protection Against Unemployment. Unemployment insurance, established as part of the federal Social Security system in 1935, is administered by the states. Within federal guidelines, each state sets its own standards for eligibility, benefits, and duration of coverage. During a typical week in 2005, about 2.7 million workers received unemployment benefits.[13]

This program, so critical to the lives of the unemployed, has several important limitations. While benefit levels vary from state to state, the program replaces only between one-third to one-half of a worker's average earnings. Moreover, only about 40 percent of the nation's unemployed workers are actually receiving benefits.[14]

Most states stop paying benefits after 26 weeks whether or not the worker has found a new job. Additionally, many states make it difficult for part-time, temporary, low-wage, and self-employed workers to qualify. Finally, the process for requesting and maintaining coverage is quite demanding, causing many eligible workers never to apply, while others fail to maintain their coverage.[15]

The nation's unemployment insurance program was an important innovation during the New Deal, and continues to be a valuable resource. But if it is to serve its original purpose, it will need to be more consistent, inclusive, accessible, and finely attuned to the work patterns of today.

Filling in the Gaps. The lower unemployment rates of the past decade reflect genuine progress for many Americans. But disparities by race and ethnicity persist, and young workers continue to have a difficult time in the job market. If we are to increase worker security, greater attention will need to be paid to the hardships of long-term unemployment, and to the importance of expanding coverage for the unemployed.

Wages

- Average weekly wages, adjusted for inflation, fell 12 percent between 1970 and 2005.

- Although women still earn less than men, the gender gap in wages has narrowed over time, reflecting both women's access to better-paying jobs and the stagnation of men's wages.

- In 2004, nearly 8 million Americans were classified as the "working poor," in that the wages they earned were insufficient to move them above the poverty line.

7.5   Average weekly wages, 1970–2005

Production or nonsupervisory workers, private, nonagricultural industries, 1982 $

Source: *Economic Report of the President*

Stalled Progress on Wages. Wages are the primary source of personal income in the United States and a critical indicator of the country's social and economic health. Given their central importance to the well-being of the nation, it is troubling to note how much ground has been lost in wage levels over the past thirty-five years.[16]

Average weekly wages, adjusted for inflation, fell from $312.94 in 1970 to $275.93 in 2005—a drop of $37.01 or 12 percent. This downward trend is particularly striking as it reverses a period of sustained improvement from 1947 to 1970, during which average weekly earnings increased by 52 percent.[17]

The 2005 wage level represents an improvement over the low point reached in 1992. But after modest increases in the late 1990s, wages flattened out, increasing by just thirty-one cents between 2000 and 2005. Overall, during the past thirty-five years, there has been a significant erosion in the one form of income upon which most American families depend.[18]

During the same period of time that average weekly wages declined by 12 percent in constant dollars, the country's gross domestic product (GDP) per capita rose dramatically. The stagnation in wage levels has meant that millions of working Americans have not benefited from the nation's economic growth.[19]

Male and Female. Male and female workers have had very different earning experiences in recent decades. In 1979, women working full-time were paid only 59.7 percent of what male workers were paid. Since then, the wage gap has narrowed, and in 2005, women's annual earnings were 77 percent of men's.[20]

7.6 Annual earnings, by gender, 1979–2005

Median earnings, full-time year-round workers, 2005 $

Source: U.S. Bureau of the Census

The narrowing of the wage gap reflects both women's increasing access to better-paying jobs and the stagnation of men's wages. Between 1979 and 2005, women's annual earnings rose from $25,293 to $31,858 in constant dollars, up by 26 percent. In contrast, male earnings declined by 2 percent, going from $42,393 to $41,386. Despite their relative gains, however, women still earn nearly $10,000 per year less than men, and have lost ground since 2002.[21]

The Working Poor. It was once assumed that poverty was primarily a problem of unemployment. However, today, as wages have declined, poverty has begun to affect growing numbers of the employed as well. In 2004, 7.8 million Americans were classified as the "working poor," in that the wages they earned were insufficient to move them above the poverty line.[22]

Women are only slightly more likely than men to be among the working poor, but poverty rates among African American and Hispanic workers far exceed those of whites. Those with less than a high school degree are almost nine times more likely than college graduates to be among the working poor. Not surprisingly, the

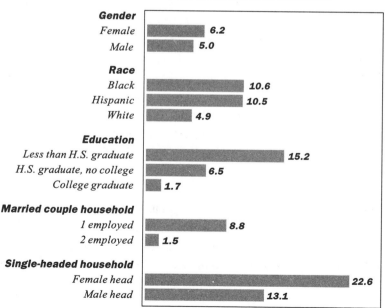

7.7 The working poor, 2004

Poverty rate, persons employed 27 weeks or more

Gender	
Female	6.2
Male	5.0
Race	
Black	10.6
Hispanic	10.5
White	4.9
Education	
Less than H.S. graduate	15.2
H.S. graduate, no college	6.5
College graduate	1.7
Married couple household	
1 employed	8.8
2 employed	1.5
Single-headed household	
Female head	22.6
Male head	13.1

Source: U.S. Bureau of the Census

lowest poverty rates are among married-couple households with two earners, while female-headed households with one earner have the highest rates.[23]

The Minimum Wage. The declining value of the federal minimum wage has helped to undermine the earnings of lower-income American workers. The minimum wage rose approximately every two years between 1972 and 1981, remained the same for nine years in the 1980s, stood still again for five years in the 1990s, and then remained at $5.15 from 1997 through early 2007. A three-stage increase, passed in 2007, is scheduled to bring the minimum wage to $7.25 by late 2009.[24]

The stagnation of the minimum wage has affected its purchasing power over time. In current dollars, the minimum wage rose from $1.60 to $5.15 between 1970 and 2006. But its real value, adjusted for inflation, declined by 26 percent. Each stretch of time when the minimum wage was held constant signified a steady loss of purchasing power for low-income workers.[25]

The federal minimum wage represents a nationally recognized floor against which other wages, particularly those for lower-income employees, tend to be calculated. For that reason it is important that it at least keep pace with inflation if it is to benefit the country's lowest-paid workers.

Middle-Class Pressures. Economic pressures today extend well beyond the working poor. Middle-class families are struggling too, faced with high prices for housing, gasoline, heating oil, tuition, and health care. This problem can be seen in the rising burden of debt. Debt among Americans has nearly doubled over the past ten years, to a total of more than 2 trillion dollars in 2005.[26]

The average American family now spends nearly 14 percent of its disposable income—one out of every seven dollars—on debt service. The strain of meeting these obligations, along with rising expenses, has contributed to a dramatic increase in the number of personal bankruptcies. Between 1987 and 2005, bankruptcies soared from 483,750 to more than 1.7 million.[27]

Working Conditions Across Nations. Among industrial nations, the U.S. hourly wage now ranks relatively low. In 2005, American production workers in manufacturing earned $23.65 per hour, less than in fourteen other countries, including Norway, Denmark, Germany, Finland, the Netherlands, Belgium, and Switzerland.[28]

7.8 Personal bankruptcies, 1987–2005

Total non-business filings

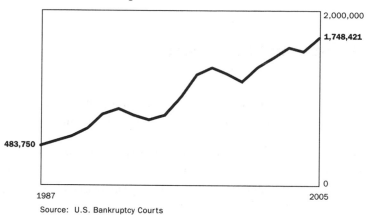

Source: U.S. Bankruptcy Courts

Americans also work unusually long hours. The Organization for Economic Cooperation and Development (OECD) reports that in 2005, Americans worked more hours per year (1,804) than workers in most other leading industrial nations. Among the countries that worked longer hours were the Czech Republic, Hungary, Poland, and Greece, while Norway and the Netherlands worked the fewest hours per year.[29]

Sharing Prosperity. National wealth has increased over the past thirty-five years, but American workers have not fully shared in that prosperity. The real value of the average weekly wage today is lower than it was in 1970. The economic strain this has caused has affected workers across the occupational spectrum.

Health Insurance Coverage

- The percentage of people without health insurance has risen steadily since 1976. In 2005, nearly one American in six had no health insurance.

- About half of American workers have employment-based insurance. Among those who do not, some work for employers who do not offer it, and some find it too expensive. Premiums for family coverage increased 60 percent between 1999 and 2005.

- Individuals at high risk for being uninsured include Hispanics, African Americans, noncitizens, young adults, and the poor.

7.9 Health insurance coverage—the uninsured, 1976–2005

Percent uninsured

Source: U.S. Bureau of the Census

More People Without Health Insurance. Health insurance coverage is much in the news today, and proposals to address the issue have come from both Congress and the states. It is broadly recognized that there is now a serious problem with the U.S. health insurance system, and that great numbers of Americans are today uninsured.

During the past three decades, the percentage of Americans without health insurance has risen sharply. In 1976, only 10.9 percent of the population was uninsured. The rate rose steadily through the 1990s, peaking in 1998 at over 16 percent. After a brief decline, the rate began to rise again. In 2005, 47 million Americans (15.9 percent) were uninsured, making it one of the worst years in three decades.[30]

Fewer People Insured Through Their Jobs. A major reason for the declining level of coverage is the deterioration of the nation's employment-based health insurance system. For many decades, this was the principal pathway to coverage, protecting workers and their families.

Today, however, only about half of American workers—53 percent—have employment-based insurance. Even full-time workers in medium and large firms have experienced a significant decline, dropping from 90 percent coverage in 1988 to 65 percent in 2005. Employees of small firms have done even more poorly. Only 43 percent were covered in 2005, down from 69 percent in 1991.[31]

Employment-based health insurance emerged in an era when a person's career often consisted of a lifelong full-time job at a single firm. Workers' experience today

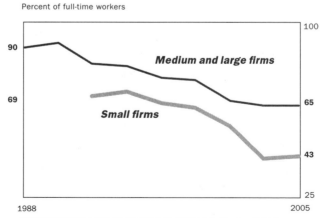

7.10 Participation in employment-based health insurance plans, by firm size, 1988–2005

Percent of full-time workers

Sources: Employee Benefit Research Institute; U.S. Bureau of the Census

is likely to include numerous job changes, as well as periods of part-time or temporary work. These circumstances greatly increase the likelihood of being uninsured.

The Cost of Employment-Based Coverage. In the past, employers paid the greater portion of health insurance costs for their workers. Over the past thirty-five years, however, rising health-care prices have caused employers to restrict eligibility, narrow the range of services covered, and require employees to pay a larger share of the cost.

Between 1999 and 2005, premiums for family coverage jumped more than 60 percent, to an average cost of about $2,900 per year in larger firms and about $3,700 per year in smaller firms. In the Census Bureau's most recent survey of uninsured workers, two-thirds of those not participating in employment-based plans said they had refused coverage because they could not afford it.[32]

Who Are the Uninsured? By race and ethnicity, Hispanic Americans, at 32.7 percent, were the group that most frequently lacked health insurance in 2005. Whites were least likely to be uninsured. Their rate, at 11.3 percent, was the lowest, followed by Asian Americans and African Americans, at 17.9 and 19.6 percent respectively.[33]

Citizenship, too, was an important factor in health insurance coverage. Among the native born, only 13.4 percent were uninsured compared to 43.6 percent of noncitizens. Naturalized citizens did considerably better than noncitizens, at 17.9 percent.[34]

Among low-income groups—those earning less than $25,000—approximately one-fourth lacked health insurance. Middle-income groups, however, were not spared. Their rates ranged from 14.1 percent to 20.6 percent. Even the wealthiest group, those with incomes of $75,000 or more, had a rate of 8.5 percent—not an insignificant number to be lacking access to health care.[35]

By age, it is young adults, ages 18 to 24, who fare the worst. Almost one-third lack health insurance, outdistancing all other age groups. The more tenuous employment status of the young makes health insurance far less accessible, and the expectation of good health may lead them to place a low priority on insurance. This gamble pays off for many, but for those who become ill, it can represent a dangerous risk.[36]

Coverage for the elderly is virtually universal, due to Medicare, and barely 1 percent are uninsured. Children, too, have done better since the State Child Health Insurance Program (SCHIP) has been implemented across the nation in recent years. Nevertheless, it is important to note that 8 million children remain uninsured.[37]

7.11 The uninsured, by race, ethnicity, citizenship, income, and age, 2005

Percent

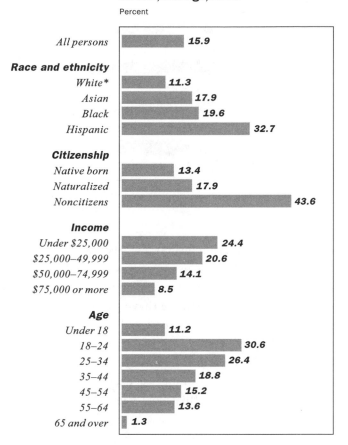

Source: U.S. Bureau of the Census
*White, non-Hispanic

Insufficient Coverage. Figures for the uninsured may still underestimate the larger health-care problems faced by Americans, since participants in the Census Bureau's annual survey are counted as insured if they were covered at some point during the previous year, even if they lacked coverage during other parts of the year.[38]

Those counted as insured also include many people whose policies cover only minimal health costs. Analysts estimate that in addition to the nearly 47 million Americans with no insurance, there are at least another 10 to 15 million whose coverage is sporadic or insufficient to meet their needs.[39]

7.12 The impact of being uninsured, 2003

Percent

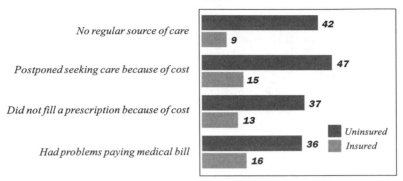

Source: Kaiser Commission on Medicaid and
the Uninsured

The Human Cost. The absence of health insurance—whether temporary or long-term—affects many aspects of life. A Kaiser Commission survey, for example, found serious health and financial problems among those lacking insurance. Many respondents who were uninsured reported having no regular source of care, postponing care or medications because of the cost, and having trouble paying their medical bills.[40]

These problems are also illustrated in a 2005 study by David Himmelstein and colleagues. The study examined the role of medical debt in forcing households to file for bankruptcy. Himmelstein reported that more than a quarter of those filing for bankruptcy specifically cited illness or injury as the principal cause of their financial problems.[41]

The majority of those going bankrupt in 2005 had health insurance when their problems began. Some lost their insurance, while others had only minimal coverage. Out-of-pocket medical costs during the year they went bankrupt averaged more than $11,000. These data suggest how central health insurance is to economic and social well-being.

The Need for Medical Security. In the U.S. health system, adequate insurance is the most reliable route to needed medical care and physical well-being. It is important that the existing disparities of coverage be reduced, and that the problems of the uninsured and underinsured be addressed.

Chapter 8
Social Indicators for the Elderly

Poverty, Ages 65 and Over
Out-of-Pocket Health Costs, Ages 65 and Over

Poverty, Ages 65 and Over

- Poverty among the elderly dropped sharply between 1970 and 2005. However, there has been no progress in the past five years.

- Persons 65 and over are the only major age group whose poverty has improved since 1970.

- Elderly women have a higher poverty rate than elderly men. Higher rates of poverty are also found among elderly African Americans, Hispanic Americans, and those who live alone.

8.1   Poverty, ages 65 and over, 1970–2005

Percent in poverty

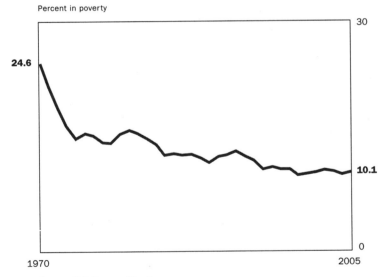

Source: U.S. Bureau of the Census

Fewer Elderly Americans in Poverty. In past generations, many Americans feared a penniless old age. They worried that when they could no longer work, they might become burdens on their families or dependent on charity. These concerns significantly diminished during the second half of the twentieth century, as the safety net this nation established began to provide a degree of economic security for the aged.

In 1970, one out of every four elderly Americans was living in poverty. Today, that figure is barely one in ten. This decline, both in actual numbers and in the poverty rate, has been dramatic, and represents one of the important success stories of American public policy.[1]

In raw numbers, while the population of the elderly has almost doubled since 1970, the number of elderly poor has declined—from 4.8 million to 3.6 million. The poverty *rate* among the elderly likewise has declined, from a high of 24.6 percent to a relatively low 10.1.[2]

The years of great progress, however, appear to be behind us. The rate of improvement first slowed, and then reversed. From 1970 to 1980, elderly poverty improved by 36 percent, from 1980 to 1990 by 22 percent, and from 1990 to 2000 by 19 percent. But from 2000 to 2005, elderly poverty worsened by 2 percent.[3]

Poverty by Age. Elderly Americans are now the only major age group whose poverty rate today is better than it was in 1970. Their rate improved by a glowing 59 percent between 1970 and 2005. Meanwhile, child poverty worsened by 15 percent, and poverty among adults, ages 18 to 64, increased by 23 percent.[4]

8.2 Poverty, ages 18–64 and ages 65 and over, 1970–2005

Percent in poverty

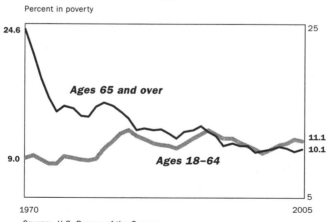

Source: U.S. Bureau of the Census

Since 1970, the elderly have benefited from a gradual expansion of the Social Security program. Today, more people are included in the program, benefits are adjusted each year for inflation (COLA), and the Supplemental Security Income program (SSI) aids those with low incomes. Medicare, with its recent drug supplement, serves as an important income protector as well, buffering the elderly against the high costs of health care.

Significant Disparities. While people ages 65 and over fare better than other age groups, there are significant disparities in poverty among the elderly themselves. The poverty rate for elderly women, for example, at 12.3 percent, continues to be far higher than for men, at 7.3 percent.[5]

Among racial groups, elderly African Americans fare the worst. Their poverty rate, at 23.3 percent today, is precisely what the rate was for elderly whites in 1969. Hispanic Americans do only slightly better, at 19.9 percent. Whites have the best elderly poverty figure, a very low 7.9 percent. It is troubling that, while poverty rates for the elderly overall have improved so sharply, the rate for minorities remains so high.[6]

Household circumstances also play a significant role in elderly poverty. Those who live alone are at the highest risk, while those living in families are much less likely to be poor. Among elderly Americans living alone in 2005, 19.1 percent were poor, while those living in families had a low poverty rate of 5.6 percent.[7]

8.3 **Poverty, ages 65 and over, by gender, race, ethnicity, and household structure, 2005**

Percent in poverty

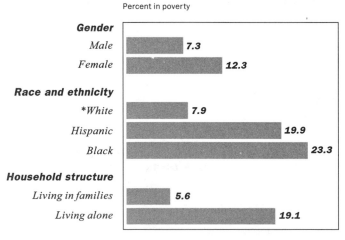

Source: U.S. Bureau of the Census
*White, non Hispanic

The Near-Poor Elderly. Although poverty has declined sharply among the elderly, many have incomes only slightly above the poverty line. These households—with incomes up to 125 percent of the poverty line—face considerable hardships. Near-poor poverty rates for the elderly are similar to those for the nation as a whole.[8]

In 2005, the near-poor poverty rate among those ages 65 and over was 16.7 percent. The rate for men was 12.4 percent—considerably lower than the rate for women, at 19.9 percent. Among those over age 75, the gender gap was even larger. Almost a quarter of women over age 75 were near-poor, compared to 13.3 percent of males.[9]

An International Perspective. The United States has not achieved the low levels of elderly poverty reached by other industrial nations. Based on the international definition of poverty—an income of less than one-half the national median income—the United States places in the lower half of industrial countries, according to the Luxembourg Income Study.[10]

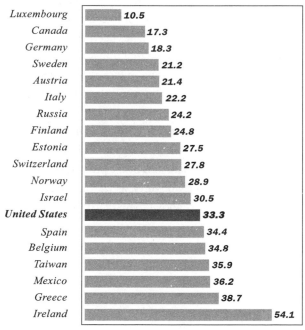

8.4 **Poverty, ages 65 and over, selected industrial countries, 2000**

Percent elderly households with income less than one-half the national median income

Luxembourg	10.5
Canada	17.3
Germany	18.3
Sweden	21.2
Austria	21.4
Italy	22.2
Russia	24.2
Finland	24.8
Estonia	27.5
Switzerland	27.8
Norway	28.9
Israel	30.5
United States	33.3
Spain	34.4
Belgium	34.8
Taiwan	35.9
Mexico	36.2
Greece	38.7
Ireland	54.1

Source: Luxembourg Income Study

Using the international definition of poverty, which is considerably higher than the poverty line defined by the United States, 33.3 percent of the nation's elderly were poor in 2000. By contrast, the best country, Luxembourg, had an elderly poverty rate of 10.5 percent. Other nations that did well were Canada, Germany, Sweden, Austria, Italy, Russia, and Finland, all with rates below 25 percent.[11]

Looking Ahead. The Institute for Innovation in Social Policy, in its National Survey of Social Health, asked adults of all ages whether they expected their retirement incomes to be sufficient to cover their needs. More than half of those surveyed, and nearly two-thirds of those with incomes below $50,000, answered "no." These worries are grounded in real trends: benefits have eroded in recent years and the current pension system is at risk.[12]

In the past, most full-time workers in the private sector were covered by "defined benefit" plans, which guaranteed a fixed retirement income, usually paid for by employers. Today, the more typical arrangement is a "defined contribution" plan, in which the amount of retirement income is not guaranteed, and much of the cost and risk is shifted to the worker. This system gives participants more control, but also leaves them more vulnerable if they contribute too little, or if their investments do poorly.[13]

Ideally, retirement benefits are augmented by a combination of savings and investments. But the groups at highest risk for late-life poverty tend to have few investments, and the savings rate in America has been declining. In 2005, personal savings moved to negative numbers for the first time since 1933, meaning that, for the first time in eighty years, Americans' debts outweighed their assets. If these trends continue, the next generation of the elderly may be less well off than the last.[14]

Finishing the Task. Seventy years ago, the nation took an impressive first step toward addressing poverty among the elderly, by passing the Social Security Act. That initial step has been furthered by many expansions of the program over time. But the lack of recent progress in reducing elderly poverty, as well as the substantial number of aging Americans with incomes just above the poverty line, indicates that there is much to be done.

Out-of-Pocket Health Costs, Ages 65 and Over

- Since the early 1980s, the percent of income the elderly have spent on their health care has increased by 44 percent.

- Approximately two-thirds of out-of-pocket health expenditures by the elderly are for specific services. The rest cover premiums—for Medicare and for private supplemental policies. These costs have risen significantly in recent years.

- The elderly poor, those with incomes of less than $10,000, spend almost a third of their incomes on health-care costs.

8.5   Out-of-pocket health-care costs, ages 65 and over, 1982–2005

Percent of income spent on health care

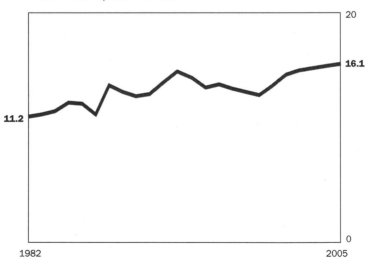

Sources: Bureau of Labor Statistics, U.S. Bureau of the Census

Eroding Elderly Income. Since 1965, when President Lyndon Johnson signed Medicare into law, elderly Americans have been substantially protected from overwhelming medical costs. But gaps in Medicare coverage have widened over time, retirement health-care benefits have grown less generous, and out-of-pocket health-care costs have taken an increasingly larger share of elderly income. This has created a significant financial burden for the elderly.[15]

Medicare pays for just under half of the total health-care costs for the elderly. In 2006 the program began to cover medication costs, with the passage of the new prescription drug program. But Medicare still does not cover major expenses for vision, hearing, dental services, or long-term care.[16]

In 2005, elderly households spent an average of $4,193 out-of-pocket on health care. As a proportion of household income, these expenses have risen every year for the past six years. Health expenditures increased from 11.2 percent of elderly income in the early 1980s, to 16.1 percent in 2005—an increase of 44 percent.[17]

Out-of-Pocket Spending. Almost two-thirds of out-of-pocket health-care expenditures by the elderly are payments for specific services. These include dentistry, home health care, long-term care, inpatient and outpatient treatments, prescription drugs, and physician fees.[18]

An additional 15 percent of expenditures go to Medicare premiums. Most beneficiaries do not pay a premium for Medicare Part A, which covers hospital care. But there is a required monthly payment for Part B, which covers nonhospital health services. These costs have climbed in recent years. In 2006 the Part B premium was $1,062 per year, an increase of nearly 100 percent in just six years.[19]

Many of the elderly also pay premiums for private health insurance plans that

**8.6   Out-of-pocket health spending by
Medicare beneficiaries, 2003**

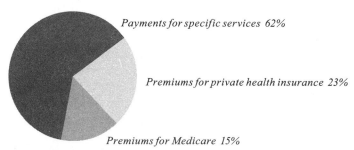

Payments for specific services 62%

Premiums for private health insurance 23%

Premiums for Medicare 15%

Source: U.S. Centers for Medicare and Medicaid Services

supplement Medicare. These policies range in cost and coverage, but here too prices have risen sharply in recent years. The costs of these policies amount to 23 percent of elderly Americans' out-of-pocket expenditures for health care.[20]

Health Care and the Elderly Poor. Medicaid, enacted at the same time as Medicare, is the government program designed to help the poor of all ages with their medical costs. However, only about one-third of the elderly poor receive Medicaid. For those who do not, medical costs can represent a heavy financial burden. [21]

Approximately one-fifth of the elderly have incomes of less than $10,000. For them, health costs are a sizable burden, amounting to 29.2 percent of their income. For those with slightly higher incomes, $10,000-$19,000, health costs are still significant, at 21.6 percent of their income. Those with incomes of $40,000 or more spend less than 10 percent on health care.[22]

Prescription Drugs. In 2006, Medicare initiated a new program to cover the cost of prescription drugs. While some elderly Americans already had drug coverage from preexisting plans, many did not. Overall, paying for drugs has represented a significant part of this age group's health-care expenditures.[23]

By the end of the initial sign-up period for the new drug program, 53 percent of Medicare beneficiaries (including the disabled) had enrolled. Another 37 percent kept their prior coverage, and 10 percent remained uncovered.[24]

The new drug coverage program is an important addition to Medicare. Yet problems remain. These include loss of coverage for some, the complexity of choices available, and the reimbursement gap, which requires recipients to pay 100 percent

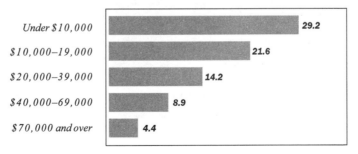

8.7 Out-of-pocket health spending, as percent of income, ages 65 and over, 2000

Percent of household income spent on health, by income level

Income level	Percent
Under $10,000	29.2
$10,000–19,000	21.6
$20,000–39,000	14.2
$40,000–69,000	8.9
$70,000 and over	4.4

Source: U.S. Centers for Medicare and Medicaid Services

of all drug costs above $2,400 until their total expenditures reach $5,451. The new Medicare plan has helped to address, but has not yet resolved, the continuing problem of prescription drug costs for the elderly.[25]

The Financial Impact. High out-of-pocket health-care expenses can have a serious impact on the economic well-being of elderly Americans. At their most extreme, they can cause debt or even bankruptcy, due to the large sums they represent.

A survey by the Commonwealth Fund found the impact of out-of-pocket costs to be serious. Among Medicare recipients, 12 percent reported that they had had to change their way of life in order to meet their medical costs, 10 percent said they were not able to pay their bills, and 8 percent had been contacted by a collection agency. Almost one in five (18 percent) reported at least one of these problems.[26]

The Health Impact. Out-of-pocket medical spending may have a serious or even life-threatening effect on the health of the elderly. When costs are too high, people may be forced to delay needed services, let prescriptions go unfilled, or forgo important medical procedures.

In 2004, Rice and Matsuoka reviewed twenty-two recent studies that assessed the impact of out-of-pocket medical costs on the health of the elderly. Most of these studies found significant evidence of poor health outcomes when coverage involved aggressive "cost-sharing"—that is, more out-of-pocket costs. The studies reviewed found higher mortality rates, poorer general health, lack of regular mammograms,

8.8 The financial impact of medical bills, Medicare beneficiaries, 2001

Percent, Medicare beneficiaries, ages 65 and over

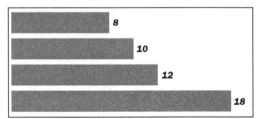

Source: Karen Davis, et al., "Medicare vs. Private Insurance," *Health Affairs*, 2002, based on Commonwealth Fund 2001 Health Insurance Survey

less use of prescribed medications, increased nursing home admissions, and more emergency room visits. Except for heart attacks, where cost levels had less impact, Rice and Matsuoka reported "near unanimity among the studies that cost-sharing has a negative effect on the appropriate use of services or health status of seniors."[27]

Looking to the Future. Out-of-pocket health-care costs represent one of the most serious problems facing the elderly. They can lead to debt and limit access to care, undermining quality of life and worsening health. This country has made a strong effort to address the health-care needs of the elderly through Medicare and the new drug benefit. But serious problems remain that have yet to be resolved.

Chapter 9
Social Indicators for All Ages

Homicides
Alcohol-Related Traffic Fatalities
Food Stamp Coverage
Affordable Housing
Income Inequality

Homicides

- The nation's homicide rate has improved over time, down from the peaks reached in the early 1980s and early 1990s. However, no progress has been made since 2000.

- Approximately one-third of murder victims and almost half of those who commit murder are younger than twenty-five.

- The homicide rate in the United States greatly exceeds the rates of most other industrial nations.

9.1 Homicides, 1970–2005

Homicides per 100,000

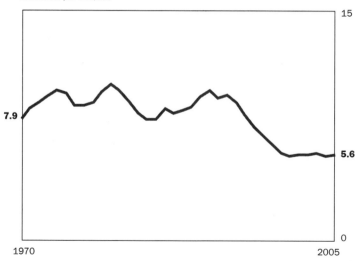

Source: FBI, Uniform Crime Reports

A Concern for Safety. Homicide is the most violent of all crimes and the one most feared by the public. When murder rates rise, communities decline. People may stay in their homes, afraid to venture out in the evening or to walk along risky streets in the daytime. Sometimes the danger may be closer, such as the threat of domestic violence or child abuse. Whatever the source, the quality of life is altered by the threat of homicide, and it is among the most important indicators of our safety and security. According to the Bureau of Justice Statistics, "no other crime is measured as accurately and precisely" as homicide. For this reason homicide is a key barometer of all violent crime.[1]

One of the most positive social trends of the past two decades has been the decline in the national homicide rate, from 7.9 per 100,000 in 1970 to a low 5.6 in 2005. Homicide peaked in 1980, at 10.2, rose nearly as high again in 1991, and then began a decade of almost uninterrupted improvement, falling to 5.5 in 2000.[2]

One cause for concern in this upbeat picture is the lack of improvement in recent years. Between 2000 and 2005, the homicide rate remained steady, between 5.5 and 5.7 per 100,00. Another troubling aspect, despite long-term improvement, is the total number of homicides in the United States. In 2005, 16,692 Americans were murdered.[3]

Impact on the Young. Young people ages 18 to 24 are killed in homicides at an annual rate of 17.1 per 100,000, a higher victimization rate than any other age group. This

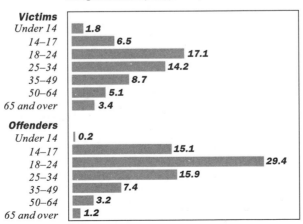

9.2   Homicides, victims and offenders, by age, 1976–2004

Average annual homicides, per 100,000

Victims	
Under 14	1.8
14–17	6.5
18–24	17.1
25–34	14.2
35–49	8.7
50–64	5.1
65 and over	3.4

Offenders	
Under 14	0.2
14–17	15.1
18–24	29.4
25–34	15.9
35–49	7.4
50–64	3.2
65 and over	1.2

Source: FBI, Supplementary Homicide Reports, 1976-2004
Note: The victims of the 9/11 attack are not included in this analysis

same age group, 18 to 24, is also disproportionately represented among those who commit homicides, with an offender rate of 29.4 per 100,000—nearly double the next highest age group. The Bureau of Justice Statistics observes that "approximately one-third of murder victims and almost half the offenders are under the age of 25." The high rate of youth involvement in homicide is a long-term problem that has not yet been resolved.[4]

Looking at cause of death by age group further illustrates the impact of homicide on the young. According to the Centers for Disease Control, homicide ranks among the top five causes of death for every age group between 1 and 34, for males and for females. Even among the youngest females, ages 1 to 4, homicide is the third most frequent cause of death. African American youth are particularly at risk. Homicide is the number one cause of death for African American males between the ages of 15 and 34, and the second most frequent cause for African American females ages 15 to 24. In 2003, homicides took the lives of more than 10,000 Americans under the age of 35.[5]

Guns and Youth. Guns are the single most important weapon in homicides, and of these, handguns are used most often. As with crime in general, the number of murders committed with guns has declined sharply during the past several decades, but guns remain the leading weapon employed. In the prime age group of 18 to 24, where both offenders and victims cluster, the use of guns in the commission of homicides has dropped sharply since the 1990s, going from a peak of 8,559 in 1993 to 5,257 in

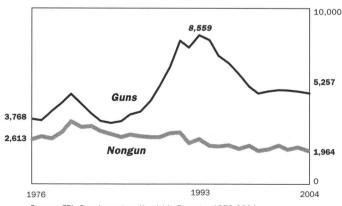

9.3 Number of homicides, by weapon, ages 18–24, 1976–2004

Number of homicides

Source: FBI, Supplementary Homicide Reports, 1976-2004

2004. But the numbers still have not returned to the lower levels of the 1980s.[6]

The Children's Defense Fund has made the impact of guns on children's lives one of their central concerns. They point out that while the average number of child gun-deaths declined from an average of 15 per day in 1994 to just under 8 per day in 2004, these numbers remain far too high. They calculate that since 1979, the total number of children and youth killed by guns is 101,413.[7]

Violent Crime. The federal Uniform Crime Reporting System tracks four types of violent crime: homicide, aggravated assault, robbery, and rape. The total violent crime rate in 2005 was 469.2 per 100,000 population. This was worse than the 1970 rate of 363.5, but far better than the peak year of 1991, when the rate hit 758.2.[8]

The rate of improvement for each of the four types of violent crime has varied. In 2005, both homicide and robbery were close to their all-time best. Assault improved by 34 percent from its worst year in 1992, and rape by 26 percent from its 1992 high. The most positive finding is that all forms of violent crime have improved since the decade of the 1990s.[9]

Homicide among Nations. For most types of violent crime—robberies, assaults, and sexual offenses—rates in the United States are comparable to those of other industrial nations. But the U.S. homicide rate is substantially higher. The homicide rate in many industrial countries is less than 2 per 100,000, while the United States' rate of 5.6 is more than double this level, and more than five times the rate of the lowest country, Norway. Other countries with low homicide rates are Denmark, Japan, Sweden, Switzerland, Spain, and Germany. Countries that, like the United States, do poorly include Hungary, New Zealand, the Czech Republic, Finland, and Bulgaria.[10]

The Death Penalty. The U.S. also differs from other nations in its use of capital punishment. Around the world the death penalty has been abolished by 89 countries, including every other industrial nation except Japan, Russia, and South Korea. In the U.S., 38 states as well as the federal government have laws allowing for the death penalty, generally for certain categories of homicide, such as first-degree murder or murder with aggravating circumstances.[11]

A series of Supreme Court decisions between 1968 and 1972 tightened the requirements for death penalty laws, ruling that they could be judged "cruel and unusual punishment" if they permitted executions that were arbitrary, too severe for the crime, offensive to society's sense of justice, or no more effective than lesser punishments. The majority of state laws were open to challenge on this standard,

9.4 Homicides, selected industrial countries

Homicides per 100,000

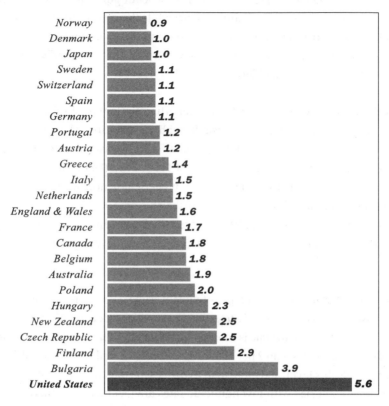

Norway	0.9
Denmark	1.0
Japan	1.0
Sweden	1.1
Switzerland	1.1
Spain	1.1
Germany	1.1
Portugal	1.2
Austria	1.2
Greece	1.4
Italy	1.5
Netherlands	1.5
England & Wales	1.6
France	1.7
Canada	1.8
Belgium	1.8
Australia	1.9
Poland	2.0
Hungary	2.3
New Zealand	2.5
Czech Republic	2.5
Finland	2.9
Bulgaria	3.9
United States	5.6

Source: "International Comparisons of Criminal Justice Statistics 2001,"
British Home Office Statistical Bulletin, 2003
Note: Data are from the most recent years available, ranging from 1999–2001

and only three executions took place between 1970 and 1980. Many states rewrote their laws, however, and during the 1980s the number of executions began to climb again, peaking at 98 in 1999. Since then executions have become somewhat less frequent; there were 53 in 2006.[12]

In the Future. During the 1990s, the homicide rate in the United States declined sharply. This is a major contribution to the quality of life in America. Yet problems persist, including a lack of improvement in recent years, the high number of homicides each year, and the disproportionate involvement of youth. These issues will need to be addressed in the coming decades.

Alcohol-Related Traffic Fatalities

- The percentage of traffic fatalities that are alcohol-related is lower today than in any year since 1977. Progress has slowed in recent years, but the overall improvement is still significant.

- Male drivers are involved in alcohol-related traffic crashes far more frequently than female drivers.

- Every year, nearly 13,000 Americans under age 25 die in motor vehicle accidents.

9.5 Alcohol-related traffic fatalities, 1977–2005

Percent of fatalities in traffic crashes involving a blood-alcohol level >.01.

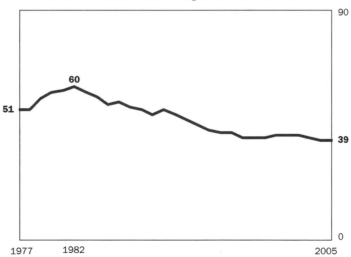

Source: National Institute for Alcohol Abuse and Alcoholism, National Highway Traffic Safety Administration

Making Progress. About 43,000 people die in traffic accidents each year, and more than a third of these accidents are alcohol-related. Driving while intoxicated thus stands at the intersection of two critical problems—alcohol abuse and unsafe driving. Each year, these two problems take thousands of lives. They affect people of all ages, and though progress has been made, they remain a significant danger to our quality of life.[13]

The standard approach to assessing the role of alcohol in traffic accidents is to measure the proportion of fatalities each year that are deemed alcohol-related, based on the blood-alcohol level of those involved. Since 1977, the proportion of alcohol-related fatalities has declined.[14]

In 2005, 39 percent of traffic fatalities were alcohol-related, the lowest proportion since the statistics began. This figure is down from 60 percent during the peak year of 1982. Unfortunately, relatively little progress has been made in the past seven years. Nevertheless, the fact that the rate has dropped 35 percent since 1982 is an important achievement.[15]

Safe Driving. Public policies encouraging safe driving helped to diminish the total number of fatal accidents between 1982 and 1992. The promotion of seat belts and lower speed limits helped to reduce traffic fatalities from 43,945 to 39,250. Since then, however, fatalities have begun to rise again. Some analysts argue that the

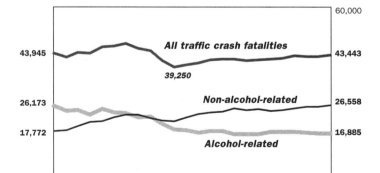

9.6   Traffic crash fatalities with and without alcohol involvement, 1982–2005

Number of fatalities

Source: National Highway Traffic Safety Administration
Note: Alcohol-related crashes involve a blood-alcohol level >.01

decision in the early 1990s to end the uniform national speed limit of 55 miles per hour has contributed to this increase.[16]

Newer initiatives have focused specifically on reducing drunk driving. National advocacy groups such as Mothers Against Drunk Driving (MADD) have urged their implementation. These programs include: revoking the license of drivers who refuse or fail a breathalyzer test, making it illegal to serve liquor to the intoxicated, and raising the minimum drinking age to 21.[17]

These policies have been effective. In 1982, the majority of traffic fatalities were alcohol-related. Since then, the percentage of traffic deaths that were alcohol-related has dropped steadily. Between 1982 and 2005, the number of traffic fatalities not related to alcohol increased by almost 10,000, while alcohol-related fatalities declined by almost exactly the same amount.[18]

The Drivers. Male drivers are involved in alcohol-related fatal traffic crashes far more frequently than female drivers. There are also clear patterns by age: 21- to 24-year-olds have the highest rates, followed by 25- to 34-year-olds. Drivers ages 65 and over account for the fewest alcohol-related fatalities. Most alcohol-related fatal accidents occur when drivers go out in the evening.[19]

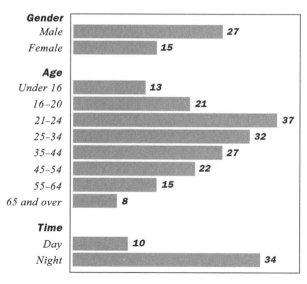

9.7   **Drivers in fatal crashes, by gender, age, and time of day, 2005**

Percent of drivers with blood-alcohol level > .01

Gender
Male — 27
Female — 15

Age
Under 16 — 13
16–20 — 21
21–24 — 37
25–34 — 32
35–44 — 27
45–54 — 22
55–64 — 15
65 and over — 8

Time
Day — 10
Night — 34

Source: National Highway Traffic Safety Administration

The Victims. Traffic fatalities, both alcohol and non-alcohol related, are the leading cause of death for both males and females, ages 5 to 24. Each year, nearly 13,000 Americans under the age of 25 die in motor vehicle accidents. Young people between 16 and 24 are at the highest risk of all—10,321 died in traffic accidents in 2005. Looking specifically at alcohol-related fatalities, 16- to 24-year-olds are also the most frequent victims. They account for about one-quarter of the deaths—the largest proportion of any age group.[20]

Youth and Alcohol Abuse. Beyond the problem of drunk driving is the broader issue of alcohol abuse by the young. Binge drinking—having more than five drinks in a row—remains a common behavior among youth. In the most recent National Survey on Drug Use and Health, 45.7 percent of young people ages 21 to 25 reported having engaged in this behavior at least once during the previous month.[21]

Binge drinking is a problem even for those under the legal drinking age of 21. Among 18- to 20-year-olds, 36.1 percent had engaged in binge drinking during the previous month, as had 19.7 percent of 16- to 17-year-olds. Within these groups, bingeing was more common among males than females, and more common among white and Hispanic youth than among African Americans.[22]

9.8 Binge drinking by gender, age, race, and ethnicity, 2005

Percent who had 5 or more drinks at a time, past month

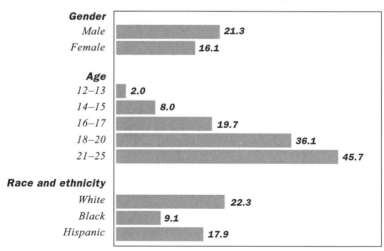

Source: Substance Abuse & Mental Health Services Administration
Note: Gender, race, and ethnicity: ages 12–20 (underage)

Counting the Cost. One approach to assessing the impact of alcohol-related traffic accidents is to measure the cost in dollars and cents. A 2002 study by the National Highway Traffic Safety Administration analyzed a broad range of associated costs, including emergency services, medical care, lost workdays, legal expenses, property damage, and—in the case of fatalities—years of lost income.[23]

The study found that alcohol-related traffic fatalities are more costly than other traffic accidents, in part because they produce a higher proportion of serious injuries and deaths. More years of income are lost because so many of the victims are young. The study concluded that alcohol-related accidents cost the nation about 51 billion dollars per year, including 40 billion from cases in which alcohol was listed as the primary cause for the crash.[24]

Another way to assess the social cost of alcohol-related traffic fatalities is to measure the years of potential life lost. The calculation—the number of people who die, multiplied by the additional years each might have lived—adds up to a loss of several hundred thousand years. Both sexes have shown some improvement in recent years, yet alcohol-related crashes continue to exact a huge toll in years lost—years in which important contributions might have been made.[25]

A Continuing Challenge. Efforts by both government and advocacy organizations have helped to moderate America's alcohol-related traffic fatalities since the 1970s. However, progress has slowed recently, and non-alcohol-related traffic fatalities have been rising for more than a decade. Thousands of lives can be saved each year—many of them young adults—if the nation's energies can be focused on both the broad challenge of reducing traffic deaths and the specific challenge of eliminating alcohol as a factor.

Food Stamp Coverage

- Food stamp participation among the poor has declined markedly over the past decade.

- In 2005, 11 percent of American households—35 million people—were defined as "food insecure" by the Department of Agriculture.

- Reports from private food banks and soup kitchens indicate that requests for emergency food assistance have increased steadily in recent years.

9.9 Food stamp participation, 1975–2004

Percent participation by poor households

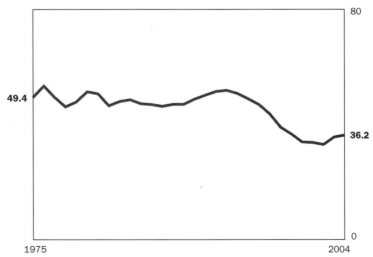

Sources: U.S. House of Representatives, Green Book; U.S. Bureau of the Census

Access to Food. Many Americans live with the threat of hunger or insufficient food. Though the media only rarely address the problem, it remains a serious concern for families and individuals throughout the nation. The federal Food Stamp Program is the nation's response to the problem. Beginning as a small surplus distribution program under President Franklin D. Roosevelt, it was phased out in the 1940s, revived as a pilot program under President John F. Kennedy, and then established as a full-fledged food assistance program under President Lyndon B. Johnson.[26]

For long-term trends, participation in the Food Stamp Program is the best available measure of food access. People with incomes below the poverty line typically need food stamps in order to purchase sufficient food. But they may be deterred from participating in the program by many obstacles, including uncertainty about eligibility, complex application procedures, long waiting periods, requirements for recertification, or citizenship status. Thus, many of the poor who are eligible for food stamps do not receive them and struggle to put food on the table as a result.[27]

Food Stamp participation among the poor has declined substantially over time. From the mid-1970s through the early 1990s, approximately half of the poor received food stamps. Participation rates then began to drop. There were modest improvements in 2003 and 2004, but the latest rate of 36.2 percent is well below the high of 51.9 percent achieved in 1993.[28]

Food Insecurity. "Food insecure" is the term the federal government now uses to characterize those who are hungry or who lack access to sufficient food. The Department of Agriculture administers an annual survey to directly measure the

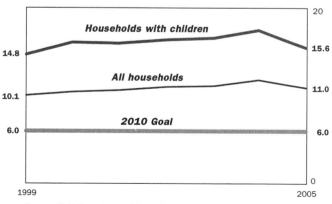

9.10 Food insecurity, 1999–2005

Percent of all households

Households with children

14.8   15.6

All households

10.1   11.0

2010 Goal

6.0   6.0

1999   2005

Source: U.S. Department of Agriculture

problem. In 2005, 11.0 percent of U.S. households experienced food insecurity.[29]

The food insecurity rate worsened each year between 1999 and 2004, but improved in 2005. There was a marked improvement among households with children in 2005, where the rate fell from 17.6 percent to 15.6. Nevertheless, the latest statistics mean that food insecurity is still a serious problem for 35.1 million people, including 12.4 million children.[30]

The Department of Agriculture also defines a category of extreme need or "very low food security" for persons whose eating patterns are disrupted and whose food intake is reduced. In 2005, 4.4 million Americans fell into this category.[31]

The federal government, in its Healthy People 2010 project, has set a goal for reducing food insecurity to 6 percent by the year 2010. That goal remains elusive. The rate worsened during five of the past six years, and remains almost double the 2010 target.[32]

Private Food Assistance. Like the Department of Agriculture studies, reports from private food banks, food pantries, and soup kitchens indicate the widespread nature of food needs in America. The annual U.S. Conference of Mayors report, for example, surveyed twenty-three cities in 2006. This study showed that organizations providing emergency food assistance saw a 7 percent increase in use over the previous year. This was the sixteenth consecutive year in which demand rose. Moreover, participating cities estimated that despite their best efforts, nearly a quarter of the need for emergency food assistance had gone unmet.[33]

America's Second Harvest—the largest private organization serving the hungry—coordinates a national network of approximately 50,000 charitable agencies that run food pantries, soup kitchens, and emergency shelters. They report that in 2005 their member agencies provided emergency hunger assistance to approximately 25 million individuals. More than half of these agencies reported that there had been an increase in demand during the past four years.[34]

Who Are the Hungry? To profile the hungry, America's Second Harvest conducted an in-depth survey of its member agency clients. From the approximately 25 million people served in 2005, more than 52,000 individuals were interviewed. The survey showed that 36 percent of those served were children under age 18, including 8 percent who were under age 6. An additional 10 percent were elderly and the remaining 54 percent were between the ages of 18 and 64.[35]

By race, about 40 percent of the recipients were white, 38 percent were African American, and the remainder belonged to other racial groups. Hispanics constituted

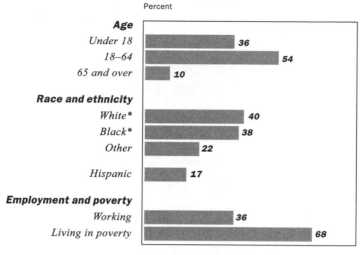

9.11 Private food assistance, client characteristics, 2005

Percent

	Percent
Age	
Under 18	36
18–64	54
65 and over	10
Race and ethnicity	
White*	40
Black*	38
Other	22
Hispanic	17
Employment and poverty	
Working	36
Living in poverty	68

Source: America's Second Harvest
*White Non-Hispanic and Black Non-Hispanic

17 percent of the total. Thirty-six percent of the households had at least one employed adult, and 68 percent had incomes below the poverty level. These findings make clear that food access is a problem experienced by Americans of every age and ethnic group. A substantial proportion are employed, reflecting the increasing problems of the working poor.[36]

Difficult Choices. For the poor, there are often harsh tradeoffs that need to be made between food and basic necessities. America's Second Harvest, in its study of member agency clients, surveyed this problem. In 2005, they found that 42 percent had to choose between paying for food and for utilities, 35 percent chose between food and housing costs, and 32 percent had to choose between food and medical care. A striking 18 percent had faced all three problems in the past 12 months.[37]

Illness and Obesity. Research has shown that among adults, hunger can result in poor nutrition or malnutrition, fostering a rise in ill health, chronic disease, and lingering disability. Equally well documented are the negative effects that inadequate nutrition can have on children, including poor cognitive functioning, lower academic achievement, behavioral and psychological problems, and a greater long-term risk of chronic disease. These outcomes make the relatively low current level of Food

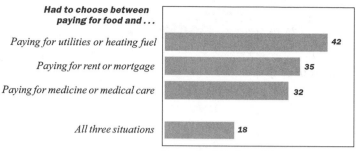

9.12 Difficult choices, private food assistance clients, 2005

Percent, past 12 months

Had to choose between paying for food and . . .

Paying for utilities or heating fuel	42
Paying for rent or mortgage	35
Paying for medicine or medical care	32
All three situations	18

Source: America's Second Harvest

Stamp participation an important concern, since participation has been shown to make a significant improvement in children's nutrition and dietary intake.[38]

Less obvious, but increasingly well researched, is the relationship between problems with food access and obesity. It might seem paradoxical that people who cannot get enough to eat should suffer from obesity, but difficulty in accessing food typically results in poor diet, with few fruits and vegetables and more high-carbohydrate, high-calorie foods, such as rice, pasta, potatoes, and bread. This type of diet can be a major factor in weight gain. The connection between food insecurity and obesity has received increasing recognition in the past several years.[39]

A National Responsibility. The American Dietetic Association asserts that "systematic and sustained action is needed to bring an end to domestic food insecurity and hunger and to achieve food and nutrition security for all in the United States." The problem of hunger affects millions of Americans, yet it is largely invisible. It will be necessary in the years ahead to accept this issue as a national responsibility, and to recognize that addressing it is a crucial investment in our country's future.[40]

Affordable Housing

- The availability of a home, as measured by the Affordability Index, has fluctuated over time, scoring best in the early 1970s, reaching its worst point in 1981, then recovering throughout the 1980s and 1990s, only to lose ground again in 2004 and 2005.

- The lower incomes of first-time buyers make the purchase of a home difficult. The Affordability Index for first-time buyers shows that during the past thirty-five years, these homebuyers have had to struggle to afford the price of a home.

- The rate of homeownership among minorities has remained consistently below that of whites.

9.13 Housing affordability, 1970–2005

Affordability Index, all buyers

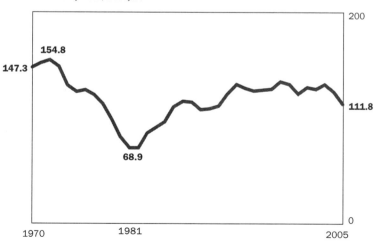

Source: National Association of Realtors

The Meaning of a Home. Shelter is a fundamental necessity for human life. Decent housing can protect and enhance a family's health, safety, and comfort; poor housing can compromise all three. A home also has emotional meaning—as an expression of personality, as a haven from outside troubles, and as a center for private life.

The financial implications of homeownership are double-edged. On the one hand, for many Americans, the purchase of a home represents the largest investment they will ever make, a family's major financial asset. Yet a mortgage may also become a significant financial burden, weighing a family down with obligations they find difficult to meet.[41]

To monitor the financial impact of housing costs over time, the National Association of Realtors has developed an Affordability Index, which tracks median house prices in relation to average family income. An Index of 100 means that the average American family has exactly the income needed to buy a median-priced house. An Index above 100 means they earn more than enough money for such a house; an Index below 100 means they earn too little.[42]

The Affordability Index has shown significant swings over the past thirty-five years. Homeownership was most affordable in 1972, when the index reached 154.8. It sank to a very poor 68.9 in 1981. It recovered, and then remained fairly stable between the mid-1990s and 2003, generally staying in a narrow band between 125 and 135. In the past two years, however, the Index dropped 19 points, indicating

9.14 Housing affordability, first-time buyers, all buyers, 1981–2005

Affordability Index

Source: National Association of Realtors

less affordability. The Index for 2005 was 111.8—its worst level since 1991. While still on the "affordable" side of 100, the sharp drop in the past two years is a cause for concern.[43]

First-Time Buyers. During the past two decades, housing prices have been relatively affordable overall. Nevertheless, many first-time buyers have had a difficult time. The National Association of Realtors' Affordability Index for First-Time Homebuyers has not reached 100 once since it was introduced. For the past decade, it has hovered in the 80s, and in 2005 it dropped to 74.0. Thus, in 2005 the average first-time homebuyer earned only about 74 percent of what was needed to buy a median-priced house—a situation that clearly put them at a disadvantage in the housing market.[44]

Undue Burdens. Another way to address the issue of affordability is to measure the "cost burden" of a dwelling—that is, the percentage of income that owners and renters spend on housing each year. Using data from the American Housing Survey, the U.S. Department of Housing and Urban Development has monitored cost burden trends over time. Their rule of thumb is that expenditures for housing should not exceed 25-30 percent of income. Spending 30-50 percent of income on housing is defined as a moderate cost burden, while spending more than 50 percent is defined as a severe burden.[45]

Using these criteria, the financial burden of a home has increased over the past twenty-five years. During this period, the percentage of households with a moderate cost burden rose from 10 to 18 percent, while the proportion of households in the severe cost burden category rose from 7 percent to 15 percent. As of 2005, one-third of American households were experiencing at least some financial burden because of their housing.[46]

International Standing. Having a home of one's own is often viewed as central to the American Dream. Yet the United States does not lead the world in ownership rates. Many other industrial nations have comparable or slightly higher rates than those in the United States.[47]

The United States ranks only moderately among industrial nations in homeownership. Greece, Iceland, Portugal, Belgium, Australia, and the United Kingdom all stand higher. Countries that do less well than the United States include Canada, Finland, Austria, France, Denmark, the Czech Republic, and Germany.[48]

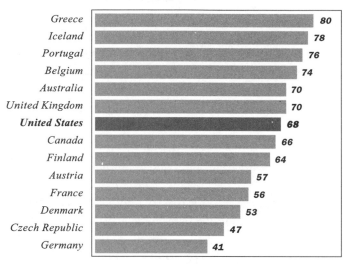

9.15 Owner-occupied housing, selected industrial countries

Percent of all housing

Country	Percent
Greece	80
Iceland	78
Portugal	76
Belgium	74
Australia	70
United Kingdom	70
United States	68
Canada	66
Finland	64
Austria	57
France	56
Denmark	53
Czech Republic	47
Germany	41

Source: Council of Mortgage Lenders, London
Note: Data are from the most recent years available,
ranging from 1999–2003

Who Owns a Home? One reason for this country's only moderate international ranking is the continuing disparity in homeownership rates by race and ethnicity. In 2005, 76 percent of white Americans owned their own homes, but fewer than 50 percent of African Americans or Hispanics did. Homeownership rates increased among all three racial and ethnic groups between 1973 and 2005, but the rate of ownership among minorities in 2005 remained only about two-thirds of the white rate—almost precisely the same percentage as in 1973.[49]

A 2005 report by the Federal Reserve Board shed light on this problem. It showed that even after controlling for such issues as borrowers' income, loan amount, and property location, minorities were denied mortgages or charged above-market rates more often than nonminority applicants.[50]

The Renters. Approximately one-third of all American households live in rental apartments. For renters, affordable housing is particularly difficult to find. The National Low Income Housing Coalition reports that in 2005, in every state in the nation, the market cost of a two-bedroom apartment required the expenditure of more than 30 percent of average renter income. This high burden is of particular concern since the American Housing Survey indicates that 41 percent of the nation's lowest-income renter households are families with children.[51]

9.16 Home ownership, by race and ethnicity, 1973 and 2005

Percent

Source: U.S. Bureau of the Census

The Homeless. In 2004, the National Law Center on Homelessness and Poverty estimated that on any given day, 840,000 Americans were either living on the street or using temporary housing. Many more—as many as 2.5 to 3.5 million—were homeless for some part of the year.[52]

The annual multi-city survey sponsored by the U.S. Conference of Mayors estimates that in 2006, single men represented 51 percent of the homeless population, followed by families with children, at 30 percent. Single women made up 17 percent of the population, and 2 percent were unaccompanied young people.[53]

The majority of cities participating in the 2006 survey reported that requests for emergency shelter were increasing, and more than three-quarters of the cities indicated that some homeless people seeking shelter had been turned away for lack of resources. The principal causes of homelessness, listed in the order identified by the participating cities, were: mental illness, lack of affordable housing, substance abuse, low-paying jobs, domestic violence, prisoner reentry, unemployment, and poverty.[54]

An Agenda for Housing. While housing has been relatively affordable over the past decade for middle-income families, the recent drop in affordability, both for all buyers and for first-time buyers, suggests a disturbing trend. The difficulties faced by low-income families, minorities, and many renters are areas in which further improvements are needed if the benefits of affordable housing are to be more widely shared.

Income Inequality

- The Gini coefficient, the standard measure of inequality, has risen since 1970, and now stands at its highest point since World War II.

- The wealthiest fifth of American households receive a larger share of the national income today than at any time since 1970.

- The U.S. rate of inequality far outpaces that of most other industrial nations.

9.17 Income inequality, 1970–2005

Gini Coefficient

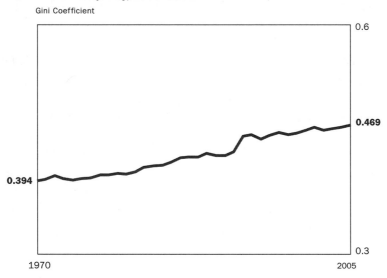

Source: U.S. Bureau of the Census

A Widening Gap. An important indicator of an equitable society is the degree to which prosperity is shared among its citizens. When economic inequality grows too great, it can weaken social cohesion, making it more difficult to sustain a sense of national purpose and community. In the United States, the gap between the rich and the poor has increased significantly over time, representing a potential harm to the larger society.

The most widely used method for measuring inequality is the Gini coefficient, which ranges from 0 to 1. If the Gini coefficient is 0, it represents total equality—everyone has the same income. If the coefficient is 1, there is total inequality—a single group or individual has all the money. The more closely a nation's Gini coefficient approaches 1, the greater the inequality.[55]

Between 1970 and 2005, America's Gini coefficient rose from .394 to .469, an increase of 19 percent. Inequality has worsened virtually every year for the past three decades. The inequality levels since 2000 are the highest recorded since World War II.[56]

Dividing the Nation. Another way to measure inequality is to look at the share of income received by each fifth (or quintile) of the population, from the lowest income group to the highest. This provides an additional perspective on how inequality has changed over time.

Between 1970 and 2005, the share of income that went to the wealthiest fifth of the nation rose from 43.3 percent to 50.4 percent, an increase of 16 percent. The four lower quintiles experienced a decline. In total, the income share that went to the lower four-fifths of the income distribution declined by 13 percent.[57]

9.18 Shares of household income, 1970–2005

Percent of total household income, by quintile

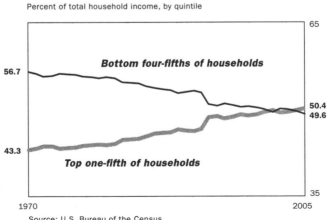

Source: U.S. Bureau of the Census

The Executive Pay Boom. From 1990 to 2004, compensation for top executives in the nation's leading corporations increased by more than 300 percent, adjusted for inflation. At the same time, average employee pay rose only 4.5 percent. As a result, the ratio between the pay of the country's top executives and the typical worker changed dramatically, from 107:1 in 1990, to 431:1 in 2004. This widening gap—between the earnings of the best-paid executives and the income earned by workers—has helped to worsen economic inequality in recent years.[58]

The Wage Shrink. Despite the boom in executive pay, wages and salaries now account for the smallest share of our national income on record. According to the Center on Budget and Policy Priorities, since 2001, wages and salaries grew by only 2 percent, while corporate profits grew by 13.7 percent. A smaller fraction of national income has gone to increases in workers' pay "than in all but one other recovery since World War II." And "for the first time on record, corporate profits have captured a larger share of the income growth . . . than wages and salaries."[59]

Minorities and Wealth. In the United States, disparities by wealth have always exceeded disparities by income. For instance, recent data show that, while the richest 10 percent of American households receive about 40 percent of the nation's household income, they hold nearly 70 percent of the nation's household wealth.[60]

The dimensions of wealth inequality are even sharper when looked at by race and ethnicity. There is a sizable gap between minority and white households in terms of

9.19 Pay ratio, average top executive to average production worker, 1990–2004

Pay Ratio

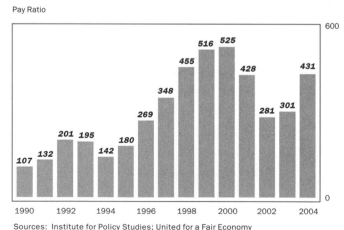

Sources: Institute for Policy Studies; United for a Fair Economy

income, and an even greater gap between the two groups in terms of wealth.[61]

The income gap between minority and white households in both 1995 and 2004 was approximately 40 percent. While both groups experienced an increase in income, the relationship between the two remained almost exactly the same.[62]

In contrast, the wealth gap between minority and white households worsened between 1995 and 2004. In 1995, the gap between minority and white net worth was 79.3 percent. By 2004, that gap had risen to 82.4 percent. This disparity can be seen in every major type of asset ownership, including real estate, businesses, retirement accounts, life insurance, stocks, and bonds.[63]

Disparities in wealth represent a critical aspect of inequality, since assets can provide a crucial safety net in periods of high expenses or reduced income. The extreme disparities by race and ethnicity represent a particularly troubling aspect of this problem.

International Measures. Compared to most industrial nations, the United States stands out for its unusually high level of inequality. In terms of the share of wealth held by the richest 10 percent of the population, the United States exceeds all nations but Switzerland. In the United States, 69.8 percent of the wealth is held by the richest

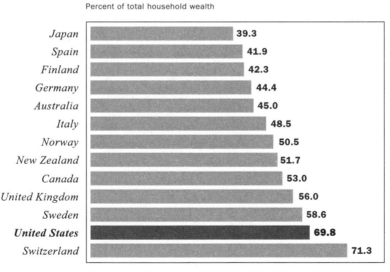

9.20 Share of household wealth, top 10 percent of households, selected industrial countries

Percent of total household wealth

Country	Percent
Japan	39.3
Spain	41.9
Finland	42.3
Germany	44.4
Australia	45.0
Italy	48.5
Norway	50.5
New Zealand	51.7
Canada	53.0
United Kingdom	56.0
Sweden	58.6
United States	69.8
Switzerland	71.3

Source: James Davies et al., *The World Distribution of Household Wealth,* World Institute for Development Economics Research, United Nations University, 2006
Note: Data are from the most recent years available, ranging from 1997–2002

one-tenth. In Switzerland, the figure is 71.3 percent. By contrast, Japan, Spain, Finland, Germany, and Australia all have a less concentrated distribution of wealth.[64]

Thinking Inequality. The widening gap between the rich and the poor has become a focus of significant research and debate during the past several years. Studies have explored the impact of inequality on health, crime, and social capital. President George W. Bush has acknowledged the problem: "I know some of our citizens worry about the fact that our dynamic economy is leaving working people behind. . . . Income inequality is real."[65] This divide worries scholars, politicians, and social analysts because it has the potential to fray the social fabric of the nation. The benefits of our national prosperity need to be shared more broadly.

Conclusion

This book is a call for change and progress. Over the past forty years, we have made relatively few inroads into accomplishing the fundamental tasks set forth in *Toward a Social Report*. The disciplined social reporting those prescient authors envisioned, leading to rational decision-making and informed debate, has clearly not come about. The nation's dialogue about its most basic social problems is still diffuse, fragmented, and sensationalistic.

New problems have emerged. The media coverage of social issues is all too frequently constrained by corporate interests. The social data we produce is so thinly spread across so many agencies, departments, and sources that it is nearly impossible to view our social health as a whole. The answer to the question "How are we doing?" now seems to have little meaning beyond our personal circumstances; the "we" of that question is even less definable today than it was in the past.

An Agenda for National Action

It is time to revive the visionary impulse of the 1960s that led a government agency like NASA to anticipate that space travel would have an impact on American society. Contracting with social scientists, NASA sought not just an analysis of the details, but a larger vision of our social world. Their research was to be, in Bertram Gross's words, "a major contribution to man's efforts to find out where he has been, where he is, and where he is going."[1] Perhaps many government agencies should be asking those kinds of questions.

We believe the federal government must take the lead in the national effort to define and assess our social health. We come to this conclusion somewhat reluctantly, as in recent years the federal government has not always been exemplary in making unbiased data judgments. No one wants a Weapons-of-Mass-Destruction debate in the social sphere.

Nevertheless, if social policies are to be crafted on a rational basis, the fundamental judgments about where we stand must have official government sanction. There is no alternative. Not-for-profit agencies and research centers can make important contributions to the effort, but they cannot carry the burden alone, nor can they bring to bear the national resources that are required.

We need a government agenda—one that a forward-thinking and imaginative administration might be willing to pursue. Following are some of the elements that might be included:

- A multi-disciplinary National Social Research Board, similar in function to a Council of Social Advisors, which would be responsible for issuing formal assessments of the nation's social health.

- An annual National Social Report, issued by this Research Board, which would comprehensively assess the nation's social well-being in terms that are accessible to the general public and the nation's media.

- A system of key national social indicators that could be monitored on a frequent and timely basis, monthly or quarterly.

- An official language and methodology for identifying *social* recessions, and a set of procedures for actively responding.

Beyond the government, there are tasks that social scientists need to pursue as well, drawing upon the lessons of economic theorists. Most fundamentally, we need to envision the social sphere as a single conceptual unity in a way that has practical import and measurable aspects.[2] A new body of social theory is needed, one that, like the governmental agenda we imagine above, would be bolder and more innovative than most academic efforts are today.

We also need a more responsive media—one that takes on the fundamental responsibility of reporting social issues in a deeper context. Greater visibility is required. Space, time, and attention need to be allocated to social concerns. Ideally, the daily paper and the morning news would allow us to shift our focus of attention from the stock market, politics, entertainment, and fashion to the larger panorama of our social life, in much the same way we look at profits, mergers, decline, and growth in the economy.

How might all these changes come about? Where do we begin? At the present time, some of the most innovative work in the nation is occurring at the local level—in the states, cities, and communities that are monitoring their social problems on a systematic basis. They have illustrated for us how to invent comprehensive social reporting systems. Local communities have demonstrated time and again that we can identify key indicators, that people do want to understand their quality of life, and that democratic and open processes can be initiated to accomplish these tasks.

At the national level, we might return to another basic democratic process—congressional hearings. When Senator Mondale's "Full Opportunity and Social Accounting Act" was first proposed in the 1960s, a remarkable series of hearings was held on how best to assess the social state of the nation. The testimony of a broad range of analysts gave a public airing to an array of ideas for social change. Hearings of this type, replicated today, might help us to forge a new consensus on how social issues could be centrally located on the nation's agenda. Conferences, public meetings, and discussions in the media might parallel such hearings, adding further impetus for change and reform.

These tasks—for the government, the academy, and the media—require a level of investment, commitment, and energy that has not been forthcoming in recent years. Yet this nation needs to envision a post-war society that is dedicated to the social well-being of its people. The projects we outline are neither so extraordinary nor so expensive that they could not be accomplished with the resources currently available to us. They merit a prominent place on the public agenda.

America's Social Health Today

In Part II of this book, we provided a brief portrait of the nation's current social state, focusing on the sixteen social indicators that make up the Index of Social Health. The larger picture they portray is reflected in the Index itself, including a long period of stagnation, some progress, and recent decline.

Among the individual narratives, a few give us hope. The improvement in high school dropouts, for example, tells us that more young people in the future may have opportunities for successful careers. Employment is better than it has been in other decades. So is crime.

Yet much of the progress that has marked this nation in the past is stalling. For almost every indicator where there has been improvement, progress has slowed in recent years:

- Infant mortality, despite long-term advances, now shows stagnation.

- Teenage drug use has shown only modest improvement in the past five years.

- The reduction in poverty among the elderly, for so long a bright note in the overall poverty picture, has come to a halt.

- Homicides declined markedly in the 1990s, but have recently remained steady, showing no additional improvement.

At the same time, several of this nation's social problems have been worsening:

- Child abuse has continued to increase sharply.

- Child poverty has grown worse since 2000.

- Income inequality continues to trend upward.

- The absence of health insurance coverage for nearly 47 million Americans is a widely acknowledged crisis in the nation.

These issues demand the attention of the nation, both because they affect millions of individuals and because we know that other industrial countries address many of these problems more effectively than we do. The industrial nations of the world provide a yardstick against which we can measure our own performance. They tell us what is possible, and provide benchmarks for our own future efforts. We have a considerable distance to travel if we are to reach those standards.

A sober and comprehensive assessment of the social health of this nation has not been forthcoming from any major institutional source. Are we approaching a social recession? Many indicators point to such a conclusion, yet such a possibility is not discussed. That could not happen in the economic sphere; it should not happen in the social sphere.

Our stalled progress on some social problems, the worsening of others, and our poor standing in the world clearly point to the need for a new public dialogue and a new public agenda highlighting these critical issues. In the midst of a long and gruesome war, it may be difficult to have a national public debate on our domestic life, but it is imperative that we begin.

Thinking Forward

This nation needs to make its social problems more visible—through greater media attention, more finely tuned social reporting, and the development of more sophisticated tools. We need to begin thinking about our social well-being as a whole, monitoring our social performance and analyzing social change in complex and multifaceted ways. Most importantly, our deepening understanding must lead to action. Where problems are emerging, we need to respond—not years after the fact, but promptly, in time to stem the tides of suffering and loss.

There is much we can do to advance the social state of the nation. This country is rich in talent and resources. We have the ability, close at hand, to improve America's social health. It is time to do so.

Notes

Introduction

1 U.S. Department of Health, Education, and Welfare, *Toward a Social Report* (U.S. Government Printing Office, 1969), iii.

2 "Full Opportunity and Social Accounting Act," Hearings before the Subcommittee on Government Research of the Committee on Government Operations, U.S. Senate, Sixtieth Congress, First Session on S. 843: A Bill to Promote the Public Welfare and to Create a Council of Social Advisors, A Social Report of the President, and a Joint Committee on the Social Report, July 19, 20, 26, 28, 1967 (U.S. Government Printing Office, 1968).

Part I
Social Reporting in American Life

Chapter 1
We Can Do Better: Toward a New Public Dialogue on Social Health

1 Eduardo Porter, "Jobs Data Indicate Economy Is Slowing," Business Day, *New York Times* (July 8, 2006).

2 Homelessness: see, for instance, National Coalition for the Homeless, "How Many People Experience Homelessness," NCH Fact Sheet #2 (June 2006), at http://www.nationalhomeless.org/publications/facts.html. Literacy: The most comprehensive survey is the National Assessment of Adult Literacy, sponsored by the National Center for Education Statistics in 1992 and 2003. For further information, see nces.ed.gov/NAAL/index.asp.

3 Current Population Survey, Historical Poverty Tables, Table 3, at www.census.gov.

4 Robert Kennedy, Address at University of Kansas, Lawrence, Kansas (March 18, 1968), at www.jfklibrary.org/Historical+Resources/Archives.

5 Raymond Bauer, ed., *Social Indicators* (M.I.T. Press, 1966).

6 Ibid., 20.

7 Ibid., vii.

8 Ibid., ix.

9 Ibid.

10 Ibid., 26.

11 Joachim Vogel, "The Future Direction of Social Indicator Research," *Social Indicators Research*, vol. 42 (1997), 108.

Chapter 2
Shaping Everyday Discourse: The News Media and Social Issues

1 Maxwell McCombs and Donald Shaw, "The Agenda-Setting Function of Mass Media," *Public Opinion Quarterly*, vol. 36 (1972), 176-187. The findings in this pioneering article, written more than thirty years ago, have been confirmed by hundreds of studies since that time. See also: Maxwell McCombs, *Setting the Agenda: The Mass Media and Public Opinion* (Policy Press, 2004).

2   See, for instance, Stephen D. Reese, Oscar H. Gandy, Jr., and August E. Grant, eds., *Framing Public Life: Perspectives on Media and Our Understanding of the Social World* (Lawrence Erlbaumb, 2003).

3   Cited in Philip Napoli, "Social Responsibility and Commercial Broadcast Television: An Assessment of Public Affairs Programming," *JMM: Journal of Multimedia*, vol. 3, no. 4 (2001), 227.

4   William A. Gamson, David Croteau, William Hoynes, and Theodore Sasson, "Media Images and the Social Construction of Reality," *American Review of Sociology*, vol. 18 (1992), 391.

5   In a 2005 survey by the Project for Excellence in Journalism, when Americans were asked to identify the two media sources they used most often for national and international news, 74 percent chose TV and 45 percent newspapers, compared to only 24 percent for the Internet, 22 percent for radio, and 5 percent for magazines. Project for Excellence in Journalism, *The State of the News Media, 2006*. Audience statistics: "Where People Go for National/International News, by Medium." Coverage issues: See Content Analysis sections under Newspapers, Online, Network TV, Cable TV, Local TV, Magazines, and Radio. All at www.journalism.org.

6   Randy Shilts, *And the Band Played On: People, Politics, and the AIDS Epidemic* (Penguin, 1987), 78, 91, 109, 110, 126, 136, 172-173, 191, 286, 301, 340, 385, 397, 536, 576, 600-601. For a comparative analysis of the coverage of AIDS and seven other diseases, 1980-1998, see Elizabeth M. Armstrong, Daniel P. Carpenter, and Marie Hojnacki, "Whose Deaths Matter? Mortality, Advocacy, and Attention to Disease in the Mass Media," *Journal of Health Politics, Policy and Law*, vol. 31, no. 4 (August 2006), 729-772.

7   Todd G. Shields, "Network News Construction of Homelessness: 1980–1993," *Communication Review*, vol. 4, no. 2 (2001), 193-218. For statistics on homelessness, see, for instance, U.S. Conference of Mayors and Sodexho, Inc., *Hunger and Homelessness Survey: A Status Report on Hunger and Homelessness in America's Cities: A 23-City Survey* (December 2006), 94.

8   On differential media attention to different social groups, see, for instance, Armstrong, Carpenter, and Hojnacki, "Whose Deaths Matter? Mortality, Advocacy, and Attention to Disease in the Mass Media," 759-760.

9   See, for instance, Herbert J. Gans, *Deciding What's News: A Study of CBS Evening News, NBC Nightly News, Newsweek, and Time* (Pantheon, 1979), 183-213; Michael Schudson, *Discovering the News: A Social History of American Newspapers* (Basic Books, 1978), 160-194; and Bill Kovach and Tom Rosenstiel, *The Elements of Journalism: What Newspeople Should Know and the Public Should Expect* (Three Rivers Press, 2001), 77.

10 Judy Peet, "Lead Poisoning: A Failed Response and Sick Children," *Nieman Reports* (Spring 2003), 20-23.

11 For other examples, see Brent Cunningham, "Across the Great Class Divide," *Columbia Journalism Review* (Issue 3, May/June 2004).

12 Gans, *Deciding What's News*.

13 James W. Tankard, Jr., Laura Handerson, Jackie Sillberman, Kriss Bliss, and Salma Ghanem, "Media Frames: Approaches to Conceptualization and Measurement," paper presented at the Association for Education in Journalism and Mass Communication, Boston (1991).

14 Angela Valdez, "Meth Madness," Willamette Week Online (April 27, 2006).

15 Kai Wright, "AIDS: Hiding in Plain Sight," *Columbia Journalism Review*, no. 2 (March/April 2004).

16 C.Z. Taylor and S.B. Sorenson, "The Nature of Newspaper Coverage of Homicide," *Injury Prevention*, vol. 8 (2002), 121-127. Crime statistics: Federal Bureau of Investigation, *Crime in the United States 2004*, at www.fbi.gov/ucr.

17 Institute for Innovation in Social Policy, unpublished data.

18 Ibid. Many of the stories in both *USA Today* and the *New York Times* dealt with the case in which entertainer Michael Jackson was accused of sexually abusing a minor. Frequency of child abuse, by type: U.S. Department of Health and Human Services, Administration for Children and Families, *Child Maltreatment 2004* (2006), 24.

19 Shanto Iyengar, *Is Anyone Responsible? How Television Frames Political Issues* (Univ. of Chicago Press, 1991).

20 John McManus, "Nutrition Report Card: Who Provides the Bay Area's Most Nutritious News?" (Grade the News, May 11, 2003) at www.gradethenews.org/dreamhost%20files.

21 John McManus and Lori Dorfman, "Youth and Violence in California Newspapers," *Issue 9* (April 2000), 7-8.

22 See, for instance, Kovach and Rosenstiel, *Elements of Journalism*, 55; and Thomas E. Patterson, *Out of Order* (Vintage, 1994), 53-93.

23 Trudy Lieberman, "Political Framing and Prescription Drugs," *Columbia Journalism Review*, no. 6 (November/December 2002).

24 Kathleen Hall Jamieson, "Newspaper and Television Coverage of the Health Care Reform Debate: January 16–July 25, 1994," report by the Annenberg Public Policy Center (August 12, 1994).

25 See, for instance, Taylor and Sorenson, "The Nature of Newspaper Coverage of Homicide," 121-127.

26 See, for instance, analysis of *New York Times* coverage in Sandra Opdycke, *Social Reporting in the United States: The Role of the Media and the Government: A Working Paper* (Institute for Innovation in Social Policy, 2001), 8-9.

27 See, for instance, *New York Times*, June 10, 2006, when the paper ran a special 10-page Health section, but covered the important story of nonprofit hospitals' failure to treat the uninsured under national news.

28 Katherine C. McAdams and Tamara M. Henry, "An Analysis of U.S. Newspaper Coverage of Early Childhood Education" (Philip Merrill College of Journalism, Fall 2004), 46.

29 For a summary of statistical activities by the federal government, see: U.S. Office of Management and Budget, *Statistical Programs of the United States Government, Fiscal Year 2005* (Washington, D.C., October 2005).

30 See, for instance, Opdycke, *Social Reporting in the United States*, 10-11.

31 U.S. Office of Management and Budget, "Schedule of Release Dates for Principal Federal Economic Indicators," at www.whitehouse.gov/omb/inforeg/statpolicy.hmtl.

32 The White House, Social Statistics Briefing Room and Economic Statistics Briefing Room, at www. whitehouse.gov/fsbr, accessed on June 15, 2006, and August 23, 2006. For greater comparability, international statistics were omitted from the analysis of economic indicators. Calculations by the Institute.

33 See, for instance, Mollyann Brodie, Elizabeth C. Hamel, Drew E. Altman, Robert J. Blendon, and John M. Benson, "Health News and the American Public, 1996-2002," *Journal of Health Politics, Policy and Law*, vol. 28, no. 5 (October 2003); Esther Thorson, "What 35 Years of Academic Research Tells Us," Poynteronline (April 9, 2003); Robert W. McChesney, *The Problem of the Media: U.S. Communication Politics in the 21st Century* (Monthly Review Press, 2004); Readership Institute, "The Power to Grow Readership: Research from the Impact Study of Newspaper Readership" (Newspaper Association of America and American Society of Newspaper Editors, April 2001).

34 Kovach and Rosenstiel, *Elements of Journalism*, 149.

35 See, for example, the curriculum for the Master's in Health Journalism offered by the University of Minnesota, at www.healthjournalism.umn.edu.

36 Larry Tye, "An Education in How to Cover the Issues," *Nieman Reports* (Spring 2003), 48-50. See also: Blue Cross/Blue Shield Foundation of Massachusetts, "The Health Coverage Fellowship," at www.bcbsmafoundation.org:80/foundationroot/index.jsp.

37 Model Social Health Page: *New York Times*, "Grades Rise, but Reading Skills Do Not" (February 23, 2007), A13; "Childhood Poverty Is Found to Portend High Adult Costs" (January 25, 2007), A19; "Violent Crime in Cities Shows Sharp Rise, Reversing Trend" (March 9, 2007), A14; "Demand for English Lessons Outstrips Supply" (February 27, 2007), 1; "To Buy or Not to Buy" (January 28, 2007), BU 2; "County Sued Over Lack of Affordable Homes" (February 4, 2007), WE 5; "Most Support U.S. Guarantee of Health Care" (March 2, 2007), "Rising Health Costs" (January 28, 2007), 20.
Social Health Digest summaries prepared by the Institute based on the following articles: "Regional Variation Seen in Heart Disease Rate" (February 16, 2007), A16; "Categorized, Compared and Displayed: Social Ills as Museum Specimens" (January 22, 2007), E3; "With Jails Full, California Eyes Other States" (February 4, 2007), 23; "To Save Later, Employers Offer Free Drugs Now" (February 21, 2007), C1; "Job Corps Plans Makeover for a Changed Economy" (February 20, 2007 (A12); Wealthy Nations Announce Plan to Develop and Pay for Vaccines" (February 10, 2007), A3; "Greater Scrutiny of Colleges and Ties to Student Lenders" (February 3, 2007), A10; "Duke Program Seeks to Expand Service Work" (February 13, 2007), A16. Photo by John Gruber.

38 See, for instance, *Columbia Journalism Review*, *Nieman Reports*, Grade the News, Poynteronline, and publications of Berkeley Media Studies.

39 This phrase appears in both the Radio Act of 1927 and the Communications Act of 1934. Cited in Advisory Committee on Public Interest Obligations of Digital Television Broadcasting, "The Public Interest Standard in Television Broadcasting" (December 18, 1998), 18.

40 Funding mechanism: Under the procedure established by the Public Broadcasting Act of 1967, Congress appropriates funds to the Corporation for Public Broadcasting (CPB), a federally chartered private entity, which in turn makes grants to public stations around the country, most of them affiliated with National Public Radio or the Public Broadcasting System. Conservative criticism: see, for instance, Laurence A. Jarvik, *PBS: Behind the Screen* (Forum/Prime Publishing, 1997). Progressive criticism: see, for instance, Steve Rendall and Peter Hart, "Time to Unplug the CPB," September/October 2005, Fairness & Accuracy in Reporting website, at www.fair.org; William Hoynes, *Public Television for Sale: Media, the Market and the Public Sphere* (Westview Press, 1994).

41 Project for Excellence in Journalism, *The State of the News Media, 2006*, "Radio: Content Analysis" "Network TV: Content Analysis," at www.journalism.org.

42 Citizens for Independent Public Broadcasting, "The CIPN Proposal for a Public Broadcasting Trust," at www.cipbonline.org.

Chapter 3
Social Reports: Institutionalizing the Reporting of Social Indicators

1 *Toward a Social Report*, U.S. Department of Health, Education, and Welfare (January 11, 1969), xii.

2 Ibid., ix.

3 Clifford W. Cobb and Craig Rixford, "Lessons Learned from the History of Social Indicators" (Redefining Progress, November, 1998), 11. See also, Denis F. Johnston, "The Federal Effort in Developing Social Indicators and Social Reporting in the United States During the 1970s," in *Social Science Research and Government: Comparative Essays on Britain and the United States*, ed. by Martin Bulmer (Cambridge University Press, 1987), 299; Marc Miringoff and Marque Miringoff, *The Social Health of the Nation: How Is America Really Doing?* (Oxford University Press, 1999), 23.

4   See, for example, Federal Bureau of Investigation, Uniform Crime Report, at www.fbi.gov/ucr/ucr. htm; Forum on Child and Family Statistics, *America's Children in Brief: Key Indicators of Well Being, 2006* (2006), at www.childstats.gov; Federal Interagency Forum on Aging-Related Statistics, *Older Americans—Update 2006: Key Indicators of Well-Being* (May 2006), at www.agingstats. gov/default.htm.

5   Children's Defense Fund, *The State of America's Children, 2005* at www.childrensdefense.org/ site/PageServer; Annie E. Casey Foundation, *Kids Count*, at http://www.aecf.org/MajorInitiatives/ KIDSCOUNT.aspx

6   *Vermont Well-Being 2006: A Social Indicators Sourcebook* (May 2006), at www.humanservices. vermont.gov.

7   Jacksonville Community Council, Inc., *Quality of Life Progress Report*, at www.jcci.org/default. aspx.

8   Gunnison County Community Indicators Project 2001, at www.hccaonline.org/page.cfm? pageid=2052.

9   Sandra Opdycke, *The Community Indicators Movement and Social Reporting: A Working Paper* (Institute for Innovation in Social Policy, 2001), 16-17.

10 Sustainable Seattle: Chantal Stevens, private communication (August 3, 2006), and Sustainable Seattle website at www.sustainableseattle.org. Communities Count Initiative Partners, *Communities Count: Social and Health Indicators Across King County*, at www.communitiescount.org.

11 New Jersey Department o Environmental Correction, Division of Science, Research, and Technology, *Living with the Future in Mind: Goals and Indicators for New Jersey's Quality of Life* (First annual update, 2000), at www.state.nj.us/dep/dsr/sustainable-state.

12 North Carolina Progress Board, *North Carolina 20/20 Update Report* (January 31, 2006), at www. ncprogress.org.

13 Minneapolis Sustainable Roundtable, *Fifty-Year Vision and Indicators for a Sustainable Minneapolis* (September 16, 2004), at www.crcworks.org/msi.html.

14 Adelphi University, *Vital Signs: Monitoring Long Island's Social Health* (2006), at www.adelphi. edu/vitalsigns.

15 Oregon Progress Board, *Achieving the Oregon Shines Vision: The 2005 Benchmark Performance Report: Is Oregon Making Progress?* Report to the Oregon Legislature and the People of Oregon (2nd Printing, April 2005), at www.oregon.gov/DAS/OPB.

16 Georgia Department of Community Affairs, Community Indicators website, at www.dca.state. ga.us/commind.

17 Atkinson Charitable Foundation, *Canadian Index of Wellbeing: Charting the Path to Progress*, at www.atkinsonfoundation.ca.

18 See, for instance, Franz Rothenbacher, "National and International Approaches in Social Reporting," *Social Indicators Research*, vol. 29 (1993), 2-3, 11-16.

19 Office of National Statistics, "National Statistics Online: Social Trends 36," at www.statistics.gov. uk/socialtrends.

20 Joachim Vogel, "Strategies and Traditions in Swedish Social Reporting: A 30-Year Experience," *Social Indicators Research*, vol. 58 (2002), 90.

21 Ibid., 102.

22 Statistics Sweden website, at www.scb.se. The principal sections of this website are available in English as well as Swedish.

23 Vogel, "Strategies and Traditions in Swedish Social Reporting," 97. See also Sten Johansson, "Conceptualizing and Measuring Quality of Life for National Policy," FIEF Working Paper Series 2001, presented at the III Conference of the International Society for Quality of Life Studies (July 2000), at swopec.hhs.se/fiefwp/papers/WP171.pdf.

24 Joachim Vogel, "The Swedish System of Official Social Surveys," EuReporting Working Paper No. 27, in *Official Social Surveys in Europe*, ed. F. Kraus and G. Schmaus (2001), 2-4, 7, at www.mzes. uni-mannheim.de/projekte/mikrodaten/wp_pf/wp_27_sweden.pdf.

25 Mahar Mangahas and Linda Luz Guerrero, "Self-Sustained Quality of Life Monitoring: The Philippine Social Weather Reports," *Social Indicators Research*, vol. 60 (2002), 123.

26 Ibid., 124.

27 Ibid.

28 Social Weather Stations website, "Mission of SWS: Objectives of the SWS Strategy," at www.sws. org.ph.

29 Ibid., "Social Weather Survey" and "Mission of SWS: SWS's Basic Functions."

30 United Nations, Department of Economic and Social Affairs, *Toward a System of Social and Demographic Statistics*, Series F, no. 19 (1975), 4.

31 See, for instance, Franz Rothenbacher, "National and International Approaches in Social Reporting," *Social Indicators Research*, vol. 29 (1993), 2-11, and Dharam Ghai, Michael Hopkins, and Donald McGranahan, "Some Reflections on Human and Social Indicators for Development," Discussion Paper No. 6 (United Nations Research Institute for Social Development, October 1988), 4-10.

32 UNICEF, *State of the World's Children 1980-81* (1980), 3, at www.unicef.org.

33 Ibid.

34 UNICEF, *State of the World's Children 2007* (2006), 137, at www.unicef.org.

35 *El Correo Catalan*, cited in *State of the World's Children 1982-83* (1982), back cover, at www.unicef. org.

36 Millennium Project, at www.unmillenniumproject.org/goals/index.htm.

37 Millennium Project, "Overview," *Investing in Development: A Practical Plan to Achieve the Millennium Development Goals* (2005), 1, at www.unmillenniumproject.org/reports/index.htm.

38 OECD, *Measuring Social Well-Being: A Progress Report on the Development of Social Indicators* (1976), at www.oecd.org; and European Commission, Statistical Office of the European Communities, "Working Group: Harmonisation of Social Statistics" (May 2, 2000).

39 *OECD Factbook 2006 — Economic, Social, and Environmental Statistics* (2006), at www.oecd.org.

40 OECD, *Society at a Glance 2005* (2005); and Andrew Sharpe and Jeremy Smith, "Measuring the Impact of Research on Well-Being: A Survey of Indicators of Well-Being," CSLS Research Report (Centre for the Study of Living Standards, February 2005), 58-60, at www.csls.ca.

41 Note, for comparison, "Convention on the Organization for Economic Cooperation and Development" (December 14, 1960); and OECD website, "The OECD: What Is It?", both at www.oecd.org.

42 U.S. version of Human Development Report: private communication from Sarah Burd-Sharps, March 26, 2007.

43 The State of the USA: The Key National Indicators Initiative, at www.keyindicators.org.

Chapter 4
Measuring Social Health:
The Index of Social Health and the National Survey of Social Health

1   The percentage decline based on rounded numbers is 19.7 percent. Carrying the Index scores to one decimal place, as is done in Appendix B, shows a decline of 19.0 percent.

2   Note: The following indicators include data projections: alcohol-related traffic fatalities; child abuse; food stamp coverage; health insurance coverage; infant mortality; out-of-pocket health costs, ages 65 and over; teenage drug abuse; teenage suicide.

3   The percentage decline based on rounded numbers is 19.7 percent. Carrying the Index scores to one decimal place, as is done in Appendix B, shows a decline of 19.0 percent.

4   U.S. Department of Labor, Bureau of Labor Statistics, "Comparative Real Gross Domestic Product Per Capita and Per Employed Person, Fifteen Countries, 1960–2005," Table 1, June 16, 2006, at www. bls.gov/fls.

5   Background of HDI: Mozaffar Quizilbash, "On the Measurement of Human Development," prepared for the UNDP Training Center, September 2002, p. 1, at hdr.undp.org.

6   United Nations Development Program, *Human Development Report 2006* (2006), 283-286, at hdr. undp.org/reports. The HDI builds on the earlier Physical Quality of Life Index, developed in the 1970s; see Morris Richard Morris, *Condition of the World's Poor: The Physical Quality of Life Index* (Pergamon Press, 1979).

7   Human Development Reports hdr.undp.org/aboutus.

8   National versions: Calvert-Henderson Quality of Life Indicators, "Overview," at www.calvert-henderson.ccom. Basic Capabilities Index: Social Watch, *Social Watch Report 2005: Roars and Whispers* (2005), 69-71, 142-143, at www.socialwatch.org.

9   Background for Genuine Progress Indicator: See, for instance, Herman E. Daly and John B. Cobb, Jr., with contributions by Clifford W. Cobb, *For the Common Good: Redirecting the Economy Toward Community, the Environment, and a Sustainable Future* (Beacon Press, 1989); Clifford W. Cobb, Ted Halstead, and Jonathan Rowe, "If the Economy Is Up, Why Is America Down?" *Atlantic Monthly* (October 1995). Latest update: Jason Venetoulis and Cliff Cobb, *The Genuine Progress Indicator, 1950-2002 (2004 Update)*, Redefining Progress (2004) at www.redefiningprogress.org.

10   United Way of America, *State of Caring Index* (2004), at national.unitedway.org/stateofcaring.

11   U.S. Department of Commerce, Bureau of the Census, Current Population Survey (CPS), a joint effort between the Bureau of Labor Statistics and the Bureau of the Census, at www.census.gov/cps.

12   U.S. Department of Commerce, Bureau of the Census, American Community Survey, at www. census.gov/acs/www. See also Bureau of the Census, News Conference on 2003 Income and Poverty Estimates from the American Community Survey (August 26, 2004); Bureau of the Census, "Fact Sheet: Differences Between the School Enrollment Estimates from the American Survey and the Annual Social and Economic Supplement to the Current Population Survey" (August 24, 2004); Bureau of the Census, "Guidance on Differences in Employment and Unemployment Estimates from Different Sources" (August 23, 2004).

13   Youth Risk Behavior Surveillance System, Data and Statistics, at www.cdc.gov/healthyyouth/yrbs.

14   U.S. Conference of Mayors–Sodexho, Inc., *Hunger and Homelessness Survey: A Status Report on Hunger and Homelessness in America's Cities, A 23-City Survey* (December 2006), at www.usmayors.org.

15   Business Cycle Dating Committee, National Bureau of Economic Research, "The NBER's Recession Dating Procedure" (October 21, 2003), at www.nber.org/cycles/recessions.html.

16 National Bureau of Economic Research, "US Business Cycle Expansions and Contractions," at www. nber.org/cycles.html.

17 Note: Child abuse, food stamp coverage, infant mortality, and teenage suicide projected for 2005 from 2004 data.

18 Kenneth C. Land, *2006 Report: The Foundation for Child Development Child and Youth Well-Being Index (CWI), 1975–2004, with Projections for 2005* (Foundation for Child Development, 2006). See also: Brookings Institution, "Event Summary: Measuring Child Well-Being: A New Index" (March 24, 2004) at www.brook.edu.

19 Linda Hoke and Sandra Johnson, *The Southern Community Index* (Southern Growth Policies Board, 2005), at www.southern.org.

20 Kentucky Long-Term Policy Research Center, "The State of the Commonwealth Index: Kentucky Makes Steady Quality-of-Life Progress," *Foresight*, no. 45 (2006) at www.kltprc.net/pubs/doctitle. htm.

21 Peace Studies Institute, *National Index of Violence and Harm* (Manchester College, December 2006) at www.manchester.edu/links/violenceindex.

22 National Conference of Citizenship, *America's Civic Health Index: Broken Engagement* (September 18, 2006), at www.civicenterprises.net.

23 U.S. Department of Health and Human Services, Centers for Disease Control and Prevention, "NHIS Survey Description" (June 2006), 6, 16, at www.cdc.gov/nchs.

24 U.S. Department of Justice, Bureau of Justice Statistics, "The Nation's Two Crime Measures" and "Violent Crimes and Property Crimes Remained at 30-Year Lows in 2004" (September 25, 2005). Both at www.ojp.usdog.gov/bjs.

25 U.S. Department of Health and Human Services, Centers for Disease Control and Prevention, National Center for Chronic Disease Prevention and Health Promotion, "Behavioral Risk Factor Surveillance System: About the BRFSS" and "Behavioral Risk Factor Surveillance System: Technical Information and Data—Survey Data Information, 2005 BRFSS Overview." Both at www.cdc.gov/nccdphp.

26 U.S. Department of Health and Human Services, Substance Abuse & Mental Health Services Administration, Office of Applied Statistics, *Results from the 2005 National Survey on Drug Use and Health: National Findings* (Sept. 2006), 10, at www.drugabusestatistics.samhsa.gov. Monitoring the Future, "Purpose and Design" and "Teen Drug Use Down But Progress Halts Among Youngest Teens" (December 19, 2005). Both at www.monitoringthefuture.org.

27 National Endowment for the Arts, "2002 Survey of Public Participation in the Arts: Research Division Report #45" (2004), 1-6, at www.arts.gov.

28 National Opinion Research Center, "General Social Survey (GSS)" at www.norc.uchicago.edu/projects, and "GSS About: Introduction to the GSS" at wwwapp.icpsr.umich.eduGSS/about/gss/about.htm.

29 Federal Reserve Board, "About the Survey of Consumer Finances" and Brian K. Bucks et al., "Recent Changes in U.S. Family Finances: Evidence from the 2001 and 2004 Survey of Consumer Finances," *Federal Reserve Bulletin*, vol. 91 (February 2006), A1-A38. Both at www.federalreserve.gov.

30 U.S. Department of Commerce, Bureau of the Census, Survey of Income and Program Participation, at www.sipp.census.gov/sipp/intro.html.

Part II

A Closer Look:
Key Indicators of Social Health

Chapter 5
Social Indicators for Children

Infant Mortality

[1] **Progress—But Slowing.** U.S. Department of Health and Human Services, Centers for Disease Control and Prevention, "Ten Great Public Health Achievements in the 20th Century." Healthier Mothers and Babies, *Morbidity and Mortality Weekly Report*, Vol. 48, no. 38 (October 1, 1999), 549, and at www.cdc.gov/od/oc/media/tengpha.htm.

[2] Infant mortality over time (deaths in first year of life, per 1,000 live births): 1970, 1975–2002—U.S. Department of Health and Human Services, Centers for Disease Control and Prevention, National Center for Health Statistics, Kenneth D. Kochanek and Joyce A. Martin, *Supplemental Analyses of Recent Trends in Infant Mortality* (2004), Table 1; 1971–1974—U.S. Department of Health and Human Services, *Vital Statistics of the United States 1992*, vol. 2, Mortality, Part A (Washington, D.C., 1994), Table 2-2; 2003–2004—U.S. Department of Health and Human Services, Centers for Disease Control and Prevention, National Center for Health Statistics, National Vital Statistics System, *E-Stats—Deaths: Final Data for 2004*, Table 1, at www.cdc.gov/nchs.

[3] **Disparities by Race Continue.** Infant mortality by race: 1970, 1975–1996—U.S. Department of Health and Human Services, Centers for Disease Control and Prevention, National Center for Health Statistics, *Deaths: Final Data for 1996*, National Vital Statistics Reports, vol. 47, no. 9 (1998), Table 25, at www.cdc.gov/nchs; 1971–1974—U.S. Department of Health and Human Services, *Vital Statistics of the United States 1992*, vol. 2, Mortality, Part A (Washington, D.C., 1994), Table 2-2; 1997–2002—U.S. Department of Commerce, Bureau of the Census, *Statistical Abstract of the United States: 2006* (2006), Table 104, at www.census.gov/compendia/statab; 2003–2004—U.S. Department of Health and Human Services, Centers for Disease Control and Prevention, National Center for Health Statistics, National Vital Statistics System, *E-Stats – Deaths: Final Data for 2004*, Table 1, at www.cdc.gov/nchs. Note 1970–1979 by race of child, 1980–2004 by race of mother.

[4] Healthy People Goals: Goal for 2000—U.S. Department of Health and Human Services, Centers for Disease Control and Prevention, National Center for Health Statistics, Maternal and Infant Health objective 14.1, "Healthy People 2000 Final Review" (Oct. 2001), Table 14, at www.cdc.gov/nchs; Goal for 2010—U.S. Department of Health and Human Services, Centers for Disease Control and Prevention, National Center for Health Statistics, Maternal and Infant Heath, Objective 16-1c, "Healthy People 2010: Midcourse Review" (2005), at www.healthypeople.gov/data.

[5] **Worsening Problems with Low Birthweight.** Low birthweight, definition: U.S. Department of Health and Human Services, Office of the Assistant Secretary for Planning and Evaluation, "Glossary of Technical Terms." *Trends in the Well-Being of America's Children & Youth 2002* (2002). Effects of low birthweight: See, for instance, U.S. Department of Health and Human Services, Centers for Disease Control and Prevention, National Center for Health Statistics, *Health, United States, 2005* (2005), Table 21, at www.cdc.gov/nchs. See also March of Dimes website, "Professionals and Researchers: Low Birthweight" at www.marchofdimes.com.

[6] Low birthweight: 1970–1980—U.S. Department of Health and Human Services, Centers for Disease Control and Prevention, National Center for Health Statistics, unpublished data; 1981–2004—U.S. Department of Health and Human Services, Centers for Disease Control and Prevention, National Center for Health Statistics, *Births: Final Data for 2004*, National Vital Statistics Reports, vol. 55, no. 1 (Sept. 29, 2006), Table 32; 2005—U.S. Department of Health and Human Services, Centers

for Disease Control and Prevention, National Center for Health Statistics, National Vital Statistics System, *Births: Preliminary Data for 2005*. All at www.cdc.gov/nchs. Disparities in low birthweight: S. Iyasu, K. Tomashek, and W. Barfield, "Infant Mortality and Low Birth Weight Among Black and White Infants—United States, 1980–2000" and "Editorial Note," *MMWR Weekly*, vol. 51, no. 27 (July 12, 2002), 589-592, at www.cdc.gov/nchs.

7 **Prenatal Care Improving.** Importance of prenatal care: see, for instance, U.S. Department of Health and Human Services, Health Resources and Services Administration, Maternal and Child Health Bureau, "A Healthy Start: Begin Before Baby's Born," at mchb.hrsa.gov/programs/womeninfants/prenatal. htm; and Greg R. Alexander and Carol C. Korenbrot, "The Role of Prenatal Care in Preventing Low Birth Weight," *Low Birth Weight*, vol. 5, no. 1 (Spring 1995).

8 Access to prenatal care: 1970–1994—U.S. Department of Health and Human Services, Centers for Disease Control and Prevention, National Center for Health Statistics, unpublished data; 1995-2003—U.S. Department of Health and Human Services, Centers for Disease Control and Prevention, National Center for Health Statistics, *Health, United States, 2005* (2005), Table 7. 2004—U.S. Department of Health and Human Services, Centers for Disease Control and Prevention, *Births: Final Data for 2004*, National Vital Statistics Reports, vol. 55, no. 1 (Sept. 29, 2006), Table 26b, both at www.cdc.gov/nchs.

9 Ibid.

10 **World Standing—Losing Ground.** International rankings: U.S. Central Intelligence Agency, *World Factbook, 2006* (2006), "Rank Order – Infant Mortality," at www.cia.gov.

11 United Nations Children's Fund (UNICEF), *The State of the World's Children 2006* (2006), Table 1, 58, and "Under-five mortality rankings," 97, at www.unicef.org.

Child Poverty

12 **No Progress.** Child poverty over time (percentage of related children under age eighteen in families with incomes below the poverty line): 1970–2005—U.S. Department of Commerce, Bureau of the Census, Current Population Survey, Historical Poverty Tables, Table 3, at www.census.gov.

13 Ibid.

14 **A Key Comparison.** Percentage of related children under age six in families with incomes below the poverty line: 1970–2005—U.S. Department of Commerce, Bureau of the Census, Current Population Survey, Historical Poverty Tables, Table 20, at www.census.gov. Percentage of persons 65 and older with incomes below the poverty line: 1970–2005—U.S. Department of Commerce, Bureau of the Census, Current Population Survey, Historical Poverty Tables, Table 3, at www.census.gov.

15 **Who Are the Poor?** U.S. Department of Commerce, Bureau of the Census, Current Population Survey, Detailed Poverty Tables, Table POV 01, at www.census.gov.

16 **Extreme Poverty.** Poverty threshold, family of three: U.S. Department of Commerce, Bureau of the Census, "Poverty Thresholds for 2005 by Size of Family and Number of Related Children Under 18 Years," at www.census.gov.

17 Children in extreme poverty (family income below 50 percent of poverty line): 1980—U.S. Department of Health and Human Services, Office of the Assistant Secretary for Planning and Evaluation, *Trends in the Well-Being of America's Children and Youth, 1996* (1996), Section ES 1.3; 2005—U.S. Department of Commerce, Bureau of the Census, Current Population Survey, Detailed Poverty Tables, Table POV 03, at www.census.gov. Extreme child poverty by race/ethnicity: 2000—U.S. Department of Commerce, Bureau of the Census, Current Population Survey, Detailed Poverty Tables, Table 2; 2005—U.S. Department of Commerce, Bureau of the Census, Current Population Survey, Detailed Poverty Tables, Table POV 03; both at www.census.gov.

[18] **The Impact of Welfare Reform.** Decline in welfare rolls: Congressional Research Service, "Welfare Reauthorization: An Overview of the Issues," CRS Issue Brief for Congress (Dec. 21, 2005), Table 1, at www.opencrs.com/rpts/IB10140_20050701.pdf. Poverty among female-headed households with children, 1996–2005: U.S. Department of Commerce, Bureau of the Census, Current Population Survey, Historical Poverty Tables, Table 4, at www.census.gov. Outcomes of welfare reform: see, for instance, Sharon Parrott and Arloc Sherman, "TANF at 10: Program Results Are More Mixed Than Often Understood" (Center on Budget and Policy Priorities, Aug. 17, 2006), at www.cbpp.org.

[19] **Child Poverty and Illness.** Lead-poisoning—effects, and current numbers affected: U.S. Department of Health and Human Services, Centers for Disease Control and Prevention, National Center for Environmental Health, Division of Emergency and Environmental Health Services, "Fact Sheet: Childhood Lead Poisoning," at www.cdc.gov. Prevalence over time and by poverty-level: Federal Interagency Forum on Child and Family Statistics, *America's Children: Key National Indicators of Well-Being 2005* (July 2005), Special Feature: Lead in the Blood of Children, and Appendix A, Table Special 2.A, at www.childstats.gov.

[20] Asthma—Prevalence over time: Federal Interagency Forum on Child and Family Statistics, *America's Children: Key National Indicators of Well-Being 2005* (July 2005), Special Feature: Asthma, and Appendix A, Table Special 1.A, at www.childstats.gov. Prevalence by poverty-level: U.S. Department of Health and Human Services, Centers for Disease Control and Prevention, Environmental Hazards and Health Effects Program, 2004 Asthma Data, Table 4-1, at www.cdc.gov. Hospitalization rates: W. Carr, L. Zeitel, and K. Weiss, "Variations in Asthma Hospitalizations and Deaths," *American Journal of Public Health*, vol. 82, no. 1 (Jan. 1992), 59-65.

[21] **U.S. Standing in the World.** U.S. international ranking: UNICEF, Innocenti Research Centre, *Child Poverty in Rich Countries 2005* (2005), Figure 1, at www.unicef-icdc.org.

Child Abuse

[22] **Rising Awareness, Rising Reports.** Effects of child abuse: see, for instance, U.S. Department of Health and Human Services, Children's Bureau, "Long Term Consequences of Child Abuse and Neglect" (2006) at www.childwelfare.gov. Child Abuse Prevention and Treatment Act of 1974 (CAPTA): U.S. Department of Health and Human Services, Administration for Children and Families, Children's Bureau, "Major Federal Legislation Concerned with Child Protection, Child Welfare, and Adoption" (2003), at www.childwelfare.gov.

[23] Child abuse over time (number of children involved in abuse/neglect reports per 1,000 population ages 0-18): 1976–1986—American Association for Protecting Children, American Humane Association, *Highlights of Official Aggregate Child Neglect and Abuse Reporting, 1987* (1989), 6; 1987–1994—National Center on Child Abuse Prevention Research, National Committee to Prevent Child Abuse, *Current Trends in Child Abuse Reporting and Fatalities: The Results of the 1996 Annual Fifty State Survey* (1997), 5; 1995–2004—U.S. Department of Health and Human Services, Administration for Children and Families, Children's Bureau, *Child Maltreatment* (annual since 1995), at www.childwelfare.gov. Note that child protective service agencies use the term "report" to designate a referral that is judged credible enough to merit further investigation. See: U.S. Department of Health and Human Services, Administration for Children and Families, Children's Bureau, *Child Maltreatment 2004* (2006), 7, at www.childwelfare.gov.

[24] Interpreting the numbers: The rate of substantiated victims per 1,000 population declined from 15.0 in 1995 to 11.9 in 2004; as percentage of total children referred, the substantiation rate declined from 35 percent to 25 percent. U.S. Department of Health and Human Services, Administration for Children and Families, Children's Bureau, *Child Maltreatment* (annual since 1995) at www.childwelfare.gov. Substantiation rates for 1995–2001 appear in "Highlights of Findings"; 2002–2004, in "Summary." Problems in confirming child abuse: See, for example, V. L. Gunn, G. B. Hickson, and W. O. Cooper, "Factors Affecting Pediatricians' Reporting of Suspected Child Maltreatment," *Ambulatory Pediatrics*,

vol. 5, no. 2 (Mar-Apr. 2005), 96-101. State procedures: U.S. Department of Health and Human Services, Administration for Children and Families, Children's Bureau, *Child Maltreatment* (2004), Appendix D, 133-162, at www.childwelfare.gov. Under-reporting of child abuse: Tessa L. Crume, Carolyn DiGuiseppi, Tim Byers, Andrew P. Sirotnak, and Carol J. Garrett, "Underascertainment of Child Maltreatment Fatalities by Death Certificates, 1990–1998," *Pediatrics*, vol. 110, no. 2 (Aug. 2002), 395-396; see also, for instance, Shelia Savell, "Child Sexual Abuse: Are Health Care Providers Looking the Other Way?" *Journal of Forensic Nursing*, vol. 1, no. 2 (Summer 2005), 78-82.

25 **Types of Maltreatment.** Definition of abuse/neglect: Cornell Law School, Legal Information Institute, U.S. Code Collection, Title 42, Chapter 65, Subchapter I, § 5106g (2), at www4.law.cornell/edu/uscode. Types of maltreatment: U.S. Department of Health and Human Services, Administration for Children and Families, Children's Bureau, "Definitions of Child Abuse and Neglect" (Jan. 2005).

26 Maltreatment, by type: U.S. Department of Health and Human Services, Administration for Children and Families, Children's Bureau, *Child Maltreatment* (2004), 24. Maltreatment type by age: U.S. Department of Health and Human Services, Administration for Children and Families, Children's Bureau, *Child Maltreatment* (2004), Table 3-11. Both at www.childwelfare.gov.

27 Ibid.

28 **Deaths from Abuse.** 2000–2003—U.S. Department of Health and Human Services, Administration for Children and Families, Children's Bureau, *Child Abuse and Neglect Fatalities: Statistics and Interventions* (2004); 2004—U.S. Department of Health and Human Services, Administration for Children and Families, Children's Bureau, *Child Maltreatment* (2004), vii. Both at www.childwelfare.gov.

29 **Who Are the Victims of Child Abuse?** Demography: U.S. Department of Health and Human Services, Administration for Children and Families, Children's Bureau, *Child Maltreatment* (2004), Tables 3-8, 3-9, 3-12, at www.childwelfare.gov. Population distribution: U.S. Department of Commerce, Bureau of the Census, *Statistical Abstract 2007*, Table 11, at www.census.gov/compendia/statab.

30 **Who Commits Child Abuse?** Gender: U.S. Department of Health and Human Services, Administration for Children and Families, Children's Bureau, *Child Maltreatment* (2004), Table 5-1. Perpetrator's relationship to child: U.S. Department of Health and Human Services, Administration for Children and Families, Children's Bureau, *Child Maltreatment* (2004), Table 5-2. Both at www.childwelfare.gov.

31 Parental relationship: U.S. Department of Health and Human Services, Administration for Children and Families, Children's Bureau, *Child Maltreatment* (2004), Table 5-1. Patterns of parental abuse: U.S. Department of Health and Human Services, Administration for Children and Families, Children's Bureau, *Child Maltreatment* (2004), Table 3-20. Both at www.childwelfare.gov.

32 **Who Reports Child Abuse?** Reporting laws: U.S. Department of Health and Human Services, Administration for Children and Families, Children's Bureau, Child Welfare Information, "Mandatory Reporters of Child Abuse and Neglect" (Mar. 2005), 1-2. Report sources: U.S. Department of Health and Human Services, Administration for Children and Families, Children's Bureau, *Child Maltreatment* (2004), Table 2-2. Both at www.childwelfare.gov.

Chapter 6
Social Indicators for Youth

Teenage Suicide

1 **A Terrible Loss.** Suicide as cause of death: U.S. Department of Health and Human Services, Centers for Disease Control and Prevention, National Center for Injury Prevention and Control, WISQARS

Leading Causes of Death Reports, at webappa.cdc.gov/sasweb/ncipc. Impact of teen suicide: see, for instance, Margarete Parrish and Judy Tunkle, "Clinical Challenges Following an Adolescent's Death by Suicide: Bereavement Issues Faced by Family, Friends, Schools, and Clinicians," *Clinical Social Work Journal*, vol. 35, no. 1 (Spring 2005), 81-102.

2   Teenage suicide over time (suicides per 100,000 population, ages 15–19): 1970–1978—U.S. Department of Health and Human Services, Centers for Disease Control and Prevention, National Center for Health Statistics, National Vital Statistics System, *Vital Statistics of the United States: Mortality* (annual); 1979–2003—U.S. Department of Health and Human Services, Centers for Disease Control and Prevention, National Center for Health Statistics, National Vital Statistics System, Mortality Tables GMWK292A and GMWKH210R at www.cdc.nchs; 2004—U.S. Department of Health and Human Services, Centers for Disease Control and Prevention, National Center for Health Statistics, National Vital Statistics System, Final Mortality Data 2004 (by email); calculations by the Institute.

3   **At Risk.** U.S. Department of Health and Human Services, Centers for Disease Control and Prevention, National Center for Health Statistics, National Vital Statistics System, Final Mortality Data 2004 (by email). Rates for Native American and Asian females should be interpreted with caution, because of the small sample size.

4   Ibid.

5   **Gender and Race Over Time.** Suicides per 100,000 population ages 15–24, by gender and race: 1970–2003—U.S. Department of Health and Human Services, Centers for Disease Control and Prevention, National Center for Health Statistics, National Vital Statistics System, Mortality Tables HIST290_6878, HIST290_7998, and GMWK12, at www.cdc.nchs; 2004—U.S. Department of Health and Human Services, Centers for Disease Control and Prevention, National Center for Health Statistics, National Vital Statistics System, Final Mortality Data 2004 (by email); calculations by the Institute.

6   Ibid.

7   **Youth Suicide Worldwide.** Global trends: American Foundation for Suicide Prevention, "International Statistics: Facts and Figures," at www.afsp.org. Data variation: Ellenor Mittendorfer-Ruiz, "Trends of Youth Suicide in Europe during the 1980s and 1990s—Gender Differences and Implications for Prevention," *Journal of Men's Health and Gender*, vol. 3, no. 3 (Sept. 2006), 251.

8   Selected industrial countries: World Health Organization Mortality Database, Table 1, at www.who.int/healthiinfo/morttables.

9   Ibid.

10 **Attempting Suicide.** Suicide attempts, and suicidal ideas and behavior: "Youth Risk Behavior Surveillance—United States," *Morbidity and Mortality Weekly Report: Surveillance Summaries*, vol. 55, no. SS-5 (June 9, 2006), Tables 16 and 18, at www.cdc.gov/HealthyYouth/yrbs. See also Danice K. Eaton, Laura Kann, Steve Kinchen, James Ross, Joseph Hawkins, William A. Harris, Richard Lowry, Tim McManus, David Chyen, Shari Shanklin, Lim Shari, Jo Anne Grunbaum, and Howell Wechsler, "Youth Risk Behavior Surveillance—United States, 2005," *Journal of School Health*, vol. 76, no. 7 (Sept. 2006), 353-359. Hispanic teenage girls: "Risk of Suicide Among Hispanic Females Aged 12 to 17," *The NHSDA Report* (Apr. 25, 2003), at www.oas.samhsa.gov. Suicidal ideas by gender, race/ethnicity, and grade-level: "Youth Risk Behavior Surveillance—United States," *Morbidity and Mortality Weekly Report: Surveillance Summaries*, vol. 55, no. SS-5 (June 9, 2006), Table 18, at www.cdc.gov/HealthyYouth/yrbs.

11 Ibid.

12 Healthy People goal: U.S. Department of Health and Human Services, Centers for Disease Control and Prevention, CDC Wonder, Data 2010: The Healthy People 2010 Database, at wonder.cdc.gov/data2010.

13 **A Continuing Problem.** Educational effects of drug abuse: see, for instance, M. Lynskey and W. Hall, "The Effects of Adolescent Cannabis Use on Educational Attainment: A Review," *Addiction*, vol. 95, no. 11 (2000), 1621-1630; D.B. Kandel and M. Davies, "High School Students Who Use Crack and Other Drugs," *Archives of General Psychiatry*, vol. 53, no. 1 (1996), 71-80. Health effects: U.S. National Institute on Drug Abuse, "Commonly Abused Drugs: Potential Health Consequences," at www.drugabuse.gov.

14 Teenage drug use over time (percentage of twelfth graders using any illicit drug in past year): L.D. Johnston, P.M. O'Malley, J.G. Bachman, and J. Schulenberg, Monitoring the Future, *National Survey Results on Drug Use, 1975–2005*, vol. 1: Secondary School Students (NIH Publication No. 06-5883, National Institute on Drug Abuse, 2006), Table 5.2, at monitoringthefuture.org. The National Survey on Drug Use and Health, administered by the federal Substance Abuse & Mental Health Services Administration, has been surveying Americans age twelve and older since 1971, but because of changes in methodology in 2002, SAMHSA advises that "2002 and later data should not be compared with 2001 and earlier data from the series to assess changes over time." U.S. Department of Health and Human Services, Substance Abuse & Mental Health Services Administration, Office of Applied Statistics, *Results from the 2005 National Survey on Drug Use and Health: National Findings* (Sept. 2006), 10, at www.drugabusestatistics.samhsa.gov.

15 Ibid.

16 **Among the Youngest.** Eighth and tenth graders: L. D. Johnston, P. M. O'Malley, J. G. Bachman, and J. Schulenberg, Monitoring the Future, *National Survey Results on Drug Use, 1975–2005*, vol. 1: Secondary School Students (NIH Publication No. 06-5883, National Institute on Drug Abuse, 2006), Table 2.2, at monitoringthefuture.org.

17 Drugs before age 13: U.S. Department of Health and Human Services, Centers for Disease Control and Prevention, National Center for Chronic Disease Prevention and Health Promotion, Youth Risk Behavior Surveillance System, Youth Online: Comprehensive Results, "Percentage of Students Who Tried Marijuana for the First time Before Age 13 Years," at www.cdc.gov/HealthyYouth/yrbs/index. htm.

18 **Who Uses Drugs?** L. D. Johnston, P. M. O'Malley, J. G. Bachman, and J. Schulenberg, *Demographic Subgroup Trends for Various Licit and Illicit Drugs, 1975–2005,* Monitoring the Future Occasional Paper No. 63 (Institute for Social Research, 2006) at monitoringthefuture.org.

19 **Which Drugs?** L. D. Johnston, P. M. O'Malley, J. G. Bachman, and J. Schulenberg, Monitoring the Future, *National Survey Results on Drug Use, 1975–2005*, vol. 1: Secondary School Students (NIH Publication No. 06-5883, National Institute on Drug Abuse, 2006), Table 5.2, at monitoringthefuture. org.

20 Ibid.

21 **Access to Drugs.** L. D. Johnston, P. M. O'Malley, J. G. Bachman, and J. Schulenberg, Monitoring the Future, *National Survey Results on Drug Use, 1975–2005*, vol. 1: Secondary School Students (NIH Publication No. 06-5883, National Institute on Drug Abuse, 2006), Tables 9.6 and 9.8, at monitoringthefuture.org. For confirmation of these findings, see U.S. Department of Health and Human Services, Substance Abuse & Mental Health Services Administration, Office of Applied Statistics, *Results from the 2005 National Survey on Drug Use and Health: National Findings* (Sept. 2006), Figure 6.7, at www.drugabusestatistics.samhsa.gov.

22 Drugs on school property: U.S. Department of Health and Human Services, Centers for Disease Control and Prevention, National Center for Chronic Disease Prevention and Health Promotion, Youth Risk Behavior Surveillance System, Youth Online: Comprehensive Results, "Percentage of Students Who Were Offered, Sold, or Given an Illegal Drug on School Property by Someone During the Past 12 Months," at www.cdc.gov/HealthyYouth/yrbs/index.htm.

23 **Perceived Risk.** Drug-use levels: L. D. Johnston, P. M. O'Malley, J. G. Bachman, and J. Schulenberg, Monitoring the Future, *National Survey Results on Drug Use, 1975–2005*, vol. 1: Secondary School Students (NIH Publication No. 06-5883, National Institute on Drug Abuse, 2006), 331-344. Perception of risk: L. D. Johnston, P. M. O'Malley, J. G. Bachman, and J. Schulenberg, Monitoring the Future, *National Results on Adolescent Drug Use, Overview of Key Findings 2005*, (NIH Publication No. 06-5882, National Institute on Drug Abuse, 2006) Table 7. Both at: monitoringthefuture.org. Other influences: U.S. Department of Health and Human Services, Substance Abuse & Mental Health Services Administration, Office of Applied Statistics, *Results from the 2005 National Survey on Drug Use and Health: National Findings* (Sept. 2006), 62-66, at www.drugabusestatistics.samhsa.gov.

High School Dropouts

24 **Dropout Rates Improving.** High school dropouts over time (status dropouts: percentage of 18- to 24-year-olds who are not enrolled in school and are not high school graduates by diploma or GED): 1970–2005—U.S. Department of Commerce, Bureau of the Census, Current Population Survey Reports, School Enrollment, Historical Tables, Table A-5a, at www.census.gov/population/www/socdemo/school.html. For a different compilation of Current Population Survey data on status dropouts, see: U.S. Department of Education, National Center for Education Statistics, "Student Effort and Educational Progress, Elementary/Secondary Persistence and Progress," Table 26-1, at nces.gov/programs/coe/2006/section3. Annual high school dropout rate (event dropouts): 1970–2005—U.S. Department of Commerce, Bureau of the Census, Current Population Survey Reports, School Enrollment, Historical Tables, Table A-4, at www.census/gov/population/www/socdemo/school.html. Graduation rates based on CPS data (percentage of persons ages 25-29 who have completed high school by diploma or GED): U.S. Department of Commerce, Bureau of the Census, Current Population Survey Reports, School Enrollment, Historical Tables, Table A-5a, at www.census/gov/population/www/socdemo/school.html. Graduation rates based on school data (percentage of ninth graders who earn a high school diploma in four years) are discussed in, for instance: Jay P. Greene, *High School Graduation Rates in the United States* (Manhattan Institute and Black Alliance for Educational Options, 2002); Christopher Swanson, *Keeping Count and Losing Count: Calculating Graduation Rates for All Students Under NCLB Accountability* (The Urban Institute, 2003). For commentary, see, for instance: Lawrence Mishel and Joydeep Roy, *Rethinking High School Graduation Rates and Trends* (Economic Policy Institute, 2006), at www.epi.org and Lyndsay Pinkus, *Who's Counted? Who's Counting? Understanding High School Graduation Rates* (Alliance for Excellent Education, 2006), at www.all4ed.org.

25 **A Profile Over Time.** Percentage of 18- to 24-year-olds who are not enrolled in school and are not high school graduates (diploma or GED), by gender, race, and ethnicity: 1970–2005—U.S. Department of Commerce, Bureau of the Census, Current Population Survey, School Enrollment, Historical Tables, Table A-5a, at: www.census.gov/population/www/socdemo/school.html.

26 Ibid. The rate for Hispanics should be interpreted with care, because the sample of 18- to 24-year-olds on whom CPS's dropout data are based includes recent immigrants from Central and South America who did not arrive in this country until they were teenagers or older. Nevertheless, the extremely high Hispanic rate suggests that even those who have been in the United States their whole lives are encountering problems in school that need to be addressed. U.S. Census Bureau microdata cited by Lawrence Mishel and Joydeep Roy, *Rethinking High School Graduation Rates and Trends* (Economic Policy Institute, 2006), 34-35, 90, at www.epi.org.

27 **The High Cost of Dropping Out.** Percentage of population 25 and over employed, by educational level: 2005—U.S. Department of Labor, Bureau of Labor Statistics, Tables from *Employment and Earnings*, annual averages, Household Data, Table 7, at stats.bls.gov/cps. Percentage of population 18 and over with health insurance, by educational level: 2005—U.S. Department of Commerce, Bureau of the Census, Current Population Survey, Historical Health Insurance Tables, Table H 101, at www.census.gov. Median earnings by educational level: 2005—U.S. Department of Commerce,

Bureau of the Census, Current Population Survey, Educational Attainment, Table 9 at www.census. gov/population/www/socdemo/educ-attn.html.

28 Educational status of state prisoners at time of incarceration: U.S. Department of Justice, Office of Justice Programs, Bureau of Justice Statistics, Special Report, *Education and Correctional Populations* (Jan. 2003), Table 1, at www.ojp.usdog.gov/bjs. Distribution of GED recipients calculated by the Institute based on data in Table 1 and text on p. 1: prisoners who earned GEDs while in prison are counted as high school dropouts at the time of incarceration; the remainder, who earned GEDs *before* they entered prison, are counted as high school graduates at the time of incarceration.

29 **Graduation Rates Among Nations.** Organization for Economic Cooperation and Development, *Education at a Glance: OECD Indicators*, 2006 edition, Table A2.1, at www.oecdbookshop. org/oecd/display.asp?K=5L9WSZPKFLVF&CID=&LANG=EN.

30 **A College Education.** Stu Woo, "U.S. Slipping in Educational Attainment Levels, Says Report Comparing OECD Countries," *Chronicle of Higher Education*, International Section, vol. 53, no. 5 (Sept. 22, 2006), 40.

31 Ibid.

32 Tuition costs: College Board, *Trends in College Pricing*, Trends in Higher Education Series (2006), Table 3a. Financial aid: College Board, *Trends in Student Aid* (2006), Trends in Higher Education Series, Table 3. Both at www.collegeboard.com/research/home. College enrollment as percentage of 18-to 24-year-old high school graduates: U.S. Department of Education, National Center for Educational Statistics, *Digest of Education Statistics 2005*, Table 184, at nces.ed.gov/programs/digest.

33 **Looking Ahead.** Cost savings from improved graduation rates: see, for instance, Alliance for Excellent Education, "Saving Futures, Saving Dollars: Five Percent Increase in Male Graduation Rate Could Lead to Savings of $5 Billion Annually," in *Straight A's: Public Education Policy and Progress*, vol. 6, no. 17 (Sept. 18, 2006), at www.all4ed.org.

Chapter 7
Social Indicators for Adults

Unemployment

1 **Changes over Time.** Measuring unemployment: U.S. Department of Labor, Bureau of Labor Statistics, *BLS Handbook of Methods* (Apr. 1997), Ch. 1, at stats.bls.gov.

2 Unemployment over time (percentage of civilian labor force unemployed, annual averages): 1970–2005—U.S. Department of Labor, Bureau of Labor Statistics, Tables from *Employment and Earnings*: Annual averages, Household Data, Table 1, at stats.bls.gov/cps.

3 Number of unemployed and long-term unemployed: 2005—U.S. Department of Labor, Bureau of Labor Statistics, Tables from *Employment and Earnings*: Annual Averages, Household Data, Table 31, at stats.bls.gov/cps.

4 **A Profile of the Unemployed.** Unemployed by race, ethnicity, gender, and educational level: 2005—U.S. Department of Labor, Bureau of Labor Statistics, Current Population Survey, Historical Data from the *Employment Situation* News Release, Tables A-1 to A-4, at stats.bls.gov/cps.

5 Ibid.

6 **Persistent Problems.** Unemployment by race and ethnicity, 1970–2005: U.S. Department of Labor, Bureau of Labor Statistics, Current Population Survey, Historical Data from the *Employment Situation* News Release, Tables A-2 to A-3, at stats.bls.gov/cps. Calculations by the Institute.

7 Ibid.

[8] Youth unemployment: *Economic Report of the President* (Feb. 2007), Table B-42, at www.gpoaccess. gov/eop/download.html.

[9] **Worker Displacement.** Displaced workers: U.S. Department of Labor, Bureau of Labor Statistics, "Worker Displacement, 2003–2005," Economic News Release (Aug. 17, 2006), Tables 3 and 7, at stats.bls.gov/cps. (Note that within the total long-tenure displaced group, 13.4 percent were officially counted as unemployed, and 16.7 percent were designated as "not in the labor force.")

[10] Ibid.

[11] **Longer Periods Out of Work.** Duration of unemployment: *Economic Report of the President* (Feb. 2007), Table B-44, at www.gpoaccess.gov/eop/download.html.

[12] Percentage of unemployed out of work 26 weeks or longer: 1970–2005—U.S. Department of Labor, Bureau of Labor Statistics, Current Population Survey, Historical Data from the *Employment Situation News Release*, Table A-9, at stats.bls.gov/cps.

[13] **Protection Against Unemployment.** Program description: U.S. Department of Labor, Employment and Training Administration, "State Unemployment Insurance Benefits: About UI" at www.work-forcesecurity.doleta.gov/unemploy. Number served: U.S. Department of Labor, Employment & Training Administration, "Characteristics of the Insured Unemployed: Distribution of Characteristics of the Insured Unemployed, Report for Calendar Year 2005," at www.workforcesecurity.doleta. gov/unemploy/chariu.asp.

[14] Benefits as percentage of usual wages: U.S. Department of Labor, Employment and Training Administration, *Unemployment Insurance Financial Data Handbook*, at workforcesecurity. doleta.gov/unemploy/hb394.asp. Coverage levels: Lori G. Kletzer and Howard Rosen, *Reforming Unemployment Insurance for the Twenty-First Century Workforce: A Discussion Paper* (Brookings Institution, September 2006), Fig. 2, 11, at www.brookings.edu.

[15] Eligibility issues: Economic Policy Institute, *Issue Guide: Unemployment Insurance*, "Unemployment Insurance: Facts at a Glance," and "Unemployment Insurance: Frequently Asked Questions," at www. epinet.org.

Wages

[16] **Stalled Progress on Wages.** Wages as percentage of personal income: U.S. Department of Commerce, Bureau of Economic Analysis, National Income and Its Disposition, Table 2.1, at www. bea.doc/bea.

[17] Wage levels over time (average weekly earnings of production and nonsupervisory workers, private nonagricultural employment, 1982 dollars) : 1970–2005— *Economic Report of the President* (Feb. 2007), Table B-47; 1947–1970—Economic Report of the President (1991), Table B-45.

[18] Ibid.

[19] Wages: *Economic Report of the President* (Feb. 2007), Table B-47. Gross domestic product: *Economic Report of the President* (Feb. 2007), Table B-1.

[20] **Male and Female.** U.S. Department of Commerce, Bureau of the Census, *Income, Poverty, and Health Insurance 2005*, Table A-2. www.census.gov. For other disparities see: U.S. Department of Labor, Bureau of Labor Statistics, National Compensation Survey: Occupational Wages in the United States (June 2005), Table 1-1, at stats.bls.gov.

[21] Ibid.

[22] **The Working Poor.** Data on working poor: U.S. Department of Labor, Bureau of Labor Statistics, *A Profile of the Working Poor, 2004* (May 2006, revised December 2006), Tables 2, 3, 5, at stats.bls. gov.

[23] Ibid.

24 **The Minimum Wage.** Minimum wage, current dollars: 1970–2006—U.S. Department of Commerce, Bureau of the Census, *Statistical Abstract 2007*, Table 633, at www.census.gov/compendia/statab. Minimum wage, constant 2006 dollars: 1970–2005—Economic Policy Institute, *EPI Issue Guide: Minimum Wage*, Table 4, at www.epi.org. 2007 legislation: Stephen Labaton, "Congress Passes Minimum Wage Legislation," *New York Times* (May 25, 2007).

25 Ibid.

26 **Middle-Class Pressures.** Household debt: 1995—U.S. Department of Commerce, Bureau of the Census, *Statistical Abstract 2006*, Table 1177, at www.census.gov/compendia/statab; 2005—Federal Reserve Board, "Consumer Credit Outstanding," Federal Reserve Statistical Release G.19 (April 2006), at www.federalreserve.gov.

27 Debt service: Federal Reserve Board, "Household Debt Service and Financial Obligations Ratios, 1980-2005" (March 9, 2006), at www.federalreserve.gov. Bankruptcies: U.S. Bankruptcy Courts, Administrative Office, Bankruptcy Statistics, "Bankruptcy Filings, 12-Month Period Ending June, by Chapter and District" (1983–2003 summary and 2004 annual), at www.uscourts.gov/bnkrpctystats.

28 **Working Conditions Across Nations.** Earnings: U.S. Department of Labor, Bureau of Labor Statistics, "International Comparisons of Hourly Compensation Costs for Production Workers in Manufacturing, 1975–2005," Supplementary Tables, Table 2, at stats.bls.gov.

29 Hours: Organization for Economic Cooperation and Development, *OECD Employment Outlook 2006*, Statistical Annex, Table F, at www.oecd.org.

Health Insurance Coverage

30 **More People Without Health Insurance.** Health insurance coverage over time (percentage of population with no health insurance): 1976–1986—Estimated percentages are based on published and unpublished data from The Center for National Health Program Studies, Harvard Medical School, based on data from the U.S. Department of Commerce, Bureau of the Census, Current Population Survey, and the National Health Interview Survey. 1987–2005—U.S. Bureau of the Census, *Income, Poverty, and Health Insurance Coverage in the United States: 2005* (Aug. 2006), Table C-1, at www.census.gov. The U.S. Census Bureau is currently revising these data back to 1995. The full ten-year revision is scheduled for release in August 2007.

31 **Fewer People Insured Through Their Jobs.** Job-based insurance: 1988–2003—Employee Benefit Research Institute, *Employee Benefit Databook*, Table 4.1a, at www.ebri.org. Part-time workers: Paul Fronstin, *Sources of Health Insurance and Characteristics of the Uninsured: Analysis of the March 2006 Current Population Survey*, Issue Brief 298 (Employee Benefit Research Institute, Oct. 2006), Figure 13, at www.ebri.org; 2005—U.S. Bureau of Labor Statistics, *National Compensation Survey: Employee Benefits in Private Industry in the United States, March 2005* (Aug. 2005), Table 2, at www.bls.gov/ncs/ebs.

32 **The Cost of Employment-Based Coverage.** Rising health costs: U.S. Department of Labor, Bureau of Labor Statistics, Consumer Price Index Detailed Report Table (annual), Table 1A, at www.bls.gov/cpi. Employers' health costs: Employee Benefit Research Institute, "Finances of Employee Benefits: Health Costs Drive Changing Trends," *Notes*, vol. 26, no. 12 (Dec. 2005), at www.ebri.org. Rising premiums: U.S. Department of Labor, Bureau of Labor Statistics, Employee Benefits Survey, "Average Employee Contribution for Family Coverage Medical Care Benefits," at stats.bls.gov. Reasons for nonenrollment: Paul Fronstin, *Sources of Health Insurance and Characteristics of the Uninsured: Analysis of the March 2006 Current Population Survey*, Issue Brief 298 (Employee Benefit Research Institute, Oct. 2006), Figure 17, at www.ebri.org.

33 **Who Are the Uninsured?** Insurance status by race, ethnicity, citizenship, and income: U.S. Department of Commerce, Bureau of the Census, *Income, Poverty, and Health Insurance Coverage in the United States: 2005* (Aug. 2006), Table 8, at www.census.gov.

34 Ibid.

35 Ibid.

36 Insurance status by age: U.S. Department of Commerce, Bureau of the Census, *Income, Poverty, and Health Insurance Coverage in the United States: 2005* (Aug. 2006), Table C-1, 69-75, at www. census.gov. SCHIP: U.S. Department of Health and Human Services, Centers for Medicare & Medicaid Services website, "State Children's Health Insurance Program," at www.cms.hhs.gov.

37 Ibid.

38 **Insufficient Coverage**. U.S. Department of Commerce, Bureau of the Census, *Income, Poverty, and Health Insurance Coverage in the United States: 2005* (2006), 20, at www.census.gov. U.S. Department of Health and Human Services, *Health Insurance Coverage: Estimates from the National Health Interview Survey* (Jan.-June 2005), 6, at www.cc.gov/nchs. See also Cathy Schoen, Michelle M. Doty, Sara R. Collins, and Alyssa L. Holmgren, "Insured but Not Protected: How Many Adults Are Underinsured?" *Health Affairs* Web Exclusive (June 14, 2005), W5 289-302, at www.healthaffairs. org; Kaiser Commission on Medicaid and the Uninsured, *Key Facts, Underinsured in America: Is Health Coverage Adequate?* (July 2002), at www.kff.org.

39 Ibid.

40 **The Human Cost**. Kaiser Commission on Medicaid and the Uninsured, *The Uninsured: A Primer — Key Facts About Americans Without Health Insurance* (Jan. 2006), 6 and 8, at www.kff.org.

41 Medical Bankruptcy: David U. Himmelstein, Elizabeth Warren, Deborah Thorne, and Steffie Woolhandler, "Illness and Injury as Contributors to Bankruptcy," *Health Affairs* Web Exclusive (Feb. 2, 2005), W 63-71, at www.healthaffairs.org. See also Elizabeth Warren, Teresa A. Sullivan, and Melissa A. Jacoby, "Medical Problems and Bankruptcy Filings," *Norton's Bankruptcy Adviser* (May 2000), at papers.ssrn.com, and Cindy Zeldin and Mark Rukavina, *Borrowing to Stay Healthy: How Credit Card Debt Is Related to Medical Expenses* (Demos and The Access Project, Jan. 2007), at www.accessprojct.org/medical.html.

Chapter 8
Social Indicators for the Elderly

Poverty, Ages 65 and Over

1 **Fewer Elderly Americans in Poverty**. Elderly poverty over time (percentage of population ages 65 and over with incomes below the poverty line): 1970–2005—U.S. Department of Commerce, Bureau of the Census, Current Population Survey, Historical Poverty Tables, Table 3, at www.census.gov.

2 Ibid.

3 Ibid.

4 **Poverty by Age**. U.S. Department of Commerce, Bureau of the Census, Current Population Survey, Historical Poverty Tables, Table 3, at www.census.gov.

5 **Significant Disparities**. Poverty by gender: U.S. Department of Commerce, Bureau of the Census, Current Population Survey, Detailed Poverty Tables, Table POV01, at www.census.gov.

6 Poverty by race and ethnicity: U.S. Department of Commerce, Bureau of the Census, Current Population Survey, Historical Poverty Tables, Table 3, at www.census.gov.

7 Poverty by household structure: U.S. Department of Commerce, Bureau of the Census, Current Population Survey, Detailed Poverty Tables, Table POV01, at www.census.gov.

8 **The Near-Poor Elderly**. U.S. Department of Commerce, Bureau of the Census, Current Population Survey, Historical Poverty Tables, Table POV01, at www.census.gov.

9   Ibid.

10 **An International Perspective**. Relative poverty rates: 2000—Luxembourg Income Study, "Relative Poverty Rates for the Total Population, Children, and the Elderly," LIS Key Figures, at www.lisproject. org/keyfigures/povertytable.htm.

11 Ibid.

12 **Looking Ahead.** Fears about retirement: Institute for Innovation in Social Policy, National Social Survey 2004 (see Appendix C); see also U.S. Department of Commerce, Bureau of the Census, *65+ in the United States: 2005* (Dec. 2005), 9-16, at www.census.gov. Social Security financing: U.S. Social Security Administration, *2006 Annual Report of the Board of Trustees of the Federal Old-Age and Survivors Insurance and Disability Insurance Trust Funds* (May 1, 2006), at www.ssa. gov/ReportsTrustFunds/; Center on Budget and Policy Priorities, "What the New Trustees' Report Shows about Social Security (June 15, 2006) at www.cbpp.org.

13 Retirement plan participation: Employee Benefit Research Institute, *EBRI Databook on Employee Benefits* (updated Nov. 2005), Chapter 4, Table 4.1a, at www.ebri.org. Types of retirement plans: U.S. Department of Labor, "Retirement Plans, Benefits and Savings: Types of Retirement Plans," at www.dol.gov. Public pension cutbacks: "Once Safe, Public Pensions Are Now Facing Cuts," *New York Times* (Nov. 6, 2006), 1.

14 Investments by income-group: Arthur B. Kenickell, *Currents and Undercurrents: Change in the Distribution of Wealth, 1989–2004*, Survey of Consumer Finances Working Paper (U.S. Federal Reserve Board, Jan. 30, 2006), Table 10, at www.federalreserve.gov. Savings rate: U.S. Department of Commerce, Bureau of Economic Analysis, National Income and Product Accounts Tables, Table 2.1, at www.bea.gov.

Out-of-Pocket Health Costs, Ages 65 and Over

15 **Eroding Elderly Income.** Number covered by Medicare, 2006: 35.6 million elderly and 6.3 million people with disabilities, totaling 41.7 million beneficiaries. U.S. Department of Health and Human Services, Centers for Medicare & Medicaid Services, *2006 Annual Report of the Boards of Trustees of the Federal Hospital Insurance and Federal Supplementary Medical Insurance Trust Funds* (May 1, 2006), 2, at www.cms.hhs.gov/ReportsTrustFunds. Percentage of elderly covered: U.S. Department of Commerce, Bureau of the Census, *Statistical Abstracts 2006* (2006), Table 142, at www.census.gov/compendia/statab.

16 Percentage of elderly health costs covered by Medicare: Kaiser Family Foundation, *Medicare at a Glance* (Sept. 2005), 1, at www.kff.org. Services covered by Medicare: U.S Department of Health and Human Services, Centers for Medicare & Medicaid Services, *Medicare and You 2006*, 12-15, at www.medicare.gov.

17 Out-of-pocket health costs over time (expenditures for health insurance, medical services, drugs, and medical supplies by households, ages 65 and over, as percentage of income): Health-care expenditures: U.S. Department of Labor, Bureau of Labor Statistics, Consumer Expenditure Survey, at stats.bls. gov/cex/home.htm. Median household income before taxes, by age-group of head of household: U.S. Department of Commerce, Bureau of the Census, Current Population Survey, Historical Income Tables, Table H10, at www.census.gov/hhes/www/income.html. Calculations by the Institute.

18 **Out-of-Pocket Spending.** Distribution of expenses: U.S. Department of Health and Human Services, Centers for Medicare & Medicaid Services, *An Overview of the U.S. Health Care System Chart Book* (Jan. 31, 2007), Table 4.15, at www.cms.hhs.gov/TheChartSeries. Distribution of out-of-pocket expenses for direct services: U.S. Department of Health and Human Services, Centers for Medicare & Medicaid Services, *Health and Health Care of the Medicare Population* (2000), Table 4, at www. medicare.gov. Medicare deductibles: U.S. Department of Health and Human Services, Centers for Medicare & Medicaid Services, *2006 Annual Report of the Boards of Trustees of the Federal*

Hospital Insurance and Federal Supplementary Medical Insurance Trust Funds (May 1, 2006), 103, at www.cms.hhs.gov/ReportsTrustFunds. Services covered by Medicare: U.S. Department of Health and Human Services, Centers for Medicare & Medicaid Services, *Medicare and You 2006*, 12-15, at www.medicare.gov.

[19] Medicare premiums: U.S. Department of Health and Human Services, Centers for Medicare & Medicaid Services, *2006 Annual Report of the Boards of Trustees of the Federal Hospital Insurance and Federal Supplementary Medical Insurance Trust Funds* (May 1, 2006), 103, at www.cms.hhs.gov/ReportsTrustFunds.

[20] Private insurance premiums: See, for instance, Kaiser Family Foundation and Health Research and Educational Trust, *Employer Health Benefits 2005, Summary of Findings* (Sept. 2005), 1, at www.kff.org.

[21] **Health Care and the Elderly Poor.** Participation in Medicaid by the elderly poor: U.S. Department of Commerce, Bureau of the Census, Current Population Survey, Historical Poverty Tables, Table POV26, at www.census.gov.

[22] Out-of-pocket expenditures by income-level: U.S. Department of Health and Human Services, Centers for Medicare & Medicaid Services, *Program Information on Medicare, Medicaid, SCHIP, and other Programs of the Centers for Medicare and Medicaid Services*, Chart Series (July 2002), Sec. III, B 5, 10, at www.medicare.gov.

[23] **Prescription Drugs.** Medicare Part D: Kaiser Family Foundation, *Policy Brief: Tracking Prescription Drug Coverage Under Medicare: Five Ways to Look at the New Enrollment Numbers* (Feb. 2006), at www.kff.org/medicare. See also Kaiser Family Foundation and Hewitt Associates, *Prospects for Retiree Health Benefits as Medicare Prescription Drug Coverage Begins: Findings from the Kaiser/Hewitt 2005 Survey on Retiree Health Benefits* (Dec. 2005), v, at www.kff.org.

[24] Ibid.

[25] Ibid.

[26] **The Financial Impact.** Karen Davis, Cathy Schoen, Michelle Doty, and Katie Tenney, "Medicare Versus Private Insurance: Rhetoric and Reality," *Health Affairs* Web Exclusive (October 9, 2002), at www.healthaffairs.org. See also The Commonwealth Fund, *Will You Still Need Me? The Health and Financial Security of Older Americans* (June 2005), 6, at www.cmwf.org.

[27] **The Health Impact.** Thomas Rice and Karen Y. Matsuoka, "The Impact of Cost-Sharing on Appropriate Utilization and Health Status: A Review of the Literature on Seniors," *Medicare Care Research and Review*, vol. 61, no. 4 (Dec. 2004), 448. Some of the studies reviewed in this article examined the link between actual out-of-pocket spending and health outcomes; others examined whether having supplemental insurance (and therefore lower obligations for out-of-pocket costs) affected recipients' health or access to health services.

Chapter 9
Social Indicators for All Ages

Homicides

[1] **A Concern for Safety.** U.S. Department of Justice, Bureau of Justice Statistics, James Alan Fox and Marianne W. Zawitz, *Homicide Trends in the U.S.* (June 2006), at www.ojp.usdoj.gov/bjs.

[2] Homicides over time (murders and non-negligent manslaughters per 100,000 population): Federal Bureau of Investigation, Uniform Crime Reports. 1970–1972—*Crime in the United States 1979* (1980); 1973–1976—*Crime in the United States 1991* (1992); 1977–1984—*Crime in the United States 1996* (1997); 1985–2005—*Crime in the United States 2005* (2006), at www.fbi.gov/ucr/ucr.htm.

3 Ibid.

4 **Impact on the Young**. Homicide victimization and offender rates per 100,000, by age, 1976–2004, annual averages: U.S. Department of Justice, Bureau of Justice Statistics, James Alan Fox and Marianne W. Zawitz, Homicide Trends in the U.S., Long Term Trends (June 2006), Trends by Age, "Homicide Type by Age, 1976–2004," at www.ojp.usdoj.gov/bjs.

5 Homicide as cause of death, by age: U.S. Department of Health and Human Services, Centers for Disease Control and Prevention, National Center for Injury Prevention and Control, WISQARS Leading Causes of Death Reports, at www/cdc/gov/ncipc/wisqars.

6 **Guns and Youth**. U.S. Department of Justice, Bureau of Justice Statistics, James Alan Fox and Marianne W. Zawitz, *Homicide Trends in the U.S.* (June 2006), Table: "Weapons Used, Homicides by Weapon and Age of Offender," at www.ojp.usdoj.gov/bjs.

7 Children's Defense Fund, "Protect Children, Not Guns," at www.childrensdefense.org.

8 **Violent Crime.** The components of violent crime: 1970–1984—U.S. Department of Commerce, Bureau of the Census, *Statistical Abstract of the United States* (annual), at www.census.gov/compendia/statab; 1985–2005—Federal Bureau of Investigation, Uniform Crime Reports, *Crime in the United States* (2005), Table 1, at www.fbi.gov/ucr/ucr.htm.

9 Ibid.

10 **Homicide Among Nations.** Gordon Barclay and Cynthia Tavares, *International Comparisons of Criminal Justice Statistics 2001* (British Home Office Statistical Bulletin, Oct. 2003), 10, at www. crimereduction.gov.uk. Data years range between 1999 and 2001.

11 **The Death Penalty.** Death penalty in other nations: Amnesty International, "Facts and Figures on the Death Penalty" and "Abolitionist and Retentionist Countries," at web.amnesty.org. U.S. death penalty laws: Death Penalty Information Center, "Facts About the Death Penalty" and "Crimes Punishable by the Death Penalty," at www.deathpenaltyinfo.org.

12 Supreme Court decisions on death penalty: Death Penalty Information Center, "Facts About the Death Penalty," at www.deathpenaltyinfo.org. Executions: 1970–2006—U.S. Department of Justice, Bureau of Justice Statistics, "Key Facts at a Glance: Executions," at www.ojp.usdoj.gov/bjs.

Alcohol-Related Traffic Fatalities

13 **Making Progress.** Alcohol-related traffic fatalities over time (deaths in alcohol-related crashes [driver, pedestrian, and/or cyclist had blood-alcohol level of .01 or higher] as percentage of all traffic fatalities): 1977–1981—Estimates based on data from National Institute for Alcohol Abuse and Alcoholism, Alcohol Epidemiologic System, Hsiao-ye Yi, Gerald D. Williams, and Michael E. Hilton, *Surveillance Report #71: Trends in Alcohol-Related Fatal Traffic Crashes, United States, 1977–2003* (Aug. 2005), Table 1, at www.niaa.nih.gov, and U.S. Department of Transportation, National Highway Traffic Safety Administration, Fatal Accident Reporting System, National Center for Statistics and Analysis, *Traffic Safety Facts 2005: A Compilation of Motor Vehicle Crash Data from the Fatality Analysis Reporting System* (Jan. 2007), Table 13, at www-nrd.nhtsa.dot.gov; calculations by the Institute; 1982-2005—U.S. Department of Transportation, National Highway Traffic Safety Administration, *Traffic Safety Facts 2005*, Table 13, at www-nrd.nhtsa.dot.gov.

14 Ibid.

15 Ibid.

16 **Safe Driving**. Policies on safe driving: U.S. Department of Transportation, National Highway Traffic Safety Administration (NHTSA), Fatal Accident Reporting System, National Center for Statistics and Analysis, *Traffic Safety Facts 2005: A Compilation of Motor Vehicle Crash Data from the Fatality*

Analysis Reporting System (Jan. 2007), Table 13, at www-nrd.nhtsa.dot.gov. Effect of speed-limit change: Insurance Institute for Highway Safety, "Q&A: Speed and Speed Limits" (Dec. 2005), at www.iihs.org.

17 Campaign against drunk driving: See, for instance, Lawrence J. Blincoe, Angela G. Seay, Eduard Zaloshnja, Ted R. Miller, Eduardo O. Romano, Stephen Luchter, and Rebecca S. Spicer, *The Economic Impact of Motor Vehicle Crashes 2000* (U.S. Dept of Transportation, National Highway Traffic Safety Administration, 2002), at www-nrd.nhtsa.dot.gov.

18 Traffic fatalities: 1982–2005—U.S. Department of Transportation, National Highway Traffic Safety Administration (NHTSA), Fatal Accident Reporting System, National Center for Statistics and Analysis, *Traffic Safety Facts 2005: A Compilation of Motor Vehicle Crash Data from the Fatality Analysis Reporting System* (Jan. 2007), Table 13, at www-nrd.nhtsa.dot.gov.

19 **The Drivers.** Driver characteristics: U.S. Department of Transportation, National Highway Traffic Safety Administration, Fatal Accident Reporting System, National Center for Statistics and Analysis, *Traffic Safety Facts 2005: A Compilation of Motor Vehicle Crash Data from the Fatality Analysis Reporting System* (Jan. 2007), Tables 15, 16, 18, at www-nrd.nhtsa.dot.gov. Underage drinking: Under the National Minimum Drinking Age Act of 1984, states are required to prohibit the purchase or public consumption of alcohol by individuals under age 21.

20 **The Victims.** Motor vehicle deaths, by age: U.S. Department of Transportation, National Highway Traffic Safety Administration, Fatal Accident Reporting System, National Center for Statistics and Analysis, *Traffic Safety Facts 2005: A Compilation of Motor Vehicle Crash Data from the Fatality Analysis Reporting System,* Jan. 2007), Table 54, at www-nrd.nhtsa.dot.gov. Cause of death by age group: U.S. Department of Health and Human Services, Centers for Disease Control, National Center for Injury Prevention and Control, WISQARS Leading Cause of Death Reports, 2003, at www.cdc. gov/ncipc/wisqars. Alcohol-related traffic fatalities, by age: U.S. Department of Transportation, National Highway Traffic Safety Administration, Fatal Accident Reporting System, National Center for Statistics and Analysis, *Traffic Safety Facts 2005: A Compilation of Motor Vehicle Crash Data from the Fatality Analysis Reporting System* (Jan. 2007), Table 81, at www-nrd.nhtsa.dot.gov.

21 **Youth and Alcohol Abuse.** U.S. Department of Health and Human Services, Substance Abuse & Mental Health Services Administration, Office of Applied Studies, *Results from the 2005 National Survey on Drug Use and Health* (2006), Table G.23 and "2005 National Survey on Drug Use and Health: National Findings," at www.drugabusestatistics.samhsa.gov/nsduh.htm.

22 Ibid.

23 **Counting the Cost.** Economic Cost: Lawrence J. Blincoe, Angela G. Seay, Eduard Zaloshnja, Ted R. Miller, Eduardo O. Romano, Stephen Luchter, and Rebecca S. Spicer, *The Economic Impact of Motor Vehicle Crashes 2000* (U.S. Dept of Transportation, National Highway Traffic Safety Administration, 2002), at www-nrd.nhtsa.dot.gov.

24 Ibid.

25 Years of potential life lost: National Institute for Alcohol Abuse and Alcoholism, Alcohol Epidemiologic System, Hsiao–ye Yi, Chiung M. Chen, and Gerald D. Williams, *Surveillance Report #76: Trends in Alcohol-Related Fatal Traffic Crashes, United States, 1977-2004* (Aug. 2006), Table 3, at www. niaa.nih.gov.

Food Stamp Coverage

26 **Access to Food.** Prevalence of hunger: See, for example, Center on Hunger and Poverty, "The Paradox of Hunger and Obesity in America," July 2003, 1, at www.centeronhunger.org; Food Stamp history: U.S. Department of Agriculture, Food and Nutrition Service, "A Short History of the Food Stamp Program," at www.fns.usda.gov/fsp/rules/Legislation/history.htm.

27 See, for example: Congressional Budget Office, "Changes in Participation in Means-Tested Programs," Economic and Budget Issue Brief (April 20, 2005) at www.cbo.gov; U.S. Government Accountability Office, "Food Stamp Program: Steps Have Been Taken to Increase Participation of Working Families, but Better Tracking of Efforts Is Needed," GAO-04-346 (March 2004), at www.gao.gov; U.S. Department of Agriculture, Economic Research Service, "Food Stamp Program Access Study: Local Office Policies and Practices," E-FAN No. 03013-1 (Dec. 2003), at www.ers.usda.gov.

28 Food Stamp coverage over time (Food Stamp participation by the poor, as a percentage of poor population): 1975–1987—Estimates based on data from *The Green Book: Background Material and Data on Programs Within the Jurisdiction of the Committee on Ways and Means*, U.S. House of Representatives, Washington, D.C., 2000, and Center on Budget and Policy Priorities, *Poverty and Income Trends, 1999: Program Participation Status of Poor Households*, calculations by the Institute. 1988–1999—Center on Budget and Policy Priorities, *Poverty and Income Trends, 1999: Program Participation Status of Poor Households*. 2000–2004—U.S. Department of Commerce, Bureau of the Census, Current Population Survey, Detailed Poverty Tables, Table POV 26, "Program Participation Status of Household—Poverty Status of People: Below Poverty," at www.census.gov.

29 **Food Insecurity.** Food insecurity definition: See U.S. Department of Agriculture, Economic Research Service, Mark Nord, Margaret Andrews, and Steven Carlson, *Household Food Security in the United States, 2005*, 4, at: www.ers.usda.gov. On the language revision from hunger to food insecurity, see for example "Brother, Can You Spare a Word," editorial, *The New York Times* (November 20, 2006), 22.

30 Food insecurity trends: U.S. Department of Agriculture, Economic Research Service, Mark Nord, Margaret Andrews, and Steven Carlson, *Household Food Security in the United States, 2005* (Nov. 2006), Tables 1A, 5, and 1B, 8. Very low food security: *Household Food Security in the United States, 2005*, 6. Both at www.ers.usda.gov.

31 Ibid.

32 2010 Goal: U.S. Department of Agriculture, Economic Research Service, Mark Nord and Margaret Andrews, "Reducing Food Insecurity in the United States: Assessing Progress Toward a National Objective," Issues in Food Assistance (May 2002), at www.ers.usda.gov.

33 **Private Food Assistance.** U.S. Conference of Mayors and Sodexho, Inc., *Hunger and Homelessness Survey: A Status Report on Hunger and Homelessness in America's Cities: A 23-City Survey* (December 2006), 3, 27, 88, at: www.usmayors.org/uscm/home.asp.

34 America's Second Harvest, "About Us," and *Hunger in America 2006* (Mar. 2006), Key Findings, at www.hungerinamerica.org.

35 **Who Are the Hungry?** America's Second Harvest, *Hunger in America 2006* (Mar. 2006), Key Findings, at www.hungerinamerica.org.

36 Ibid.

37 **Difficult Choices.** America's Second Harvest (Mar. 2006), *Hunger in America 2006*, Key Findings, at www.hungerinamerica.org.

38 **Illness and Obesity.** Effect on children: See, for example: John T. Cook, Deborah A. Frank, Suzette M. Levenson, Nicole B. Neault, Tim C. Heeren, Maurine M. Black, Carol Berkowitz, Patrick H. Casey, Alan F. Meyers, Diana B. Cutts, and Mariana Chilton, "Child Food Insecurity Increases Risks Posed by Household Food Insecurity to Young Children's Health," *Journal of Nutrition,* vol. 136, no. 4 (Apr. 2006), 1073-1076; Katherine Alaimo, Christine Olson, and Edward Frongillo, Jr., "Food Insufficiency and American School-Aged Children's Cognitive, Academic, and Psychosocial Development," *Pediatrics*, vol. 108, no. 1 (July 2001), p. 44; John T. Cook, Deborah A. Frank, Carol Berkowitz, Maureen M. Black, Patrick H. Casey, Diana B. Cutts, Alan F. Meyers, Nieves Zaldivar, Anne Skalicky, Suzette Levenson, Tim Heeren, and Mark Nord, "Food Insecurity Is Associated with

Adverse Health Outcomes Among Human Infants and Toddlers," *Journal of Nutrition*, vol. 134, no. 6 (April 2003), 1432-1438.

39 Food Insecurity and Obesity: Parke Wilde and Jerusha N. Peterman, "Individual Weight Change Is Associated with Household Food Security Status," *Journal of Nutrition,* vol. 136, no. 5 (May 2006), 1395-1400; see also Elizabeth J. Adams, Laurence Grummer-Strawn, and Gilberto Chavez, "Food Insecurity Is Associated with Increased Risk of Obesity in California Women," *The Journal of Nutrition*, vol. 133, no. 4 (April 2003), 1070-1075; Center on Hunger and Poverty, "The Paradox of Hunger and Obesity in America," July 2003, at www.centeronhunger.org/pubs.html#HF.

40 **A National Responsibility.** American Dietetic Association, "Position Paper on Food Insecurity and Hunger in the United States," at www.eatright.org/cps/rde/xchg/ada/hs.xsl/advocacy_adar1202_ENU_HTML.htm.

Affordable Housing

41 **The Meaning of a Home.** Houses as proportion of net worth: Arthur B. Kennickell, *Currents and Undercurrents: Changes in the Distribution of Wealth, 1989-2004*, Survey of Consumer Finances, (Federal Reserve, Jan. 30, 2006), Table 11a, at www.federalreserve.gov.

42 Affordable housing over time: Housing Affordability Index—one-quarter of median family income, as percentage of the funds necessary to qualify for an 80 percent mortgage on a median-price home: 1970–2005—National Association of Realtors, Realtor Research, unpublished data; see also monthly postings of Housing Affordability Index, at www.realtor.org/Research.nsf/Pages/HousingInx.

43 Ibid.

44 **First-Time Buyers.** Housing Affordability Index for First-Time Home Buyers—one-quarter of median family income of first-time home buyers, as percentage of the funds necessary to qualify for an 80 percent mortgage on a median-priced home. 1981–2005—National Association of Realtors, Realtor Research, unpublished data; see also monthly postings of First-Time Housing Affordability Index, at www.realtor.org/Research.nsf/Pages/HousingInx.

45 **Undue Burdens.** Guidelines on housing cost as percentage of income: See, for instance: National Association of Realtors, Methodology for Affordability Index, at www.realtor.org/Research. nsf/Pages/HousingInx; and National Low Income Housing Coalition, *Out of Reach 2005* (Dec. 2005), at www.nlihc.org.

46 Cost burden over time: U.S. Department of Housing and Urban Development, Office of Policy Development and Research. 1978, 1987—*Affordable Housing Needs: A Report to Congress on the Significant Need for Housing* (December 2006), Table A-2b; 1991–2005— *Affordable Housing Needs 2005: A Report to Congress on the Significant Need for Housing (May 2007),* Table A-2b. Both at www.huduser.org.

47 **International Standing.** International comparison: Kathleen Scanlon and Christine Whitehead, *International Trends in Housing Tenure and Mortgage Finance* (Council of Mortgage Lenders: London, Nov. 2004), at www.cml.org.uk.

48 Ibid.

49 **Who Owns a Home?** Ownership by race and ethnicity. U.S. Department of Commerce, Bureau of the Census, Housing Vacancies and Homeownership, Annual Statistics 2005, "Homeownership Rates by Race and Ethnicity of Householder: 1994 to 2005," at www.census.gov.

50 Disparities in lending practices: Robert B. Avery, Glenn B. Canner and Robert E. Cook, "New Information Reported Under HMDA and Its Application in Fair Lending Enforcement," *Federal Reserve Bulletin*, vol. 9, no. 3 (Summer 2005), 344-394, at www.federalreserve.gov.

51 **The Renters.** Renters as percentage of total households: U.S. Department of Housing and Urban Development, Office of Policy Development and Research, *Affordable Housing Needs: A Report to Congress on the Significant Need for Housing*, Annual Compilation of Worst Case Housing Needs Survey (Dec. 2005), Table A-2a, at www.huduser.org. Renters' ability to pay: National Low Income Housing Coalition, *Out of Reach 2005* (Dec. 2005), at www.nlihc.org. State populations: U.S. Department of Commerce, Bureau of the Census, National and State Population Estimates, April 1, 2000, to July 1, 2005, at www.census.gov. Families with children: U.S. Department of Housing and Urban Development, *Affordable Housing Needs*, Table A-6b, 64, at www.huduser.org.

52 **The Homeless.** Number of homeless: National Law Center on Homelessness and Poverty, *Homelessness in the United States and the Human Right to Housing* (Jan. 14, 2004), 7, at www.nlchp.org.

53 Characteristics of the homeless: United States Conference of Mayors – Sodexho, Inc., *Hunger and Homelessness Survey: A Status Report on Hunger and Homelessness in America's Cities, A 23-City Survey* (Dec. 2006), 66, 88, at www.usmayors.org.

54 Ibid.

Income Inequality

55 **A Widening Gap.** Gini coefficient over time: 1967–2005— U.S. Department of Commerce, Bureau of the Census, *Income, Poverty, and Health Insurance Coverage 2005* (Aug. 2006), Table A-3, at www.census.gov. The sharp increase in inequality in 1993 is due to a change that year in Census Bureau procedure, designed to make the measurement of inequality more accurate.

56 Income inequality: 1970–2005—U.S. Department of Commerce, Bureau of the Census, *Income, Poverty, and Health Insurance Coverage 2005* (Aug. 2006), Table A-3. 1947–1966—U.S. Department of Commerce, Bureau of the Census, Current Population Survey, *The Changing Shape of the Nation's Income Distribution, 1947-98* (2000), Figure 1. Both at www/census.gov/hhes.

57 **Dividing the Nation.** Income share by quintile: U.S. Department of Commerce, Bureau of the Census, *Income, Poverty, and Health Insurance Coverage 2005* (Aug. 2006), Table A-3, at www/census. gov/hhes. Federal tax receipts by type: Economic Policy Institute, *The State of Working America, 2006/2007* (2006), Table 1.17, at www.stateofworkingamerica.org. Tax liability by income class: Congressional Budget Office, *Historical Effective Federal Tax Rates: 1979–2003* (December 2005), Table 2. Income shares before and after taxes: Congressional Budget Office, *Historical Effective Federal Tax Rates: 1979–2003* (December 2005), Appendix Table 4C, at www.cbo.gov. See also U.S. Department of the Treasury, Internal Revenue Service, Michael Strudler and Tom Petska, *Further Analysis of the Distribution of Income and Taxes, 1979–2002* (Oct. 2005), 2, 4, 6, 9, at www.irs. gov/taxstats.

58 **The Executive Pay Boom.** Executive pay and pay ratio: Sarah Anderson, John Cavanagh, Scott Klinger, and Liz Stanton, *Executive Excess 2005* (Institute for Policy Studies and United for a Fair Economy, Aug. 30, 2005), 13, 14, at www.faireconomy.org. Based on *Business Week* annual survey; includes salary, bonus, restricted stock, payouts on other long-term incentives, and the value of options exercised. National income shares: U.S. Department of Commerce, Bureau of Economic Analysis, National Income and Product Accounts Table, Table 1.12, at www.bea.gov/bea.

59 **The Wage Shrink.** Center on Budget and Policy Priorities, Aviva Aron-Dine and Isaac Shapiro, "In First Half of 2006, Wages and Salaries Captured Smallest Share of Income on Record, Share of Income Going to Corporate Profits at Highest Level Since 1950" (October 6, 2006), at www.cbpp.org. Note: Wages and salaries, and corporate profits are "average annual rates."

60 **Minorities and Wealth.** Distribution of Income: Congressional Budget Office, *Historical Effective*

Federal Tax Rates: 1979–2003 (December 2005), Appendix Table 4C, at www.cbo.gov. Distribution of Wealth: Arthur B. Kennickell, *Currents and Undercurrents: Changes in the Distribution of Wealth, 1989-2004*, Survey of Consumer Finance Working Paper (U.S. Federal Reserve Board, June 2006), Table 11a, at www.federalreserve.gov.

61 Wealth and income by race/ethnicity: Brian K. Bucks, Arthur B. Kennickell, and Kevin B. Moore, "Recent Changes in U.S. Family Finances: Evidence from the 2001 and 2004 Survey of Consumer Finances," *Federal Reserve Bulletin*, vol. 92 (Feb. 2006), A4-A5, A8, A22, at www.federalreserve. gov.

62 Ibid.

63 Ibid.

64 **International Measures.** Global wealth distribution, 2000: James B. Davies, Susanna Sandstrom, Anthony Shorrocks, and Edward N. Wolff, *The World Distribution of Household Wealth* (World Institute for Development Economics Research, United Nations University, Dec. 2006), Table 10a. Wealth distribution by country: James Davies, et al., *The World Distribution of Household Wealth* (World Institute for Development Economics Research, United Nations University, Dec. 2006), Table 9; data are from 1997–2000. Both at www.wider.unu.

65 **Thinking Inequality.** Studies on inequality: See, for example, Ichiro Kawachi and Davd Kennedy, *The Health of Nations: Why Inequality Is Harmful to Your Health* (New Press, 2006); Richard Wilkinson, *The Impact of Inequality: How to Make Sick Societies Healthier* (New Press, 2006); Grace Budrys, *Unequal Health, How Inequality Contributes to Health or Illness* (Rowman and Littlefield), 2003. Quote from President Bush: Greg Ip and John D. McKinnon, "Bush Reorients Rhetoric, Acknowledges Income Gap," *Wall Street Journal* (March 26, 2007).

Conclusion

1 Raymond Bauer, ed., *Social Indicators* (MIT Press, 1966), ix.

2 A few sociologists have moved in this direction in the past, notably Talcott Parsons with his vision of a "social system." But Parsons' multi-layered construct had far less policy relevance than is currently needed, and did too little to incorporate social change. See Talcott Parsons, *The Social System* (Routledge, 1991).

List of Tables and Graphs

Appendix A

Selected Social Indicator Data Over Time

Infant Mortality

	Infant deaths	Infant mortality rate		
		All	White	Black
1970	74,667	20.0	17.8	32.6
1971	67,981	19.1	17.1	30.3
1972	60,182	18.5	16.4	29.6
1973	55,581	17.7	15.8	28.1
1974	52,776	16.7	14.8	26.8
1975	50,525	16.1	14.2	26.2
1976	48,265	15.2	13.3	25.5
1977	46,975	14.1	12.3	23.6
1978	45,945	13.8	12.0	23.1
1979	45,665	13.1	11.4	21.8
1980	45,526	12.6	10.9	22.2
1981	43,305	11.9	10.3	20.8
1982	42,401	11.5	9.9	20.5
1983	40,627	11.2	9.6	20.0
1984	39,580	10.8	9.3	19.2
1985	40,030	10.6	9.2	19.0
1986	38,891	10.4	8.8	18.9
1987	38,408	10.1	8.5	18.8
1988	38,910	10.0	8.4	18.5
1989	39,655	9.8	8.1	18.6
1990	38,351	9.2	7.6	18.0
1991	36,766	8.9	7.3	17.6
1992	34,628	8.5	6.9	16.8
1993	33,466	8.4	6.8	16.5
1994	31,710	8.0	6.6	15.8
1995	29,583	7.6	6.3	15.1
1996	28,487	7.3	6.1	14.7
1997	28,045	7.2	6.0	14.2
1998	28,371	7.2	6.0	14.3
1999	27,937	7.1	5.8	14.6
2000	28,035	6.9	5.7	14.1
2001	27,568	6.8	5.7	14.0
2002	28,034	7.0	5.8	14.4
2003	28,025	6.9	5.7	14.0
2004	27,936	6.8	5.7	13.8

Infant deaths: Deaths in the first year of life.

Infant mortality rate: Deaths in the first year of life per 1,000 live births.

Sources: U.S. Department of Health and Human Services, Centers for Disease Control, National Center for Health Statistics, National Vital Statistics System. 1970, 1975–2002—"Supplemental Analyses of Recent Trends in Infant Mortality," by Kenneth D. Kochanek and Joyce A. Martin (2004), Table 1; 1971–1974 —*Vital Statistics of the United States 1992*, vol. 2, Mortality, Part A (1994), Table 2-2; 2003–2004—*E-Stats Deaths: Final Data for 2004*, Table 1, at www.cdc.nchs.

Note: 1970–1979 by race of child, 1980–2004 by race of mother.

Child Poverty

	Number of children in poverty (000s)	Child poverty rate				Number of children in poverty (000s)
		Related children in families				Total children
		All	White*	Black	Hispanic	
1970	10,235	14.9	10.5	41.5		10,440
1971	10,344	15.1	10.9	40.4		10,551
1972	10,082	14.9	10.1	42.7		10,284
1973	9,453	14.2	9.7	40.6	27.8	9,642
1974	9,967	15.1	9.3	39.6	28.6	10,156
1975	10,882	16.8	10.5	41.4	33.1	11,104
1976	10,081	15.8	9.6	40.4	30.1	10,273
1977	10,028	16.0	9.7	41.6	28.0	10,288
1978	9,722	15.7	9.4	41.2	27.2	9,931
1979	9,993	16.0	9.6	40.8	27.7	10,377
1980	11,114	17.9	11.3	42.1	33.0	11,543
1981	12,068	19.5	12.4	44.9	35.4	12,505
1982	13,139	21.3	13.8	47.3	38.9	13.647
1983	13,427	21.8	14.4	46.2	37.7	13,911
1984	12,929	21.0	13.1	46.2	38.7	13,420
1985	12,483	20.1	12.3	43.1	39.6	13,010
1986	12,257	19.8	12.2	42.7	37.1	12,876
1987	12,275	19.7	11.2	44.4	38.9	12,843
1988	11,935	19.0	10.5	42.8	37.3	12,455
1989	12,001	19.0	10.9	43.2	35.5	12,590
1990	12,715	19.9	11.6	44.2	37.7	13,431
1991	13,658	21.1	12.4	45.6	39.8	14,341
1992	14,521	21.6	12.4	46.3	39.0	15,294
1993	14,961	22.0	12.8	45.9	39.9	15,727
1994	14,610	21.2	11.8	43.3	41.1	15,289
1995	13,999	20.2	10.6	41.5	39.3	14,665
1996	13,764	19.8	10.4	39.5	39.9	14,463
1997	13,422	19.2	10.7	36.8	36.4	14,113
1998	12,845	18.3	10.0	36.4	33.6	13,467
1999	11,678	16.6	8.8	32.8	29.9	12,280
2000	11,005	15.6	8.5	30.9	27.6	11,587
2001	11,175	15.8	8.9	30.0	27.4	11,733
2002	11,646	16.3	8.9	32.1	28.2	12,133
2003	12,340	17.2	9.3	33.6	29.5	12,866
2004	12,473	17.3	9.9	33.4	28.6	13,041
2005	12,335	17.1	9.5	34.2	27.7	12,896

Child poverty rate: Percentage of related children under age 18 in families with incomes below the poverty line.

Source: U.S. Department of Commerce, Bureau of the Census, Current Population Survey, Historical Poverty Tables, Table 3, at www.census.gov.

* 1970–1973: White; 1974–2005: White non-Hispanic.

Child Abuse

	Children involved in child abuse reports		Child abuse fatalities
	Number of children	Child abuse rate	
1976	669,000	10.1	
1977	838,000	12.8	
1978	836,000	12.9	
1979	988,000	15.4	
1980	1,154,000	18.1	
1981	1,225,000	19.4	
1982	1,262,000	20.1	
1983	1,477,000	23.6	
1984	1,727,000	27.3	
1985	1,928,000	30.6	810
1986	2,086,000	32.8	1,002
1987	2,157,000	34.0	1,042
1988	2,265,000	35.0	1,092
1989	2,435,000	38.0	1,095
1990	2,559,000	40.0	1,099
1991	2,684,000	42.0	1,233
1992	2,909,000	45.0	1,129
1993	2,967,000	45.0	1,216
1994	3,074,000	46.0	1,278
1995	3,120,000	43.0	1,248
1996	3,126,000	43.5	1,046
1997	2,923,000	42.0	1,196
1998	2,806,000	41.5	1,100
1999	2,823,000	42.4	1,082
2000	2,939,000	40.6	1,330
2001	3,058,000	41.2	1,420
2002	3,135,000	43.8	1,450
2003	2,856,000	45.9	1,400
2004	3.424,000	47.8	1,490
2005	3,598,000	48.3	1,460

Child abuse rate: Number of children involved in abuse/neglect reports per 1,000 population ages 0-18.

Sources: 1976–1986—American Association for Protecting Children, American Humane Association, Highlights of Official Aggregate Child Neglect and Abuse Reporting, 1987 (1989), 6; 1987–1994—National Center on Child Abuse Prevention Research, National Committee to Prevent Child Abuse, Current Trends in Child Abuse Reporting and Fatalities: The Results of the 1996 Annual Fifty State Survey (1997), 5; 1995–2005—U.S. Department of Health and Human Services, Administration for Children and Families, Children's Bureau, Child Maltreatment (annual since 1995), at www.childwelfare.gov.

Note: For the more recent years of data, revisions are anticipated.

Teenage Suicide

	Ages 15-19	Ages 15-24				
		All	White male	White female	Black male	Black female
1970	5.9	8.8	13.9	4.2	10.5	3.8
1971	6.5	9.3	14.4	4.5	9.7	4.8
1972	6.8	10.1	15.4	4.5	14.7	4.7
1973	6.9	10.5	17.3	4.3	12.7	3.3
1974	7.1	10.8	17.6	4.7	11.1	3.4
1975	7.5	11.7	19.3	4.9	12.7	3.2
1976	7.2	11.5	18.9	4.8	13.0	3.7
1977	8.7	13.3	22.4	5.4	13.0	3.7
1978	7.9	12.1	20.4	4.9	13.0	2.7
1979	8.4	12.4	20.5	4.9	14.0	3.3
1980	8.5	12.3	21.4	4.6	12.3	2.3
1981	8.6	12.2	21.1	4.9	11.2	2.4
1982	8.7	12.1	21.2	4.5	11.3	2.3
1983	8.6	11.8	20.4	4.5	11.5	2.7
1984	8.9	12.4	21.8	4.7	11.2	2.4
1985	9.9	12.8	22.3	4.7	13.3	2.0
1986	10.1	12.9	23.1	4.7	11.4	2.3
1987	10.2	12.7	22.2	4.6	12.9	2.5
1988	11.1	12.9	22.7	4.5	14.5	2.6
1989	11.1	13.0	22.5	4.3	16.6	2.9
1990	11.1	13.2	23.2	4.2	15.1	2.3
1991	11.0	13.1	23.0	4.2	16.4	1.6
1992	10.8	13.0	22.7	3.8	18.0	2.2
1993	10.9	13.5	23.1	4.3	20.1	2.7
1994	11.1	13.8	24.1	3.8	20.6	2.7
1995	10.5	13.3	23.5	3.9	18.0	2.2
1996	9.7	12.0	20.9	3.8	16.7	2.3
1997	9.5	11.4	19.5	3.7	16.0	2.4
1998	8.9	11.1	19.3	3.5	15.0	2.2
1999	8.2	10.1	17.5	3.2	14.3	1.9
2000	8.2	10.2	17.9	3.1	14.2	2.2
2001	7.9	9.9	17.6	3.1	13.0	1.3
2002	7.4	9.9	17.7	3.1	11.3	1.7
2003	7.3	9.7	16.9	3.1	12.1	2.0
2004	8.2	10.3	17.9	3.8	12.2	2.2

Suicide rate: Suicides per 100,000 population.

Sources: U.S. Department of Health and Human Services, Centers for Disease Control and Prevention, National Center for Health Statistics, National Vital Statistics System. Suicides ages 15-19: 1970–1978— *Vital Statistics of the United States: Mortality* (annual); 1979–2003—Mortality Tables GMWK292A and GMWKH210R; 2004—Final Mortality Data 2004 (personal communication). Suicides ages 15-24: 1970–2003—Mortality Tables HIST290_6878, HIST290_7998, and GMWK12, at www.cdc. nchs; 2004—Final Mortality Data 2004 (by email).

Teenage Drug Abuse

	Percentage using any illicit drug in past year				
	12th graders	10th graders	8th graders	Ages 12-17	Ages 18-25
1975	45.0				
1976	48.1				
1977	51.1				
1978	53.8				
1979	54.2			24.3	45.5
1980	53.1				
1981	52.1				
1982	49.4				
1983	47.4				
1984	45.8				
1985	46.3			20.7	37.4
1986	44.3				
1987	41.7				
1988	38.5			14.9	29.1
1989	35.4				
1990	32.5			14.1	26.1
1991	29.4	21.4	11.3	13.1	26.6
1992	27.1	20.4	12.9	10.4	24.1
1993	31.0	24.7	15.1	11.9	24.2
1994	35.8	30.0	18.5	15.5	24.6
1995	39.0	33.3	21.4	18.0	25.5
1996	40.2	37.5	23.6	16.7	26.8
1997	42.4	38.5	22.1	18.8	25.3
1998	41.4	35.0	21.0	16.4	27.4
1999	42.1	35.9	20.5	19.8	29.1
2000	40.9	36.4	19.5	18.6	27.9
2001	41.4	37.2	19.5	20.8	31.9
2002	41.0	34.8	17.7	22.2	35.5
2003	39.3	32.0	16.1	21.8	34.6
2004	38.8	31.1	15.2	21.0	33.9
2005	38.4	29.8	15.5	19.9	34.2

Illicit drug use rate: Persons reporting using any illicit drug, as percentage of population.

Sources: By grade-level: L.D. Johnston, P.M. O'Malley, J.G. Bachman, and J.Schulenberg, Monitoring the Future, *National Survey Results on Drug Use, 1975–2005*, vol. 1 (NIH Publication No. 06-5883, National Institute on Drug Abuse, 2006), Table 5.2, at monitoringthefuture.org. By age group: U.S. Department of Health and Human Services, Substance Abuse and Mental Health Services Administration, Office of Applied Statistics, National Survey on Drug Use and Health (annual), at www.oas.samhsa.gov/WebOnly.htm#NHSDAtabs.

	Status dropouts: Percentage of persons ages 18-24 who have not finished high school and are not enrolled in school						Event dropouts: % of 10th-12th graders dropping out per year
	All	Male	Female	White	Black	Hispanic	All
1970	17.3	16.8	17.8	15.2	33.3		5.7
1971	17.0	16.8	17.2	15.4	28.8		5.4
1972	16.6	16.2	16.9	15.2	26.2	40.4	6.2
1973	15.7	15.3	16.1	14.2	26.5	38.9	6.3
1974	15.9	15.9	15.8	14.5	25.1	37.1	6.7
1975	15.6	15.2	16.0	13.9	27.3	34.9	5.8
1976	15.9	16.2	15.6	14.7	24.2	36.5	5.9
1977	15.8	16.4	15.2	14.7	23.9	38.7	6.5
1978	15.9	16.4	15.3	14.6	24.6	39.2	6.7
1979	16.3	17.1	15.6	14.9	25.5	39.2	6.7
1980	15.6	16.9	14.3	14.4	23.5	40.3	6.0
1981	15.6	17.2	14.1	14.7	21.7	38.5	5.9
1982	15.6	16.5	14.7	14.6	22.0	37.0	5.4
1983	15.4	17.0	13.9	14.3	21.5	37.5	5.2
1984	14.8	15.9	13.7	14.1	18.4	34.2	5.0
1985	13.9	15.3	13.0	13.5	17.6	31.5	5.2
1986	13.9	14.9	12.9	13.4	16.8	34.4	4.3
1987	14.5	15.4	13.5	14.2	17.0	32.8	4.1
1988	14.6	15.6	13.5	14.2	17.7	39.6	4.8
1989	14.4	15.7	13.2	14.1	16.4	37.7	4.5
1990	13.6	13.9	13.3	13.5	15.1	37.3	4.0
1991	14.2	15.0	13.4	14.2	15.6	39.6	4.0
1992	12.7	13.5	11.9	12.2	16.3	33.9	4.3
1993	13.1	13.7	12.5	12.7	16.4	32.8	4.3
1994	13.3	14.4	12.3	12.7	15.5	34.7	5.0
1995	13.9	14.5	13.4	13.6	14.4	34.7	5.4
1996	12.8	13.2	12.3	12.5	16.0	34.5	4.7
1997	13.0	14.1	11.8	12.4	16.7	30.6	4.3
1998	13.9	15.8	12.0	13.7	17.1	34.4	4.4
1999	13.1	14.9	12.1	12.8	16.0	33.9	4.7
2000	12.4	13.8	11.1	12.2	15.3	32.3	4.5
2001	13.0	15.1	11.0	13.4	13.8	31.7	4.7
2002	12.3	14.0	10.6	12.2	14.5	30.1	3.3
2003	11.8	13.7	9.9	11.6	14.2	28.4	3.8
2004	12.1	13.9	10.4	11.9	15.1	28.0	4.4
2005	11.3	13.2	9.5	11.3	12.9	27.3	3.5

Status dropout rate: Percentage of 18- to 24-year-olds who are not enrolled in school and are not high school graduates (diploma or GED).

Event dropout rate: Annual dropouts, as percentage of enrolled students, grades 10 to 12.

Sources: U.S. Department of Commerce, Bureau of the Census, Current Population Survey, School Enrollment Historical Tables. Status dropouts: Table A-5a. Event dropouts: Table A-4. Both at www.census.gov/population www/socdemo/school.html.

Unemployment

			Unemployment rate		
	Total	White	Black	Hispanic	Youth (ages 16-19)
1970	4.9	4.5			15.3
1971	5.9	5.4			16.9
1972	5.6	5.1	10.4		16.2
1973	4.9	4.3	9.4	7.5	14.5
1974	5.6	5.0	10.5	8.1	16.0
1975	8.5	7.8	14.8	12.2	19.9
1976	7.7	7.0	14.0	11.5	19.0
1977	7.1	6.2	14.0	10.1	17.8
1978	6.1	5.2	12.8	9.1	16.4
1979	5.8	5.1	12.3	8.3	16.1
1980	7.1	6.3	14.3	10.1	17.8
1981	7.6	6.7	15.6	10.4	19.6
1982	9.7	8.6	18.9	13.8	23.2
1983	9.6	8.4	19.5	13.7	22.4
1984	7.5	6.5	15.9	10.7	18.9
1985	7.2	6.2	15.1	10.5	18.6
1986	7.0	6.0	14.5	10.6	18.3
1987	6.2	5.3	13.0	8.8	16.9
1988	5.5	4.7	11.7	8.2	15.3
1989	5.3	4.5	11.4	8.0	15.0
1990	5.6	4.8	11.4	8.2	15.5
1991	6.8	6.1	12.5	10.0	18.7
1992	7.5	6.6	14.2	11.6	20.1
1993	6.9	6.1	13.0	10.8	19.0
1994	6.1	5.3	11.5	9.9	17.6
1995	5.6	4.9	10.4	9.3	17.3
1996	5.4	4.7	10.5	8.9	16.7
1997	4.9	4.2	10.0	7.7	16.0
1998	4.5	3.9	8.9	7.2	14.6
1999	4.2	3.7	8.0	6.4	13.9
2000	4.0	3.5	7.6	5.7	13.1
2001	4.7	4.2	8.6	6.6	14.7
2002	5.8	5.1	10.2	7.5	16.5
2003	6.0	5.2	10.8	7.7	17.5
2004	5.5	4.8	10.4	7.0	17.0
2005	5.1	4.4	10.0	6.0	16.6

Unemployment rate: Percentage of civilian labor force unemployed (annual average).

Sources: U.S. Department of Labor, Bureau of Labor Statistics, Historical Data from the *Employment Situation* News Release, Tables A-1, A-2, and A-3, at stats.bls.gov/cps.

Wages

	Average weekly earnings (1982 dollars)	Median annual earnings, year-round full-time workers (2005 dollars)			Value of minimum wage	
		Male	Female	Female as % of male	Current dollars	Constant dollars (2006)
1970	$312.94	$39,036	$23,175	59.4	$1.60	$7.14
1971	318.05	39,181	23,315	59.5	1.60	6.84
1972	331.59	41,258	23,872	57.9	1.60	6.63
1973	331.39	42,573	24,110	56.6	1.60	6.24
1974	314.94	41,080	24,136	58.8	2.00	6.64
1975	305.16	40,800	23,998	58.8	2.10	6.88
1976	309.61	40,694	24,495	60.2	2.30	7.13
1977	310.99	41,582	24,501	58.9	2.30	6.70
1978	310.41	42,877	25,486	59.4	2.65	7.40
1979	298.87	42,393	25,293	59.7	2.90	7.41
1980	281.27	41,763	25,125	60.2	3.10	7.13
1981	277.35	41,558	24,617	59.2	3.35	7.04
1982	272.74	40,819	25,204	61.7	3.35	6.65
1983	277.50	40,685	25,873	63.6	3.35	6.38
1984	279.22	41,515	26,427	63.7	3.35	6.14
1985	276.23	41,866	27,035	64.6	3.35	5.94
1986	276.11	42,919	27,584	64.3	3.35	5.83
1987	272.88	42,638	27,791	65.2	3.35	5.64
1988	270.32	42,266	27,916	66.0	3.35	5.44
1989	267.27	41,552	28,535	68.7	3.35	5.22
1990	262.43	40,086	28,708	71.6	3.80	5.48
1991	258.34	41,123	28,728	69.9	4.25	5.93
1992	257.95	41,175	29,146	70.8	4.25	5.94
1993	258.12	40,453	28,932	71.5	4.25	5.80
1994	259.97	40,201	28,932	72.0	4.25	5.68
1995	258.43	40,064	28,617	71.4	4.25	5.54
1996	259.58	39,819	29,371	73.8	4.75	5.56
1997	265.22	40,843	30,289	74.2	5.15	6.07
1998	271.87	42,274	30,932	73.2	5.15	6.31
1999	274.64	42,629	30,827	72.3	5.15	6.18
2000	275.62	42,228	31,130	73.7	5.15	5.98
2001	275.38	42,209	32,218	76.3	5.15	5.82
2002	278.83	42,801	32,786	76.6	5.15	5.73
2003	278.72	43,158	32,605	75.5	5.15	5.60
2004	277.61	42,160	32,285	76.6	5.15	5.46
2005	275.93	41,386	31,858	77.0	5.15	5.28

Average weekly earnings: production and nonsupervisory workers, private nonagricultural employment.

Sources: Average weekly earnings: *Economic Report of the President 2007* (Feb. 2007), Table B-47. Male and female annual median income, year-round full-time workers: U.S. Department of Commerce, Bureau of the Census, *Income, Poverty, and Health Insurance 2005* (Aug. 2006), Table A-2, at www. census.gov. Minimum wage, current dollars: 1970–2006—U.S. Department of Commerce, Bureau of the Census, *Statistical Abstract 2007,* Table 633, at www.census.gov/compendia/statab; Minimum wage, constant 2006 dollars: Economic Policy Institute, *EPI Issue Guide: Minimum Wage,* Table 4, at www.epi.org.

Health Insurance Coverage

	Number of uninsured (millions)	Uninsured, as percentage of population			
		All	White*	Black	Hispanic
1976	23.2	10.9			
1977	23.8	11.1			
1978	24.3	11.3			
1979	24.4	11.0			
1980	24.6	10.9			
1981	27.1	12.0			
1982	28.9	12.6			
1983	30.6	13.2			
1984	31.9	13.7			
1985	32.6	13.8			
1986	31.9	13.7			
1987	31.0	12.9	9.8	19.9	30.7
1988	32.7	13.4	10.2	19.6	31.8
1989	33.4	13.6	10.3	19.2	33.4
1990	34.7	13.9	10.7	19.7	32.5
1991	35.4	14.1	10.8	20.7	31.5
1992	38.6	15.0	11.5	20.2	32.9
1993	39.7	15.3	11.9	20.5	31.6
1994	39.7	15.2	11.5	19.7	33.7
1995	40.6	15.4	11.5	21.0	33.3
1996	41.7	15.6	11.5	21.7	33.6
1997	43.4	16.1	12.0	21.5	34.2
1998	44.3	16.3	11.9	22.2	35.3
1999	40.2	14.5	11.0	19.8	33.0
2000	39.8	14.2	9.6	18.8	32.9
2001	41.2	14.6	10.0	19.0	33.2
2002	43.6	15.2	10.7	20.2	32.4
2003	45.0	15.6	11.1	19.6	32.7
2004	45.3	15.6	11.2	19.3	32.3
2005	46.6	15.9	11.3	19.6	32.7

Uninsured: Percentage of population with no health insurance.

Sources: 1976–1986—Estimates are based on published and unpublished data from the Center for National Health Program Studies at Harvard Medical School, based on data from the U.S. Department of Commerce, Bureau of the Census, Current Population Survey, and the National Health Interview Survey. 1987–2005—U.S. Department of Commerce, Bureau of the Census, *Income, Poverty, and Health Insurance Coverage in the United States: 2005* (August 2006), Table C-1, 60, at www.census.gov.

*White non-Hispanic

Note: The U.S. Census Bureau is currently revising these data back to 1995. The new data will be incorporated into the Index when the full ten-year revision is released in August 2007.

Poverty, Ages 65 and Over

	Percentage, ages 65 and over, living in poverty				Percentage, ages 65 and over, living below 125 percent of poverty
	Total	White	Black	Hispanic	
1970	24.6	22.6	48.0		
1971	21.6	19.9	39.3		
1972	18.6	16.8	39.9		
1973	16.3	14.4	37.1	24.9	
1974	14.6	12.8	34.3	28.9	
1975	15.3	13.4	36.3	32.6	25.4
1976	15.0	13.2	34.8	27.7	25.0
1977	14.1	11.9	36.3	21.9	24.5
1978	14.0	12.1	33.9	23.2	23.4
1979	15.2	13.3	36.2	26.8	24.7
1980	15.7	13.6	38.1	30.8	25.7
1981	15.3	13.1	39.0	25.7	25.2
1982	14.6	12.4	38.2	26.6	23.7
1983	13.8	11.7	36.0	22.1	22.0
1984	12.4	10.7	31.7	21.5	21.2
1985	12.6	11.0	31.5	23.9	20.9
1986	12.4	10.7	31.0	22.5	20.5
1987	12.5	10.6	32.4	27.5	20.2
1988	12.0	10.0	32.2	22.4	20.0
1989	11.4	9.6	30.7	20.6	19.1
1990	12.2	10.1	33.8	22.5	19.0
1991	12.4	10.3	33.8	20.8	19.7
1992	12.9	11.0	33.5	22.1	20.5
1993	12.2	10.7	28.0	21.4	19.7
1994	11.7	10.2	27.4	22.6	18.7
1995	10.5	9.0	25.4	23.5	17.7
1996	10.8	9.4	25.3	24.4	18.4
1997	10.5	9.0	26.0	23.8	17.0
1998	10.5	8.9	26.4	21.0	16.8
1999	9.7	8.3	22.8	20.5	15.7
2000	9.9	8.7	21.8	20.9	16.7
2001	10.1	8.9	21.9	21.8	16.6
2002	10.4	9.1	23.8	21.4	16.9
2003	10.2	8.8	23.7	19.5	16.9
2004	9.8	8.3	23.8	18.4	16.5
2005	10.1	8.7	23.3	19.9	16.7

Poverty rate, ages 65 and over: Percentage of persons ages 65 and over with incomes below the poverty line.

Source: U.S. Department of Commerce, Bureau of the Census, Current Population Survey, Historical Poverty Tables, Tables 3 and 12, at www.census.gov.

Out-of-Pocket Health Costs, Ages 65 and Over

	Householders, ages 65 and over		
	Median household income	Average out-of-pocket health costs	Percentage of income spent on health care
1973	$ 4,583	$ 507	11.1
1982	11,041	1,237	11.2
1983	11,718	1,336	11.4
1984	12,799	1,493	11.7
1985	13,254	1,652	12.5
1986	13,845	1,720	12.4
1987	14,443	1,650	11.4
1988	14,923	2,099	14.1
1989	15,771	2,135	13.5
1990	16,855	2,208	13.1
1991	16,975	2,257	13.3
1992	17,135	2,474	14.4
1993	17,751	2,733	15.4
1994	18,095	2,678	14.8
1995	19,096	2,648	13.9
1996	19,448	2,759	14.2
1997	20,761	2,855	13.8
1998	21,729	2,936	13.5
1999	22,797	3,019	13.2
2000	23,083	3,247	14.1
2001	23,118	3,493	15.1
2002	23,152	3,586	15.5
2003	23,787	3,741	15.7
2004	24,516	3,899	15.9
2005	26,036	4,193	16.1

Out-of-pocket health costs: Expenditures for health insurance, medical services, drugs, and medical supplies.

Sources: Median household income before taxes: U.S. Department of Commerce, Bureau of the Census, Current Population Survey, Historical Income Tables, Table H-10, at www.census.gov/hhes/www/income.html. Health-care expenditures: U.S. Department of Labor, Bureau of Labor Statistics, Consumer Expenditure Survey, at stats.bls.gov/cex/home.htm. Calculations by the Institute.

Homicides

		Rate per 100,000 population				
		Victims of homicide				All violent
	Homicides	Male	Female	White	Black	crime
1970	7.9					363.5
1971	8.6					396.0
1972	9.0					401.0
1973	9.4					417.4
1974	9.8					461.1
1975	9.6					487.8
1976	8.8	13.6	4.2	5.1	37.1	467.8
1977	8.8	13.7	4.2	5.4	36.2	475.9
1978	9.0	14.0	4.1	5.6	35.1	497.8
1979	9.7	15.4	4.4	6.1	37.5	548.9
1980	10.2	16.2	4.5	6.3	37.7	596.6
1981	9.8	15.6	4.3	6.2	36.4	594.3
1982	9.1	14.1	4.3	5.9	32.3	571.1
1983	8.3	12.8	3.9	5.3	29.4	537.7
1984	7.9	12.1	3.9	5.2	27.2	539.9
1985	7.9	12.2	4.0	5.2	27.6	558.1
1986	8.6	13.2	4.1	5.4	31.5	620.1
1987	8.3	12.6	4.2	5.1	30.7	612.5
1988	8.5	12.9	4.2	4.9	33.5	640.6
1989	8.7	13.6	4.0	5.0	35.1	666.9
1990	9.4	15.0	4.0	5.4	37.6	729.6
1991	9.8	15.7	4.2	5.5	39.3	758.2
1992	9.3	14.9	4.0	5.3	37.2	757.7
1993	9.5	15.0	4.2	5.3	38.7	747.1
1994	9.0	14.4	3.8	5.0	36.4	713.6
1995	8.2	12.9	3.7	4.8	31.6	684.5
1996	7.4	11.7	3.3	4.3	28.3	636.6
1997	6.8	10.7	3.0	3.9	26.0	611.0
1998	6.3	9.7	3.0	3.8	23.0	567.6
1999	5.7	8.8	2.7	3.5	20.5	523.0
2000	5.5	8.6	2.6	3.3	20.5	506.5
2001	5.6	8.8	2.6	3.4	20.4	504.5
2002	5.6	8.8	2.6	3.3	20.8	494.4
2003	5.7	9.0	2.5	3.4	20.9	475.8
2004	5.5	8.7	2.4	3.3	19.7	463.2
2005	5.6					469.2

Homicide: Murder and non-negligent manslaughter.

Sources: Homicide and violent crime rates: Federal Bureau of Investigation, Uniform Crime Reports. 1970–1972— *Crime in the United States 1979* (1980); 1973–1976—*Crime in the United States 1991* (1992); 1977–1984—*Crime in the United States 1996* (1997); 1985–2005—*Crime in the United States 2005* (2006), at www.fbi.gov/ucr/ucr.htm. Homicide victimization rates: Federal Bureau of Investigation, *Supplementary Homicide Reports, 1976-2004*, at www.ojp.usdoj.gov/bjs.

Alcohol-Related Traffic Fatalities

	Total traffic fatalities	Fatal Accident Reporting System: National Highway Traffic Safety Administration (NHTSA)		Alcohol Epidemiological Data System: National Institute of Alcohol Abuse and Alcoholism (NIAAA)	
		Alcohol-related traffic fatalities (driver, pedestrian, and/or cyclist)		Alcohol-related traffic fatalities (driver only)	
		Number	Percentage of total fatalities	Number	Percentage of total fatalities
1977	47,715			17,414	36.5
1978	50,327			18,362	36.5
1979	51,084			20,245	39.6
1980	51,077			21,114	41.3
1981	49,268			20,662	41.9
1982	43,945	26,173	60	18,622	42.6
1983	42,589	24,635	58	17,847	41.9
1984	44,257	24,762	56	18,523	41.9
1985	43,825	23,167	53	18,040	41.2
1986	46,087	25,017	54	20,038	43.5
1987	46,390	24,094	52	19,918	42.9
1988	47,087	23,833	51	19,303	41.0
1989	45,582	22,424	49	18,381	40.3
1990	44,599	22,587	51	18,279	41.0
1991	41,508	20,159	49	16,231	39.1
1992	39,250	18,290	47	14,684	37.4
1993	40,150	17,908	45	14,225	35.5
1994	40,716	17,308	43	13,693	33.6
1995	41,817	17,732	42	13,881	33.2
1996	42,065	17,749	42	13,557	32.4
1997	42,013	16,711	40	12,870	30.6
1998	41,501	16,673	40	12,663	30.5
1999	41,717	16,572	40	12,547	30.1
2000	41,945	17,380	41	13,050	31.1
2001	42,196	17,400	41	12,864	30.5
2002	43,005	17,524	41	13,068	30.5
2003	42,884	17,105	40	12,766	29.9
2004	42,836	16,919	39	16,919*	39.5*
2005	43,443	16,885	39		

Alcohol-related: Blood-alcohol level of .01 or higher.

Sources: Total traffic fatalities and alcohol-related fatalities (NIAAA): 1977–2004—National Institute for Alcohol Abuse and Alcoholism, Alcohol Epidemiologic System, *Surveillance Report #71* (Aug. 2005), Table 1, and Surveillance Report #76 (August 2006), Table 1, at www.niaaa.nih.gov. Alcohol-related traffic fatalities (NHTSA): 1982–2005—National Highway Traffic Safety Administration, Fatal Accident Reporting System, National Center for Statistics and Analysis, *Traffic Safety Facts 2005: A Compilation of Motor Vehicle Crash Data from the Fatality Analysis Reporting System* (Jan. 2007), Table 13, at www-nrd.nhtsa.dot.gov.

* Starting with 2004 data, NIAAA, like NHTSA, includes the alcohol involvement of pedestrians and/or cyclists in its definition of alcohol-related crashes.

Food Stamp Coverage

	Participation in Food Stamp Program		Percentage of households that are food insecure
	All participants, as percentage of poor population	Poor participants, as percentage of poor population	
1975	63.0		
1976	68.1		
1977	63.1		
1978	58.8		
1979	61.0		
1980	65.6		
1981	64.7		
1982	59.3		
1983	61.2		
1984	62.0		
1985	60.2		
1986	59.9		
1987	59.1		
1988	58.9	47.0	
1989	59.6	47.0	
1990	59.6	48.8	
1991	63.3	50.2	
1992	68.9	51.5	
1993	68.7	51.9	
1994	72.1	50.8	
1995	73.0	48.9	
1996	69.8	46.9	
1997		43.6	
1998		39.0	
1999		36.6	10.1
2000		33.8	10.5
2001		33.6	10.7
2002		32.9	11.1
2003		35.5	11.2
2004		36.2	11.9
2005			11.0

Food insecure: Families that are uncertain of having, or are unable to acquire, enough food for all the members of their households.

Sources: Total food stamp participation, as percentage of poor population: *The Green Book: Background Material and Data on Programs Within the Jurisdiction of the Committee on Ways and Means,* U.S. House of Representatives (2000). Food stamp participation by the poor, as percentage of poor population—1988–1999—Center on Budget and Policy Priorities, *Poverty and Income Trends, 1999: Program Participation Status of Poor Households* (1999); 2000–2004—U.S. Department of Commerce, Bureau of the Census, Current Population Survey, Detailed Poverty Tables, Table POV 26, at www.census.gov. Food insecurity: U.S. Department of Agriculture, Economic Research Service, Mark Nord, Margaret Andrews, and Steven Carlson, *Household Food Security in the United States,* 2005 (Nov. 2006), Section 1, Table 1B, at www.ers.usda.gov.

	Housing Affordability Index		Housing cost-burden (Percentage of households paying more than 30 percent of their income for housing)		
	All buyers	First-time buyers	All households	Owner households	Renter households
1970	147.3				
1971	151.9				
1972	154.8				
1973	147.9				
1974	130.3				
1975	123.5				
1976	125.8				
1977	120.6				
1978	111.4		17.3	31.3	8.1
1979	97.2				
1980	79.9				
1981	68.9	50.7			
1982	69.5	50.6			
1983	83.2	59.4			
1984	89.1	64.9			
1985	94.8	68.3			
1986	108.9	75.6			
1987	114.2	79.0	23.5	38.1	15.2
1988	113.5	77.7			
1989	106.4	70.8			
1990	107.5	71.6			
1991	110.3	73.3	24.8	37.3	17.8
1992	121.7	80.8			
1993	130.5	86.6	25.4	39.2	17.9
1994	127.6	84.7			
1995	125.0	82.9	27.2	40.0	20.4
1996	125.9	83.5			
1997	126.5	83.8	27.5	39.6	21.2
1998	133.2	88.3			
1999	130.9	86.9	27.2	39.5	21.2
2000	121.9	80.9			
2001	128.1	84.9	28.7	39.5	23.6
2002	126.4	83.7			
2003	130.7	86.4	29.4	41.5	23.7
2004	123.9	82.0			
2005	111.8	74.0	32.9	45.3	27.3

Housing Affordability Index for All Buyers and First-Time Buyers: One-quarter of median family income (all families or first-time buyers), as percentage of the funds necessary to qualify for an 80 percent mortgage on a median-price home.

Sources: Housing Affordability Index, 1970–2005, and First-Time Housing Affordability Index, 1981–2005: National Association of Realtors, Realtor Research, unpublished data. Cost-burden: U.S. Department of Housing and Urban Development, *Affordable Housing Needs: A Report to Congress on the Significant Need for Housing* (December 2006, May 2007), Table A-2b, at www.huduser.org.

Income Inequality

	Gini Coefficient	Shares of aggregate household income received by:		
		Top fifth	Middle three-fifths	Bottom fifth
1970	0.394	43.3	52.6	4.1
1971	0.396	43.5	52.4	4.1
1972	0.401	43.9	51.9	4.1
1973	0.400	43.9	51.9	4.2
1974	0.395	43.5	52.2	4.3
1975	0.397	43.6	52.1	4.3
1976	0.398	43.7	52.0	4.3
1977	0.402	44.0	51.8	4.2
1978	0.402	44.1	51.7	4.2
1979	0.404	44.2	51.6	4.1
1980	0.403	44.1	51.7	4.2
1981	0.406	44.3	51.6	4.1
1982	0.412	45.0	51.0	4.0
1983	0.414	45.1	50.9	4.0
1984	0.415	45.2	50.8	4.0
1985	0.419	45.6	50.4	3.9
1986	0.425	46.1	50.2	3.8
1987	0.426	46.2	50.0	3.8
1988	0.426	46.3	49.8	3.8
1989	0.431	46.8	49.3	3.8
1990	0.428	46.6	49.5	3.8
1991	0.428	46.5	49.7	3.8
1992	0.433	46.9	49.4	3.8
1993	0.454	48.9	47.6	3.6
1994	0.456	49.1	47.3	3.6
1995	0.450	48.7	47.6	3.7
1996	0.455	49.0	47.4	3.6
1997	0.459	49.4	47.1	3.6
1998	0.456	49.2	47.2	3.6
1999	0.458	49.4	47.0	3.6
2000	0.462	49.8	46.7	3.6
2001	0.466	50.1	46.3	3.5
2002	0.462	49.7	46.9	3.5
2003	0.464	49.8	46.9	3.4
2004	0.466	50.1	46.6	3.4
2005	0.469	50.4	46.2	3.4

Gini coefficient: Measure of the income shares received by households at various levels of the income distribution; ranges from 0 (total equality) to 1 (total inequality).

Source: U.S. Department of Commerce, Bureau of the Census, *Income, Poverty, and Health Insurance Coverage 2005* (Aug. 2006), Table A-3, at www/census.gov/hhes.

Appendix B
Technical Note on the Index of Social Health

The Index of Social Health was designed by Marc L. Miringoff, Marque-Luisa Miringoff, and Sandra Opdycke in 1985–1986, and has been released annually since 1987. It consists of the following indicators:

> Children
>> Infant mortality
>> Child poverty
>> Child abuse

> Youth
>> Teenage suicide
>> Teenage drug abuse
>> High school dropouts

> Adults
>> Unemployment
>> Wages
>> Health insurance coverage

> The Elderly
>> Poverty, ages 65 and over
>> Out-of-pocket health costs, ages 65 and over

> All Ages
>> Homicides
>> Alcohol-related traffic fatalities
>> Food stamp coverage
>> Affordable housing
>> Income inequality

The sixteen indicators were selected based on the following guidelines:

- They have been measured reliably and consistently over time by government or recognized private research organizations. All of the indicators included have been documented on a systematic basis for an extended period of time.

- They represent a distribution over the age spectrum. The chosen indicators reflect conditions of children, youth, adults, the elderly, and some that affect all age groups.

- They reflect a balance between social and socioeconomic dimensions. The selected indicators address social concerns such as health, education, and public safety, as well as issues of socioeconomic well-being such as poverty, wages, and unemployment.

- They address issues that have long been at the center of public concern and policy debate, and are monitored consistently by government or leading research organizations because of their significance to the nation.

- They have been studied in sufficient depth over time to make possible an assessment of their performance in terms of race, ethnicity, gender, age, class, and other relevant demographic categories.

- They are indicators that have undergone significant change over time and thus merit systematic monitoring.

A single index score is calculated for each year, based on rating each indicator's performance that year against its best recorded performance since 1970. For example, the best (or lowest) child poverty rate between 1970 and 2005 was the 14.2 percent achieved in 1973. That becomes the indicator's standard, and would be scored 10 on a 0-10 scale. To calculate the overall Index for a given year, the scores for all sixteen indicators are totaled, and expressed as a percentage of the best possible score (a 10 on every indicator). Each year's index is computed in that way, making it possible to track the nation's social performance over time.

A more detailed description of the index methodology can be found in the following article prepared by Institute staff: Marc Miringoff, Marque-Luisa Miringoff, and Sandra Opdycke, "Monitoring the Nation's Social Performance: The Index of Social Health," in *Children, Families, and Government: Preparing for the Twenty-First Century,* ed. Edward Zigler, Sharon Lynn Kagan, and Nancy W. Hall (Cambridge University Press, 1996).

The Index of Social Health is revised periodically, as new or revised data become available. For the most current version of the Index, see the Institute website, at iisp. vassar.edu. As this book went to print, the numbers for the Index (1970–2005) were as follows:

1970	65.7	1988	48.4
1971	65.4	1989	49.3
1972	67.5	1990	48.5
1973	69.6	1991	46.4
1974	66.5	1992	46.6
1975	60.8	1993	43.2
1976	64.9	1994	45.1
1977	61.3	1995	48.9
1978	60.5	1996	50.7
1979	55.3	1997	52.5
1980	50.2	1998	54.0
1981	46.6	1999	59.6
1982	41.6	2000	60.0
1983	44.2	2001	56.4
1984	48.8	2002	54.9
1985	48.5	2003	54.8
1986	48.1	2004	53.5
1987	51.6	2005	53.2

Sources

Infant mortality. Deaths in first year of life, per 1,000 live births: 1970, 1975–2002––U.S. Centers for Disease Control, National Center for Health Statistics, National Vital Statistics System, Kenneth D. Kochanek and Joyce Martin, "Supplemental Analyses of Recent Trends in Infant Mortality" (2004), Table 1; 1971–1974—U.S. Department of Health and Human Services, *Vital Statistics of the United States 1992,* vol. 2, Mortality, Part A (Washington, D.C.), Table *2-2; 2003–2004—E-Stats Deaths: Final Data for 2004,* Table 1. At www.cdc.nchs.

Child poverty. Percentage of related children under age 18 in families with incomes below the poverty line: 1970–2005—U.S. Department of Commerce, Bureau of the Census, Current Population Survey, Historical Poverty Tables, Table 3, at www.census.gov.

Child abuse. Number of children involved in abuse/neglect reports per 1,000 population ages 0-18: 1976-1986—American Association for Protecting Children, American Humane Association, *Highlights of Official Aggregate Child Neglect and Abuse Reporting, 1987* (1989), 6; 1987–1994—National Center on Child Abuse

Prevention Research, National Committee to Prevent Child Abuse, Current Trends in Child Abuse Reporting and Fatalities: The Results of the 1996 Annual Fifty State Survey (1997), 5; 1995-2005—U.S. Department of Health and Human Services, Administration for Children and Families, Children's Bureau, Child Maltreatment (annual since 1995), at www.childwelfare.gov.

Teenage suicide. Suicides per 100,000 population ages 15-19: U.S. Centers for Disease Control and Prevention, National Center for Health Statistics, National Vital Statistics System. 1970-1978—*Vital Statistics of the United States: Mortality* (annual); 1979-2003—Mortality Tables GMWK292A and GMWKH210R at www.cdc.nchs; 2004—Final Mortality Data 2004 (by email).

Teenage drug abuse. Percentage of twelfth graders using any illicit drug in past year, 1975-2005—L.D. Johnston, P.M. O'Malley, J.G. Bachman, and J. Schulenberg, Monitoring the Future, *National Survey Results on Drug Use, 1975-2005*, vol. 1: Secondary School Students (NIH Publication No. 06-5883, National Institute on Drug Abuse, 2006), Table 5.2, at monitoringthefuture.org.

High school dropouts. Percentage of 18- to 24-year-olds who are not enrolled in school and are not high school graduates (diploma or GED): 1970-2005—U.S. Department of Commerce, Bureau of the Census, Current Population Survey Reports, School Enrollment. Historical Tables, Table A-5a., at www.census.gov/population/www/socdemo/school.html.

Unemployment. Percentage of civilian labor force unemployed (annual average): 1970-2005—U.S. Department of Labor, Bureau of Labor Statistics, Historical Data from the *Employment Situation* News Release, Tables A-1, at stats.bls.gov/cps.

Wages. Average weekly earnings, production and nonsupervisory workers, private nonagricultural employment: 1970-2005—*Economic Report of the President* (Feb. 2007), Table B-47.

Health insurance coverage. Percentage of population with no health insurance: 1976-1986—Estimates are based on published and unpublished data from The Center for National Health Program Studies at Harvard Medical School, based on data from the U.S. Department of Commerce, Bureau of the Census, Current Population Survey, and the National Health Interview Survey. 1987-2005 —— U.S.

Department of Commerce, Bureau of the Census, *Income, Poverty, and Health Insurance Coverage in the United States: 2005* (August 2006), Table C-1, 60, at www.census.gov. The U.S. Census Bureau is currently revising these data back to 1995. The new data will be incorporated into the Index when the full ten-year revision is released in August 2007.

Poverty, ages 65 and over. Percentage of population ages 65 and over with incomes below the poverty line: U.S. Department of Commerce, Bureau of the Census, Current Population Survey, Historical Poverty Tables, Table 3, at www.census.gov.

Out-of-pocket health costs, ages 65 and over. Expenditures for health insurance, medical services, drugs, and medical supplies by elderly households, as percentage of income: Expenditures: U.S. Department of Labor, Bureau of Labor Statistics, Consumer Expenditure Survey. stats.bls.gov/cex/home.htm. Median household income before taxes: U.S. Department of Commerce, Bureau of the Census, Current Population Survey, at www.census.gov/hhes/www/income.html. Calculations by the Institute.

Homicides. Murder and non-negligent manslaughter per 100,000 population: Homicide and violent crime rates: Federal Bureau of Investigation, Uniform Crime Reports. 1970-1972—*Crime in the United States 1979* (1980); 1973-1976—*Crime in the United States 1991* (1992); 1977-1984—*Crime in the United States 1996* (1997); 1985-2005—*Crime in the United States 2005* (2006), at www.fbi.gov/ucr/ucr. htm.

Alcohol-related traffic fatalities. Deaths in alcohol-related crashes (driver, pedestrian, and/or cyclist had blood-alcohol level of .01 or higher), as percentage of all traffic fatalities: 1977-1981 – Estimates based on data from National Institute for Alcohol Abuse and Alcoholism, Alcohol Epidemiologic System, Hsiao-ye Yi, Gerald D. Williams, and Michael E. Hilton, *Surveillance Report #71: Trends in Alcohol-Related Fatal Traffic Crashes, United States, 1977-2003* (Aug. 2005), Table 1, at www.niaa.nih.gov, and U.S. Department of Transportation, National Highway Traffic Safety Administration, Fatal Accident Reporting System, National Center for Statistics and Analysis, *Traffic Safety Facts 2005: A Compilation of Motor Vehicle Crash Data from the Fatality Analysis Reporting System* (Jan. 2007), Table 13, at www-nrd.nhtsa.dot.gov; calculations by the Institute. 1982-2005 — National Highway Traffic Safety Administration, *Traffic Safety Facts 2005*, Table 13, at www-nrd.nhtsa.dot.gov.

Food stamp coverage. Food stamp participation by the poor, as a percentage of poor population: 1975-1987—Estimates based on data from *The Green Book: Background Material and Data on Programs Within the Jurisdiction of the Committee on Ways and Means*, U.S. House of Representatives, Washington, D.C., 2000, and Center on Budget and Policy Priorities, *Poverty and Income Trends, 1999: Program Participation Status of Poor Households* (1999); 1988-1999—Center on Budget and Policy Priorities, *Poverty and Income Trends, 1999*; 2000-2004—U.S. Department of Commerce, Bureau of the Census, Current Population Survey, Detailed Poverty Tables, Table POV 26, at www.census.gov.

Affordable housing. Housing Affordability Index (one-quarter of median family income, as percentage of the funds necessary to qualify for an 80 percent mortgage on a median-price home): 1970-2005—National Association of Realtors, Realtor Research, unpublished data; see also monthly postings of Housing Affordability Index, at www.realtor.org/Research.nsf/Pages/HousingInx.

Income inequality. Gini coefficient: 1970–2005—U.S. Department of Commerce, Bureau of the Census, *Income, Poverty, and Health Insurance Coverage 2005* (Aug. 2006), Table A-3, at www.census.gov.

Note: Missing years are projected based on available data.

Appendix C
Technical Note on the National Survey of Social Health

The National Survey of Social Health evolved from two major projects undertaken by the Institute for Innovation in Social Policy. The first was the Working Group on Social Indicators sponsored by the Ford Foundation; the second was the Working Group on the Arts and Humanities sponsored by the Rockefeller Foundation.

The Working Group on Social Indicators met over a two-year period, from 1997 to 1998, to consider how to advance the field of social reporting and social indicators. Participants included twenty-two members from a diverse array of fields, including medicine, economics, education, law, sociology, psychology, demography, and public health. In the course of their deliberations, participants affirmed the need for a national social survey and proposed indicators in areas such as work, income, and health.

At the same time, at the request of the Rockefeller Foundation, the Institute organized a second two-year working group, on the topic of the Arts and Humanities. Meeting from 1998 to 1999, this working group included artists, philosophers, and representatives from the humanities. The group further advanced the notion of a national social survey by proposing a set of key indicators designed to assess the contributions of creativity and culture to the social health of the nation.

Building on this work, Institute staff designed the National Survey on Social Health. It was pre-tested in Philadelphia with funding from the John S. and James L. Knight Foundation, and then administered nationwide in 2000, with the support of the Ford and Rockefeller Foundations. The survey has been administered twice since then, in 2002 and 2004, with the support of the Nathan Cummings Foundation and the Rockefeller Foundation.

The latest edition of the National Survey of Social Health was conducted by Quinley Research and fielded in April 2004. The full survey had 1,601 respondents, with subsections having smaller samples. The section on arts and culture had 801 respondents and a margin of error of +/− 3.1 percent. Data were weighted by age, education, marital status, gender, race, ethnicity, and region to achieve a nationally representative sample.

Detailed Results of the National Survey of Social Health

Numbers represent percentages.
Figures may not add up to 100 because of rounding.
Groupings of response categories presented in the text may differ slightly because of rounding.

Key Deficits: Income, Health Care, and Safety

Income

During the past 12 months:

Had to cut down on some important food items, such as cereal, meat, fresh fruit, or vegetables, because of their high cost.
Yes 32; No 68; Not sure 1.

Had to work extra hours or an extra job in order to make ends meet.
Yes 39; No 60; Not sure <1.

Sometimes found their rent, mortgage, or utilities were difficult to pay, because of the pressures of other needs.
Yes 42; No 58; Not sure <1.

Expect retirement income will be sufficient to cover needs and allow a good quality of life?
Will not cover needs 54; Will cover needs 39; Not sure 7.

Think it is very easy / fairly easy / fairly hard / or very hard for average Americans to provide for themselves and their families today.
Very easy 5; Fairly easy 19; Fairly hard 43; Very hard 31; Not sure 1.
[Pie chart based on those answering.]

Health Care

During the past 12 months:

Did not get medical care because could not afford it or because it would have been too difficult to get.
Yes 23; No 77; Not sure 1.

Worried about paying for the cost of medications.
Yes 34; No 65; Not sure 1.

Worried about paying for the cost of dental care.
Yes 37; No 63; Not sure <1.

Worried they would not be able to cover health-care costs.
Yes 38; No 61; Not sure 1.

Sometimes felt rushed, as if the doctor was watching the clock.
Strongly agree 26; Somewhat agree 23; Somewhat disagree 19; Strongly disagree 30; Not sure 2.

Sometimes felt treated like just a number, not a person.

Strongly agree 25; Somewhat agree 25; Somewhat disagree 22; Strongly disagree 25; Not sure 3.

Sometimes not quite clear about something the doctor said.

Strongly agree 19; Somewhat agree 29; Somewhat disagree 19; Strongly disagree 31; Not sure 2.

Considered changing doctor or health-care provider because dissatisfied with some aspect of treatment,

Yes 29; No 70; Not sure 1.

Safety

During the past 12 months:

Decided not to go somewhere at night because of concerns over safety.

Yes 34; No 66; Not sure <1. *Male:* Yes 22; No 78; Not sure 0. *Female:* Yes 45; No 54; Not sure 1. *Income:* <$35,000 Yes: 47; No 52; Not sure 1. $35,000-50,000 Yes 30; No 70; Not sure 0. $50,000-75,000 Yes 25; No 74; Not sure 1. $75,000+ Yes 24; No 76; Not sure 0. *Education:* H.S. or less Yes 39; No 61; Not sure <1. Some college Yes 33; No 66; Not sure 1. College graduate + Yes 24; No 75; Not sure <1. *Race and ethnicity:* Hispanic Yes 39; No 61; Not sure 0. Black Yes 39; No 61; Not sure 0. White Yes 33; No 67; Not sure 1.

Worried about the safety of family and friends.

Strongly agree 38; Somewhat agree 27; Somewhat disagree 13; Strongly disagree 21; Not sure <1.

Generally felt uneasy opening the door to strangers.

Strongly agree 45; Somewhat agree 24; Somewhat disagree 17; Strongly disagree 13; Not sure 1.

Generally kept doors locked when at home.

Strongly agree 64; Somewhat agree 12; Somewhat disagree 14; Strongly disagree 10; Not sure <1.

Key Assets: Arts and Culture

The Significance of Arts and Culture

How important is it to you that your child be involved in the arts?

Very important 44; Fairly important 40; Not very important 13; Not important at all 1; Not sure 2.

How important to your child is:

Reading?

Very important 58; Fairly important 23; Not very important 13; Not important at all 4; Not sure 2.

Doing creative work?

> Very important 51; Fairly important 33; Not very important 14; Not important at all 1; Not sure <1.

Listening to music?

> Very important 50; Fairly important 31; Not very important 15; Not important at all 4; Not sure 1.

Do you sometimes wish you had had more chance to go to artistic events or live performances when you were young?

> Yes, very much 37; Yes, somewhat 29; Just a little 12; Not at all 21; Not sure 1.

Do you sometimes wish you had had more chance to do creative work when you were young?

> Yes, very much 38; Yes, somewhat 25; Just a little 13; Not at all 23; Not sure 1.

During the past twelve months, how often have you had a discussion with someone about...
Your own creative work?

> Very often 32; Fairly often 32; Not very often 26; Not at all 9; Not sure <1.

A movie?

> Very often 29; Fairly often 34; Not very often 18; Not at all 20; Not sure 0.

A book, a poem, or a story?

> Very often 27; Fairly often 25; Not very often 24; Not at all 23; Not sure <1.

A musical performance, live or recorded?

> Very often 19; Fairly often 26; Not very often 27; Not at all 28; Not sure 0.

A play or other dramatic performance?

> Very often 8; Fairly often 17; Not very often 32; Not at all 43; Not sure 0.

An art show or work of art?

> Very often 6; Fairly often 12; Not very often 32; Not at all 49; Not sure 0.

Arts Participation

Approximately how often during the past twelve months have you...
Listened to music at home?

> Very often 58; Fairly often 19; Not very often 14; Not at all 8; Not sure 0. *2002 survey:* Very often 68; Fairly often 18; Not very often 10; Not at all 3; Not sure 0.

Read any books just for pleasure?

> Very often 31; Fairly often 26; Not very often 21; Not at all 22; Not sure <1. *2002 survey:* Very often 32; Fairly often 21; Not very often 25; Not at all 21; Not sure <1.

Done any creative work yourself?

> Very often 32; Fairly often 27; Not very often 14; Not at all 26; Not sure <1. *2002 survey:* Very often 33; Fairly often 28; Not very often 21; Not at all 19; Not sure <1.

Been to the movies?

Very often 7; Fairly often 14; Not very often 45; Not at all 33; Not sure <1. *2002 survey:* Very often 15; Fairly often 22; Not very often 32; Not at all 32; Not sure <1.

Attended any live performances?

Very often 7; Fairly often 15; Not very often 33; Not at all 45; Not sure 1. *2002 survey:* Very often 9; Fairly often 22; Not very often 33; Not at all 36; Not sure 0.

Went to art shows or museums?

Very often 4; Fairly often 11; Not very often 26; Not at all 59; Not sure <1. *2002 survey:* Very often 3; Fairly often 12; Not very often 28; Not at all 57; Not sure <1.

Would read books more often if. . .

They were cheaper to buy Yes 35; No 62; Not sure 2. There were more libraries closer to home or work Yes 30; No 60; Not sure 2. Library hours were more convenient Yes 38; No 68; Not sure 1.

Would listen to music more often if. . .

Tapes and CDs were cheaper Yes 52; No 46; Not sure 2. Had more information on what is available Yes 40; No 58; Not sure 2. Had more time Yes 56; No 43; Not sure 1.

Would go to the movies more often if. . .

Tickets were cheaper Yes 58; No 40; Not sure 2. Had more information about them Yes 30; No 70; Not sure <1. They were located closer to home or work Yes 37; No 63; Not sure <1.

Would go to live performances more often if. . .

Tickets were cheaper Yes 52; No 46; Not sure 2. Had more information about them Yes 38; No 60; Not sure 2. They were located closer to home or work Yes 48; No 50; Not sure 2.

Would go to art shows or art museums more often if. . .

Admissions were cheaper Yes 29; No 69; Not sure 2. More information about them Yes 42; No 56; Not sure 2. Located closer to home or work Yes 41; No 59; Not sure 1.

Would do creative work more often if. . .

Had more money to spend on it, such as buying supplies or paying for lessons Yes 45; No 52; Not sure 3. Had better or more convenient space to do it in Yes 44; No 54; Not sure 2. Had more information about different kinds of creative work Yes 43; No 55; Not sure 3.

During past 12 months, was kept from going to arts activities by:

Physical or health problems Yes 12; No 88; Not sure <1. Not having enough time Yes 54; No 44; Not sure 2. Not having someone to go with Yes 21; No 78; Not sure 1.

(Answers are, in order: <$35,000; $35,000 to <$50,000; $50,000 to <$75,000; $75,000 and over.)

Approximately how often during the past twelve months have you. . .

Gone to any art shows or museums?

Very often 4,4,3,6; Fairly often 7,8,18,17; Not very often 20,31,33,36; Not at all 69,57,47,40; Not sure <1,0,0,0.

Gone to any live performances?
Very often 4,5,14,6; Fairly often 12,14,23,21; Not very often 25,40,37,48; Not at all 58,41,27,25; Not sure 1,0,0,0.

Been to the movies?
Very often 5,7,6,11; Fairly often 17,14,22,11; Not very often 37,40,51,65; Not at all 40,40,21,13; Not sure <1,0,0,1.

Read any books just for pleasure?
Very often 34,32,36,29; Fairly often 19,29,25,36; Not very often 19,23,22,22; Not at all 27,17,17,13; Not sure <1,0,0,0.

Done any creative work yourself?
Very often 35,30,37,33; Fairly often 27,32,29,35; Not very often 17,18,12,13; Not at all 22,21,22,19; Not sure 0,0,0,0.

Listened to music at home?
Very often 58,63,62,59 ; Fairly often 16,15,20,28; Not very often 14,13,15,11; Not at all 11,10,2,2; Not sure 0,0,0,0.

Index

About the Institute

The Institute for Innovation in Social Policy devotes its full capacity to the analysis and publication of social indicators. Established in 1985, the Institute has worked on social indicators at the national, state, and international levels as a way to improve the reporting and understanding of social conditions. The Institute's work has had significant impact on public policy, public education, and the academic community.

Since its inception, the Institute has released numerous social indicator reports and working papers. Staff members have collaborated on a book, entitled *The Social Health of the Nation: How America Is Really Doing* (1999), as well as articles in journals and other publications. In addition, over the past decade, the Institute has conducted eight national conferences on social health and social indicators.

The Institute monitors social trends at the national level by means of its Index of Social Health, which has been released annually since 1987, and its National Survey of Social Health, which has been administered three times, in 2000, 2002, and 2004. Findings from early years of the index and survey are summarized in the Institute's *Social Report*, published in 2001 and 2003.

At the state level, the Institute has published two editions of *The Social Health of the States*, in 2001 and in 2003. A third edition will be released in 2007. Twelve editions of *The Social State of Connecticut* were produced by the Institute, from 1994 to 2005, with the support of the Connecticut State Legislature and the William Caspar Graustein Foundation. The Institute developed an Index of the Social Health of Connecticut for this project, based on its Index of Social Health methodology.

The Institute also has examined indicators of culture and creativity based on data from its National Survey of Social Health. These are summarized in *Arts, Culture, and the Social Health of the Nation*, published in 2003 and 2006.

Director: Marque-Luisa Miringoff, Ph.D.
Associate Director: Sandra Opdycke, Ph.D.
Vassar College, Box 529
Poughkeepsie, NY 12604

Information about the Institute can be found at: http://iisp.vassar.edu

About the Authors

Marque-Luisa Miringoff, Ph.D., is Professor of Sociology at Vassar College, Poughkeepsie, NY. She has served as Chair of the Sociology Department and Director of the Urban Studies Program. She has been a member of the Institute for Innovation in Social Policy since 1985 and its Director since 2004. Her writings include *The Social Health of the Nation: How America Is Really Doing* (1999) with Marc Miringoff and Sandra Opdycke, *The Social Costs of Genetic Welfare* (1991), and numerous articles on health and social indicators.

Sandra Opdycke, Ph.D., has been Associate Director of the Institute for Innovation in Social Policy since 1985. Her writings include *The Routledge Historical Atlas of Women in America* (2000), *Placing a Human Face on the Uninsured* (2000), *The Social Health of the Nation: How America Is Really Doing* (1999) with Marc Miringoff and Marque-Luisa Miringoff, *No One Was Turned Away: The Role of Public Hospitals in New York City Since 1900* (1999), and *American Social Policy: Reassessment and Reform* (1986) with Marc Miringoff. She previously taught at Vassar College.